Reclaiming the Author

Figures and Fictions

from Spanish America

Lucille Kerr

Duke University Press

Durham and London   1992

Contents

Preface

"The Spanish Americans are actually *doing* what the French are only talking about." This bemused assessment was made some years ago by a colleague in French who had only recently begun to read contemporary Spanish American fiction. The statement intrigued me for a number of reasons. It provoked me to consider what it might mean to posit a relationship between Spanish American narrative and French literary theory, and how any such comparative statement might resonate for Spanish American culture as a whole. For one might take this statement either as an obsequious or as a condescending comment; one might see it as situating the Spanish American tradition as ahead of or behind, above or below, the French enterprise. Moreover, one might take it either as a spontaneous, touristic remark or as a studied, critical observation; one might see in it a momentary interest in cultures and currents viewed as relatively exotic from a European or Anglo-

American perspective, or hear it as the voicing of a persistent sense of loss in contemporary Western culture.

Whatever its cultural resonances, the statement seemed to me to raise questions about the relation between modern critical concepts and contemporary literary production. It became a reminder of the problematical nature of the opposition (that is, between "doing" and "talking about" literature) proposed within it. In fact, such a dichotomy or division is precisely what contemporary Spanish American fiction puts into question. Spanish American narratives suggest that the apparently discrete doing of literature is also always a way of talking about it. My study aims to examine the figure of the author as one of the concepts about which the Spanish Americans talk as they do literature. It also aims to demonstrate how, in raising questions about critical figures such as the author, the Spanish Americans have directed attention to how works of narrative fiction, as a whole, get read.

It is well known that contemporary Spanish American writers have received considerable recognition for work regarded as experimental and even revolutionary. Spanish American narratives have appeared to challenge conventions of narrative fiction. They have also helped to redirect thinking about the formal categories of analysis (for example, author, narrator, character, reader, plot, and story) that shape the reading of traditional and experimental texts alike, and about reading practices more generally. One of those categories—the author—has seemed to me particularly intriguing, given the kind of attention it has received at least since the 1960s and the complex production of Spanish American narratives around it.

As I began to consider this critical concept in relation to Spanish American fiction, I tried to address a variety of issues. I thought about what the word "author" has come to mean within contemporary critical vocabulary, and considered how the critical as well as etymological relationship between the terms "author" and "authority" might figure in the development of modern critical concepts. I reflected on the possible relationship between the analysis of implied or fictional author-figures and the consideration of the empirical authors assumed to be responsible for their invention. I considered the models of authorship and the authorial roles or responsibilities proposed by contemporary fiction, and how they might revise or reaffirm traditional conceptions of the author. I came to view the poetics of contemporary Spanish American fiction as giving new life to the figure of the author while also attesting to its "death." But I also wondered what the different figures of the revitalized author might look like.

To focus on such matters, I realized, was to consider the place of the author as a privileged place, and this would run counter to the thinking prevalent in many contemporary critical circles. Talk about the author's death, followed by, for example, a burgeoning of interest in the reader, has made discussion of the author not only problematical but also polemical. Indeed, such developments seem to have virtually stripped "the author" (that is, the author as a critical concept) of its authority. Nevertheless, it seemed to me that, even while it appeared justifiable to talk (as many have done) about the author's death, disappearance, or self-effacement in any number of texts, something else was also happening with Spanish American fiction. It seemed that the author's demise had often been misread when the notion was taken far beyond the context for which it had been proposed initially.

I turned to the writing of some well-known Spanish American authors with these problems in mind, precisely because their narratives seem to pose questions about authorial identity, activity, and authority through the different figures of the author they propose. Their questions dovetail with questions posed by modern critical theory, and bear on problems inherent in current critical vocabulary. Moreover, Spanish American fiction has us consider not only how one might conceive of the author as a personal or textual figure, but also how one is inevitably led to confound radically different figures and concepts to which the term author might be applied.

Here I mean to explore, through concrete examples (that is, through readings of individual texts), how the Spanish Americans have shaped and situated the figure of the author in recent years, and how their work has called into question concepts that would strive to contain or constrain it as a uniform or unitary figure. I am arguing that Spanish American writers have developed a critique of the author (and by critique I mean analysis or critical discussion) that both complements and contradicts notions set forth outside works of fiction. Moreover, their writing has developed a radical, but also curiously recuperative, poetics of authorial activity—one that involves a competition, a dialogue of critical concepts that refuses to close off the question of the author.

In approaching the Spanish Americans' work in this way, I also want to suggest how the reading of modern narrative has been conditioned by their writing, how prevailing critical vocabulary is constantly being tested (and further complicated) by their fiction. Spanish American narratives have a good deal to say about critical and literary concepts. To read modern Spanish American fiction, it seems to me, is to read in two directions at once. It is to move, either explicitly or implicitly, from problems of exegesis to issues in poetics and criticism, and back again.

However, as I suggest above, the kind of reading I have in mind is not one that would subordinate the works of Spanish American fiction to a group of theoretical or critical texts (such as the French theory referred to by my colleague) that might be taken as models to be illustrated or followed. Though in the opening chapter I refer to well-known and exemplary essays by Barthes and Foucault, as well as to a famous text by Borges, the central portion of this study intends to demonstrate how particular works of narrative fiction reconfigure a variety of images of the author. I present those texts as asking questions about the author in terms that derive from their own terrain, not from a foreign (either "literary" or "theoretical") territory that would be imposed upon them.

The texts I have chosen engage the question of the author in distinctive and yet related ways. They represent a number of (but by no means all) the ways that such a question has been posed by Spanish American narrative. Further, I have chosen authors whose status in contemporary Spanish American culture is of some significance. Though some names may be more recognizable than others to different audiences (undoubtedly, the names of Cortázar, Donoso, Fuentes, Puig, and Vargas Llosa are better known than that of Poniatowska, especially to readers outside Hispanism), all have by now achieved positions of some, if not consequential, importance within the Spanish American tradition. The work of these writers obviously represents substantial trends in modern Spanish American literature.

(That Cortázar, Donoso, Fuentes, Puig, and Vargas Llosa are as often as not identified as boom authors and that their work—as well as that of other well-known literary figures—has come to form the modern canon of Spanish American fiction is obvious. That Poniatowska, among other perhaps less well-known writers, might also be situated among them as an established figure or that a so-called testimonial novel might be situated with, rather than separated from, examples of the new narrative, may well be less evident. The juxtaposition of authors and texts in this study is intended to cast doubts on such divisions and to serve as a reminder about the continued readjustments that have shaped—and will continue to give shape to—the Spanish American canon.)

The choice of writers who might be regarded as having already received ample recognition has been made with at least two other considerations in mind. First, the authors whose writing I have chosen to discuss are among those whose texts and real-world appearances have come to represent "the Spanish American author" in recent years. One must, of necessity, turn to their texts to consider the status of the author in modern Spanish American writing and to view the images of the author projected by such well-known figures. Even though there are other (one might say, less canonical) images of the author offered by a variety of currents that have been shaping Spanish American narrative in the last several decades or so, the literary production of many of these prominent authors still stands at center stage. Second, the texts of established boom and post-boom authors develops an unsettling (and, in my view, truly significant) encounter among critical concepts and authorial figures within and around their own borders. Indeed, the encounter staged by their writing is unsettling precisely because it would also have one reconsider the canonical positions and critical concepts often associated with the writing of celebrated authors.

To be sure, other writers and currents have come along to challenge some of the figures of the author generated by the boom. I would argue that such a challenge is already present within the writing of some of these established figures—within texts such as those I have chosen to discuss in this study of "the author." Therefore, given that the work of many of the renowned authors has come to represent, if not also to redefine or even resist, the institutionalization of the author in modern Spanish American culture, how such texts figure authorial activity (if not also authorial authority) becomes of critical interest. I will explore some of the ways in which Spanish American texts from the sixties onward put into question the privilege and powers of any author while they still reinvest the figure(s) of the author with a great deal of authority.

The matter of recognition may be significant for other reasons. In fact, when I began to work on this project, I was intrigued by the idea that an apparent recovery of authority by contemporary figures of the author in Spanish America has more or less coincided with an apparent loss of authority suffered by certain concepts of the author in European and Anglo-American contexts. I noticed that most of the

Spanish American authors in whose writing such a recovery seemed to have been produced were precisely those who seemed to have contributed to the author's demise. I even puzzled about whether one might make some connection between the potential, though admittedly precarious, resurrection of the author as a figure of authority and the rise to positions of stardom of many Spanish American authors. However, intriguing as the celebrated real-world figure may be, the focus of the present study has situated the author-superstar beyond its frame. For I primarily wanted to see how Spanish American narratives have reclaimed different, and to my mind rather vital, figures of the author, at the same time that they have acknowledged the author's death. That is, I wanted to demonstrate how a variety of Spanish American texts provide evidence of the extremely complex situation of "the author" in recent years.

As I devised these readings I modified some of my initial ideas about the revitalization of the author. As I suggest above, I see contemporary Spanish American fiction not so much as returning the author (either as a textual or personal figure) to an unequivocally authoritative or privileged position but as staging a competition of critical figures of potentially comparable, though shifting, authority. I see the Spanish Americans as developing a dialogue of concepts that no one theory or text can contain or contest completely. My selection of texts, therefore, aims to provide representative examples of how this competitive staging is developed and how the question of the author continues to be raised in contemporary fiction.

The first chapter's objective is to reframe such questions, to introduce some of the ways in which the concept of the author has developed in this century, and to serve as a reminder of ideas that issue from past eras. There I am interested in suggesting how the question of the author persists (even when it may appear to have disappeared) rather than in plotting out a definitive or exhaustive history of concepts and vocabulary. The chapters that follow focus on the question of the author as it is posed within different works of Spanish American fiction and also around them. The discussion of each of these texts follows their order of publication. I begin with Julio Cortázar's *Rayuela* (1963) and end with Mario Vargas Llosa's *El hablador* (1987). Between those chapters, I deal with Elena Poniatowska's *Hasta no verte Jesús mío* (1969), Carlos Fuentes's *Terra nostra* (1975), Manuel Puig's *Pubis angelical* (1979), and José Donoso's *El jardín de al lado* (1981). However, by adhering to chronology I do not mean to suggest that there has been a discernible and definitive evolution of thinking about this question in Spanish American fiction. Rather, I want to propose that from the 1960s, when Spanish American narrative seemed to flourish as it never had before and when modern criticism brought renewed attention to the concept of the author, the question of the author has persistently been raised by the Spanish Americans. And, in different ways, they have continued to renew and resituate that question.

My readings, therefore, turn in several directions. As in Kerr, *Suspended Fictions: Reading Novels by Manuel Puig* (1987), where I first formulated some general ideas about the author in contemporary Spanish American fiction, I have attempted to focus first one way, then another, on texts that turn their own gaze toward the figure of the author. Thus, in some cases I have focused principally on an individual text, reading it closely while also speculating more generally from time to time about the concept (or concepts) of the author formulated by it (the chapters on Fuentes, Donoso, and Vargas Llosa). In others, I have moved from a particular text to additional writings by the same or by different authors, and I have tried to construct a dialogue of texts and authorial figures around that work as well as around issues related to the question of the author (the chapters on Cortázar, Poniatowska, and Puig). Everywhere, however, I have aimed to keep "the author" in view. For I want to view the question of the author, as it has been raised by Spanish American fiction, as crucial to the reading of contemporary narrative and to the development of narrative poetics and criticism.

The research and writing of this study have been assisted by a grant from the Joint Committee on Latin American Studies of the Social Science Research Council and the American Council of Learned Societies with funds provided by the National Endowment for the Humanities and the Ford Foundation. I wish to express my appreciation for their support.

Chapters four and six have been adapted and substantially revised or expanded from articles that previously published in PMLA ("The Paradox of Power and Mystery: Carlos Fuentes' *Terra nostra*," vol. 95, 1980) and *Criticism* ("Authority in Play: José Donoso's *El jardin de al lado*," vol. 25, 1983; copyright 1983 by Wayne State University Press), respectively; chapter three has appeared in similar form and with the same title in MLN (vol. 106, 1991). I wish to thank the publishers of those journals for granting permission to use that material.

My thanks go to a number of colleagues and friends whose generosity and goodwill have made all the difference to this book. For their support at the grant proposal stage, I thank Gerald L. Bruns, John S. Brushwood, John W. Kronik, and Enrique Pupo-Walker. For their willingness to share bibliographic information, or to talk about texts or topics not entirely within my own realm of expertise, or to discuss issues taken up by a particular chapter, I thank Peter Allen, Barbara E. Kurtz, Lillian Manzor-Coats, Carmen Silva-Corvalán, Greg Thalman, Peter Starr, and Nancy J. Vickers, and for their occasional interest in my research for this book, I give thanks to Vincent Farenga and Dragan Kujundžić. For reading an individual chapter at an early stage of this project, I thank Carlos J. Alonso, Andrew P. Debicki, and Peggy Kamuf. For his reading of the completed manuscript and his valuable critical observations and editorial suggestions, I offer thanks to Djelal Kadir; for his careful scrutiny of the entire manuscript as well as his lucid comments on critical and theoretical points, I very gratefully acknowledge Michael du Plessis; for his inventive suggestions about titular phrases, I am indebted to Alexander Argyros. And, last, but by no means least—for their friendship and support during every phase of this project, I give special thanks to Marjorie Perloff and to Suzanne R. Pucci.

I would also like to express my gratitude to LaVonne Wuertz, of the University of Southern California's Doheny Memorial Library, for her generous assistance with the research for this project. My thanks also go to Reynolds Smith, of Duke University Press, whose goodwill and good humor were much appreciated throughout the publishing process.

1

Situating the Author
Notions Old and New

A discussion of the figure of the author in contemporary Spanish American fiction seems to require a recapitulation of some of the statements that have been made about the author, especially over the last twenty-five or thirty years. Indeed, it seems appropriate to remind readers of the commonplaces surrounding this figure and of the questions that might still be raised about it. To my mind, certain texts by Borges, Barthes, and Foucault have exemplary value for such a discussion, which would also need to turn, albeit in a schematic fashion, toward some of the ideas and terminology that have informed thinking about this critical figure over the years. Here, I would like to frame the readings of works by Cortázar, Poniatowska, Fuentes, Puig, Donoso, and Vargas Llosa with a review of some concepts, exemplary texts, and terms that might not only pursue but also anticipate the problematical turns taken by contemporary Spanish American fiction around the figure of the author.

"No sé cuál de los dos escribe esta página" ["I don't know which of the two is writing this page"] (808; translation mine).[1] Thus ends "Borges y yo" ["Borges and I"], one of Borges's best-known texts and one that openly addresses the question of the author. In a characteristically perplexing (and recognizably Borgesian) manner "Borges y yo" remarks upon the complexity of that question instead of providing a definitive answer to the dilemmas of identity raised by it. Indeed, this text, first published in 1957, presents the author as a complex figure whose appearance and disappearance now as one kind of figure, now as another, would also embody the critical and literary vicissitudes of the author in recent decades. This text's ending, therefore, seems an appropriate place to begin to talk about the author. For, it opens up, rather than closes off, questions also associated with the work of other Spanish American authors who have pursued further the suggestive directions proposed by Borges.[2]

The final sentence of Borges's text is problematical for a number of reasons. It closes off the rumination about the relation between the two figures of its title with a remark that would grammatically transform them from a pair both united and divided as two into a group of three ("yo" ["I"] and the two others, one of whom presumably "escribe esta página" ["writes this page"]). The sentence thus generates a proliferation of authorial figures (all, it seems, potential referents for the name "Borges") and sites of authorship. At the text's conclusion the problematical relation between the title's two differentiated but conjoined figures seems to slip beyond the control of any one speaker or author. This final statement of undecidability about the source of the text, and about its authorship, thus effects a disappearance of the author as a univocal and stable authority or origin.[3] Yet, this dispersion of authorial subjectivity would also confer upon each of the figures in "Borges y yo" something of an authorial position. The suggestion that the author cannot be found in any single site potentially situates the author's figure everywhere. The seemingly final authorial disappearance in this last sentence also opens up the possibility of an inevitable return, and the eventual reappearance of the author.

Indeed, the final sentence proposes an undecidable question (the question of who is writing the text, of who is its subject and author). By virtue of being unanswerable, this question insinuates itself as a query that endures, as a question that insists upon returning. Though it may have come to be viewed over the last few decades as a question of limited urgency or legitimacy, it appears at the end of "Borges y yo" as a residual record of the persistence with which the author's figure asserts itself even in contemporary writing. The final question remains also as a question of reading which may be posed as much by the text's unidentified reader as by its anonymous writer. It may well be that one can't stop asking this question, as Borges's text proposes it. Indeed, it seems that, following in his path, contemporary Spanish American fiction has continued to pose it in ever more problematical ways.

Borges's final, and implicitly interrogative, sentence appears to conclude a brief but complex text that also effects a conflation, or consolidation, of authorial figures. In "Borges y yo" the figure of the author as a biographical person and private entity ("yo") is confounded with that of the author as a literary personage and public character ("Borges"). Much as those different figures would initially be distinguished in grammatical or thematic terms, they are finally drawn together and identified with each other. In fact, any talk about the one sounds like talk about the other, any identification of the one looks like identification of the other. It is precisely this dialectical, symbiotic relation of seemingly distinct figures of the author (grammatically figured by the conjunction "y" ["and"] in the text's title) that is proposed by the text and that its final sentence would also repeat.

"Borges y yo" thus distinguishes and confounds different figures of the author. The text implicitly warns against confusing the biographical author with the textual author-figure. But it also appears to undermine the idea of the author as anything but a literary or linguistic construct. It seems that the biographical figure who "lives" ("yo vivo, yo me dejo vivir" ["I live, I let myself live"]) is absorbed into the literary figure who writes ("Borges . . . [trama] su literatura" ["Borges . . . weave[s] his tales and poems"]) (808/279). But at the text's end—if not already at its beginning, where the author virtually appears in the title of one of his own texts—the name Borges still designates, while balancing in dialectical identification, the one and the other figure.

(It ought to be noted that the word author does not appear in the text itself. It is inferred from the appearance of the name Borges and the identification of the figure to which it refers as the producer of literary texts. Indeed, it could be argued that the disappearance of the author is literally a verbal disappearance, but that, having left its mark, its figure continues to suggest itself everywhere, under both the proper name and the pronoun that would mark the place[s] of this text's confounding authorial subject.)

The competition, so to speak, between these initially disparate figures of the author is, moreover, refigured as a competition of reading. In reading "Borges y yo" one also reads different and competing ways of reading the author: either as a biographical entity or as a textual subject; either as an idiosyncratic and individual figure or as a figure identical to others; either as a disappearing figure or as a figure that returns and reappears. In fact, "Borges y yo" may be read as a critical parable about the difficulty of stabilizing the figure of the author, or of deciding on an unequivocal concept that the term author would designate or describe. It may be taken as a fable about this figure's resistance to either a singularly historical or uniquely literary existence— that is, as an allegory of the competing readings developed around the critical concept called the author.[4]

Moreover, in "Borges y yo," Borges maps out notions with which his name has become associated and because of which his writing has been regarded as bearing as much of a theoretical as a literary significance. But Borges's writings about matters that might be called theoretical are not set apart from his texts that might be identified as literary. Borges's writing has come to be appreciated also for the way it questions such discursive and generic distinctions. Borges's formative position in the history of modern Spanish American literature, and his considerable influence in Western literary currents as well, result in some measure from such unsettling propositions and performances, for which other contemporary Spanish American authors continue to be recognized.[5]

Indeed, as we shall see, the questions raised by Borges's "Borges y yo" are questions that insinuate themselves in contemporary Spanish American narrative more generally. The poetics of fiction proposed by many of those texts resituates the figure of the author in ways that both complement and contradict theories about the author put forward especially by European literary critics. Though, on the one hand one may see in Spanish American fiction exemplary cases of the author's death or disappearance, on the other hand one may also discover how the author resists the declarations of its demise and how it returns, or is reclaimed, in a somewhat altered form perhaps, as a striking and vital figure.

Oddly, such a return of the author, or the refusal of the author to disappear, may well be evident even in some of the texts considered to be pivotal to any discussion of the author in modern literary studies— that is, precisely in those texts that would seem to dispose of the author as a viable critical category or concept. I am thinking, of course, of Barthes's "The Death of the Author" (1968), and "From Work to Text" (1971), and also of Foucault's "What Is an Author?" (1969)—texts for which Borges's "Borges y yo" may well be taken as a revealing "precursor."[6] Indeed, in addition to serving as watershed texts, Barthes's and Foucault's essays also return to the question with which Borges's essay ends.

As we recall, Barthes's essays aim to dismantle a specific concept of the author, represented by the term in its upper-case form (that is, "Author") in the first of the two essays. The title "The Death of the Author" has already become a catch phrase that has functioned as both "a shorthand for a nonhermeneutic thinking about texts and as a label against which to react in the name of the historical subject" (Kamuf 5). Barthes puts into question not the existence of an empirical entity that would be referred to as the author but, rather, a certain way of reading the relation between such a person and the literary texts he or she writes.

According to Barthes, the concept of the Author would position the author as a privileged, paternal figure, as the authoritative "father" or divine creator in whom meaning would be seen to originate. His attack on the "reign" of the Author is thus also a critique of the grounding assumptions of a critical practice that would find in authors and their writing mutually reinforcing identities and expressions. His call for the "death" of the Author, and the concomitant "birth" of the reader ("The Death of the Author" 148), is thus a call for renouncing a model of reading associated with many of the historically or biographically oriented critical currents that prevailed in literary scholarship well into the current century.

As Barthes questions this traditional notion of authorship, his critique would also appear to disengage the author-as-person from the literary text as such. But if, in fact, Barthes's proposal produces such a disengagement it is not so much in the undermining of the Author as a valid critical trope or concept as in the characterization of writing itself as "the destruction of every voice, of every point of origin" ("The Death of the Author" 142). It is perhaps mostly in this latter characterization that the emphasis of Barthes's critique lies, as his two essays' terminological and conceptual substitutions ("modern scriptor" for "Author," "text" for "work") and ideological shifts (dethronement of the Author to empowerment of the reader) may well illustrate.

We remember that Barthes not only questions the model of textual filiation, and thus the temporal logic (the author as anteriority), that empowers the notion of the Author. He also proposes an alternate way of conceiving of the author—that is, as a figure within and simultaneous with, rather than outside and prior to, the literary text. The proposed shift to a set of critical notions that might substitute for (but not erase entirely) some of the Author's traditional supports suggests an essentially textual relationship. Moreover, Barthes's use of the term "scriptor" ("The Death of the Author" 145–47), and also his reference to the author as a "guest" or "paper author" ("From Work to Text" 78), not only depersonalize the concept of the author. They also seem to weaken, if not destroy, the authority of any kind of position that may be understood as authorial.

One might consider that to redefine the role of the author as that of a modern scriptor is to preempt the author's original authority and responsibility—that is, to deny him or her the position of a modern *auctor*. The author's role as a scriptor, like that of his medieval or ancient counterpart, would be that of a writer who holds little, if any, authority. For such a writer would not "inspire," "found," or "originate" anything, but would merely repeat, by writing or reinscribing, the text into which he also incorporates himself.[7] Moreover, this text, which "is made of multiple writings, drawn from many cultures and entering into mutual relations of dialogue" ("The Death of the Author" 148), would become the site in which "if the author is a novelist, he inscribes himself . . . as one of his characters, as another figure sewn into the rug" ("From Work to Text" 78).[8]

Barthes's shift in terminology, then, dislodges the Author, or the idea of the external author-as-person, and instates the author-as-textual-figure. The shift to the phrase "modern scriptor" would seem to detach the author-as-person from the history associated with the concept of the author, whose evolution is tied to the question of authority and traditional (that is, filiative) models of authorship. For the use of the word scriptor in the oppositional role suggested by Barthes evokes a model of writing within which there seems to be no place for the writer as author-person, and therefore no space for the concept of the Author. And in this model, the new term would turn the reading of literary texts not so much against the idea of the author as a person, as against the idea of the author as a person who becomes identified as the origin of and, consequently, the authority on the work's meaning. Moreover, the terminological shift constitutes a transfer of authority from the Author to the reader. The figure of the reader thus has a new importance and privilege conferred upon it by Barthes's essay.[9]

The revised critical vocabulary proposed by Barthes places the author in an apparently unoriginal position, where the one who writes is but the one who repeats, quotes, and filters the discourse of others. This shift in terminology would also propose that one reconsider the kind of authority that may be exercised by any author, that one shift one's thinking about the author as an authority. At the same time, however, it leads one to consider the ways in which a text inscribes within itself the figure of the author, which in practice, as we shall see later, may oddly solidify as well as subvert its own position of privilege. The matter of disentangling the one notion from the other, or even the one term from the other, may, however, present some problems.

Indeed, it could be argued that, while this reading of the situation proposes to undermine both the privilege of the author's biography, intentions, and interpretations and the authority of the author's name, it does not entirely dispel the personal image of the "new" author—that is, the author-turned-scriptor. Either notion—that of the scriptor as well as that of the author—may well retain within itself, and thus reinforce, the idea of a person engaged in an activity of literary production that also sustains the author's personal identity and image.

In fact, near the beginning of his well-known attempt to answer the question "What Is an Author?" Foucault suggests that, in spite of the developments in thinking about writing generally, certain "notions [for example, the 'work' and 'writing'] . . . intended to replace the privileged position of the author actually seem to preserve that privilege and suppress the real meaning of his disappearance" ("What Is an Author?" 143). As we recall, Foucault's review of the special properties of the author's name leads to the proposal that such a name "characterize[s] a certain mode of being of discourse" (147)—the "author-function," which is "characteristic of the mode of existence, circulation, and functioning of certain discourses within a society" (148).

Foucault's discussion of the author-function takes up the situation not only of authors of individual works but also of authors in "transdiscursive" positions (for example, Marx, Freud; 153–56). Foucault's consideration of the problems surrounding the concept of the author both retains the figure of the author as a person and resituates the author's activity as a function of discourse. The author, though an historical subject, is no longer to be viewed as an originator but rather as a "functional principle" and "ideological product" (159).[10] Arguably, questions about authenticity, originality, or authorial identity and meaning have no place in such formulations about the author (160), which articulate further the features and possible consequences of the Author's not-so-recent death.

Foucault's observations about the name of the author and his proposal for viewing the author as a function and figure of discourse raise points that differ somewhat from those in Barthes's essay, while also confirming their insights. Foucault's consideration of the special properties of the author's name is a reminder that the name of the author and, therefore, also the word author have a variety of meanings for our modern critical idiom, in which use of the term, as well as of authors' names, often brings together (and sometimes confounds) disparate senses. Though the name of the author shares certain properties with other proper names (both are "situated between the two poles of description and designation" [146]), it also possesses a "paradoxical singularity": "the author's name, unlike other proper names, does not pass from the interior of a discourse to the real and exterior individual who produced it; instead, the name seems always to be present, marking off the edges of the text, revealing, or at least characterizing, its mode of being" (147).

It would appear that the author's name is to be understood as performing certain related functions, according to Foucault. It would designate certain properties of discourses characterized by the author-function, describe the instances of discourse through which a particular author or form of authorial activity reveals itself, and establish relations among the texts, practices, or positions which can be attributed to individual authors. As such, that name could also be taken as "the label of [a text's] stylistic individuality" (Steiner [summarizing Tynianov] 133). That individuality would be understood not as personal but rather as textual, as the author's name would refer to a literary rather than to a biographical figure (Steiner [summarizing Tynianov] 134).[11]

Foucault's discussion of the author's name also suggests other problems. For example, inasmuch as that name (which is associated with the texts presumed to have been written by a particular author whose virtual signature appears on them) also seems to duplicate and yet differ from the name of a person who functions as an author, the possibilities for confounding the different senses of that name may well persist when attention is turned to the figure of the author.[12] In its capacity as a description of a person and as a designation of an authorial function, that name may call up (alternately and simultaneously) different meanings. In addition, inasmuch as the biographical referent always seems ready to return from within or behind that name, and potentially to stake a claim to it, the differentiation neatly marked off in theory may seem in practice ever ready to slip out of control. And, such slippage would allow the reentry, as it were, of more traditional ways of reading the figure and function of the author. (It is precisely such a slippage that is orchestrated by "Borges y yo.") Indeed, the proximity of the author-as-person suggests the threatening presence of the Author, whose recuperation remains imminent in the practice of reading works of fiction, if not in the theories informing how they get read.

Barthes's and Foucault's proposals suggest that a depersonalization of the author would shortcircuit the possibility of attributing traditional forms of authority to individual authors or of viewing the author's name as an authoritative or authenticating marker. The author deprived of individual identity and dispossessed of the role of creator, or of that of originator of meaning, would also be stripped of a position of authority. Whether viewed as ultimately divine or human in one era or another, such a position (and the authority it brings with it) would necessarily be exterior to the work, both anterior and posterior to its production. The various shifts in critical conceptions of the author, then, would place the theoretical entity somewhere within the production of discourse, within the frame of the literary text, rather than outside or prior to it.

When these discussions propose the exclusion of the empirical author as a locus of meaning or arbiter of interpretation from such a framework, they also seem to distance the author within the text (the author as projection of authorial activity outside or as textualized figure produced by it) from the exercise of authority. The author's figure would appear less as that of an authoritative author. It would appear or project itself less as a figure of authority the farther inside the text it would seem to be situated. Thus, as the authority of the Author is dismantled, the author (in either personal or textual form) would no longer appear to be the master-figure from which any kind of knowledge or meaning could be derived or around which any kind of textual design would seem to develop. Indeed, the authorial subject or author-figure in fiction becomes, as recalled from Barthes's statements, but another "character"—a figure divested of responsibility for and authority over the text. With the demise of the Author, and also the acceptance of the idea of the author-function, then, the concept of the author is divested of its former interpretive privilege, of its position as gateway to reliable, if not authoritative, reading.[13]

Barthes's presentation of the author (that is, under the term scriptor) as a textualized figure and Foucault's proposal to consider the author principally as a discursive function mark a widely accepted shift in recent thinking about the author. However, the turn toward the textual figure and away from the biographical entity may also appear ready to turn back on itself through the same questions that seem to propel it. That is, Barthes's and Foucault's essays, as suggested above, also return to the very same question that returns at the end of "Borges y yo." Indeed, it is precisely this question that virtually initiates and ends their texts as well, and which, oddly enough, also holds open, as it opens for interrogation, the place of authority associated with other, more traditional figures of the author.

As we recall, both Barthes and Foucault raise the question "who is speaking?" and the answers they give propose additional questions about "the author." Barthes invokes the query as a quasi-rhetorical question about Balzac's *Sarrasine* ("The Death of the Author" 142) and provisionally answers it ("No one, no 'person', says it" [147]) as he begins to conclude his discussion. Foucault poses the same question as part of a question he borrows from Beckett, asking "What does it matter who is speaking?" at both the beginning and the end of his text ("What Is an Author?" 141, 160). Barthes suggests that the question deserves an answer only insofar as that answer does not bring back the Author. Although Foucault concedes that there are a number of ways to both ask and answer the question, at the same time he would make the answer to that question the point of departure for a radical inquiry into the institutions of discourse rather than about individuals.

The question thus becomes a question that can be taken literally (as a question one might answer but to which one is not to pay direct attention) or rhetorically (as a strategic query one is not expected to answer but to which one might nonetheless reply, as do Barthes and Foucault, with different, though related, ideas about the concept of the author).[14] Whether one takes this question as essentially rhetorical or tries to read it in literal terms, however, it remains, even in a negative form, as a reminder of its own potential for resituating the matter of the author in both familiar and foreign terms.

Indeed, the question seems to endure as a query whose literal possibilities may well resist the pull of its rhetorical effects. By asking the question—either implicitly (Borges) or explicitly (Barthes and Foucault)—the wrong answer, so to speak, also manages to persist. Or, rather, by asking this question, Borges, Barthes, and Foucault would also open up a space (albeit a negative space) for the reappearance of the figure whose denegation that question (or one of its answers) might propose. For the question contains within itself the place within which this disappearing figure still finds a place to appear. Oddly, then, the question of the author may well linger as an unanswered question as much in the proposals of figures such as Barthes or Foucault as in the texts of writers such as Borges.

There emerges from this question a competition of concepts, figures, and images one may take now as appropriate, now as inappropriate referents for "the author." However, such a contest, which I shall consider later as one suggested by a good many works of modern Spanish American fiction, is inherent in the development of twentieth-century literary criticism more generally. As we are well aware, the theories of literature supported by different critical trends also assume different perspectives on, as well as definitions of, the author. And, since disparate models of reading remain in competition today, different theories of authorship, different notions about the author, implicitly confront one another from one arena to another.

If one were to attempt to tell the story of "the author" as part of the development of modern critical theory, however, one would inevitably recall that the apparent watershed reached by Barthes's and Foucault's essays is neither a completely radical departure from all previous proposals nor a mere repetition of the formulations of other twentieth-century thinkers. Indeed, the overall history of the author unfolds not so much as a linear progression but as a variform development that moves from the idea of the author as a person to the idea of the author as a textual and/or discursive phenomenon, and back again.[15]

Moreover, this history also reveals that neither of these notions is as monolithic or homogeneous as it might appear from its apparently oppositional relation to the other. To think of the author as a person has not always meant that the relation between that person and his or her text is conceived of in the same way; to think of the author as a figure within a text has not always meant the complete abandonment of the idea of the author as a person nor the assumption of a single way of reading such an authorial figure. Indeed, the vicissitudes of and variations on the concept of the author in our own century should serve as reminders of the complexity of this critical term, as well as of the complex relations among the different reading models proposed by twentieth-century critical thought.

It would appear that, while different critical schools would situate the author (of any sort) in different positions of more or less importance for the reading of literary texts, the figure with which they have most often been concerned is that of the empirical author. The questions about the author raised by much of twentieth-century criticism seem to address the matter of how (if at all) criticism is to take into account or to focus attention (if any) on the author-as-person: whether the author's life, or intentions, or personality, or psychology, or "consciousness," or social class is to be given any importance for the reading of literature; whether the question of a text's meaning, or design, is a question that can (or cannot) be answered through reference to the empirical or biographical author.

The critical models assumed by Russian Formalism and, later, Anglo-American New Criticism—models known for their abandonment of assumptions underlying the positivistic scholarship predominant when they began to emerge—are the earliest and perhaps the first well-known responses to the question of the author in modern literary study. A similar reaction against the positivistic conception of the author underlies the positions taken by later proposals about the author as an essentially textual phenomenon or discursive effect, such as those of Barthes and Foucault.

As we recall, the Formalists' view of literature generally precludes discussion of authorial intention, biography, or psychology, responding critically as their views do to the genetic fallacy characteristic of the critical trends prevalent around their time.[16] Indeed, by viewing the development of literature as the independent and internal evolution of literary devices and forms rather than as the consequences of the activities of individual authors who might be viewed as genius-figures, the Formalists' theory of literature virtually erases the author as an individual creator or literary source of critical significance.[17]

Likewise, New Criticism deemphasizes the author as an object of critical attention (for example, Wimsatt and Beardsley's "intentional fallacy"), as its practitioners develop the "intrinsic" strategies of close reading that have become associated with that school.[18] And, though in the work of some of the current's earlier critics the literary text may be viewed as an expression of authorial consciousness, New Criticism's predominant thinking virtually severs the text from its author, as well as from its sociohistorical context.[19] Thus, while for both Russian Formalism and Anglo-American New Criticism the term author continues to refer to the person identified as a work's creator, the reading of literature is not to be directed at the activities, identity, or intentions of any such person. Consequently, these critics begin to erode the authority of the "real" author, insofar as that author cannot be regarded as an external origin of a text's meaning.

Though semiological theories of literature, which develop out of formalist and linguistic paradigms, propose a sender-receiver model to explain how literary texts are produced and received, the sender is not so much a person (that is, the empirical author) as a system of signs or set of codes out of which the text is generated and within which meaning is produced. That is, though the real author may be cast in the role of the text's "sender," that role—or the author himself or herself—is to be understood as manifested only in textual form, as a style or "textual strategy" (Eco 10–11). The quintessential structuralist statement found in Barthes's essay makes patently viable the empirical figure's loss of authority, the transformation of the author into a textual figure or "paper author" (as noted above). The author-person is at best a mediating or filtering subject through whom cultural conventions rather than personal intentions are manifested.[20]

Deconstruction pushes things even further. The term author would at most designate an effect of discourse, not a point of original reference or authoritative intention that might be represented by writing or seen to govern its production or meaning.[21] Indeed, the problematizing of the concept of the author within deconstruction amounts to a questioning of the institution of authorship and the vocabulary and concepts that have persisted and upheld its privilege within Western culture.[22]

Another way of taking attention away from any kind of author- or sender-figure is to focus on the reader, and that is precisely what reader-response criticism has aimed to do. This apparent reaction to the author's disempowerment (among the many responses provoked by Barthes's pronouncement in "The Death of the Author") proposes to install the reader in the place of privilege vacated by the dead figure of the author. Though the question of precisely which concept of the reader prevails in reader-response criticism may emerge as a problematical issue (by reader, does one refer to a "real" or to a textualized or inscribed reader-figure),[23] which further complicates this critical shift from one "side" of the text to the other, such an emphatic transfer of attention virtually removes "the author" from view.[24]

This gradual and seemingly inexorable erosion of the empirical author's authority for the interpretation of literary texts, this curtailment of attention given to the personal activity or identity of the author, does not, as we know, represent the only direction in which thinking about literature has developed in this century. Indeed, the positions proposed by phenomenology (from which, as we remember, reader-oriented theory and criticism first emerge) and by hermeneutics, or by some Marxist and feminist critics, or by currents such as the New Historicism, for example, take things in other directions. And depending on whether the authority or privilege of the author-as-person is viewed as having been forcefully attacked but not destroyed, or as having been completely dismantled, these trends could be regarded as fostering either the retention or the reemergence of a place of considerable importance for the concept(s) of the author.

For example, by conceiving of the critic's activity as an act of identification with and recuperation of the author's consciousness within the work, Poulet (as a representative of modern phenomenology) posits the author as both an empirical entity (the person who writes) and a textual figure (a figure perceived as a consciousness, not a personal biography, within the text).[25] And, the defense of authorial meaning, undertaken most forcefully by Hirsch (and associated with currents in hermeneutics), restores to the author not only the status of person but also the position of authoritative and intentional creator.[26]

The writings of many Marxist critics have emphasized the idea of the author as a person situated within a particular sociohistorical or cultural reality or relationship. Yet such emphasis does not necessarily lead in identical directions nor does it preclude consideration of the author in terms of the textual or discursive spaces in which any authorial figure might be situated. Consider, for example, the diversity of assumptions underlying Lukács's writings about authors' works and the artistic reflection of reality, or Goldmann's positioning of the author as the representative of a social group's "mental structure," or Macherey's idea of the author as a "producer" rather than as a "genius" or "creator," or the Marxist appropriation of Bakhtin's view of the author as a discursive position or "style" in dialogue with other, sometimes opposing, discourses representative of the cultural realities inherent in language.[27]

Likewise, the work of critics such as Gilbert and Gubar represents some currents in Anglo-American feminist criticism that view women authors as well as female literary characters within the parameters of cultural, biographical, and historical contexts.[28] On the other hand, the work of someone such as Cixous would represent some tendencies followed by many European critics and writers, who take up the matter of "l'Ecriture féminine" and for whom the term author would describe not only a culturally determined empirical entity but also a textual or linguistic phenomenon, a writing subject and discursive figure.[29] And, some critics associated with New Historicism, which aims to refocus attention on both the biographical framework and the historical conditions of literary production, seem to orchestrate another recuperation of the author-as-person. Yet they might also resituate the idea of the author as an individual creator, by considering the origins of texts' production to be determined by a variety of historical, social, and cultural (rather than strictly personal or biographical) factors.[30]

The implicit or explicit assumptions about concepts of the author that are characteristic not only of different modern currents, but also of different tendencies within such currents, thus seem to take things in a number of directions at once. And one senses that neither the recent questioning of the subject[31] at one end of critical theory, nor the apparent recuperation of the empirical, historical, or intending person at the other, is able to contain (that is, to control or to encompass) the author in any kind of position, or within any lexicon, where it might be domesticated and apprehended in a stable, unproblematical form. And, as we shall see, it is precisely the uncontainable quality of the figure of the author and the uncontrollable as well as overlapping senses subsumed by the term author that Spanish American fiction brings into view.

Such diversity of critical assumptions about the author would still seem to lead away from the positions assumed by the scholarly practices in the early part of the century, and from their antecedents as well. However, it may well be that even the very earliest senses of "the author" may not have been completely discarded or entirely discredited by the shifts that generally characterize much recent critical theory, as well as modern literary production.

Indeed, any concept of the author seems to bear within itself a considerable amount of authority—and with good reason. For the term is inseparable from its own history, and that history has bound it to the idea of authority ("author," as we recall, derives from auctor[32]; the auctores were writers taken as authorities[33]). And it is precisely this idea that remains embedded within the word author, and that, consequently, inheres in the critical concept. Indeed, as I shall suggest later, the poetics of fiction formulated by a good deal of contemporary narrative reinforces the idea of the author as an authority, even though such poetics also seem to disconnect it from the idea of originality. It is precisely the former concept that lingers in these contemporary figures of the author, and which, oddly enough, also leads back to some early notions inherent in "the author."[34]

Whether the idea of the author as a textual figure rather than a person seems so radical or not, one may nevertheless wonder how, or in what forms, the author-as-person or the author's name came to be held in such high regard (and to wield considerable authority) in Western culture.[35] It is tempting to return to Foucault's "What Is an Author?" to consider how the question of the author has shifted during eras prior to our own and how its story might be told. Though one might not yet be able to tell the kind of tale he suggested ought to be told (that is, the one about discursive forms and functions), one could follow somewhat the story he begins to tell, the story of the different literary and cultural concepts that have prevailed in the past. To be sure, one would get some very different answers to (and a less than completely tidy narrative around) the titular question his essay poses.

Indeed, if one were to tell the most dominant version of the story of "the author" one would have to tell what is first a European and eventually also an Anglo-American story. On the other hand, if one were to tell other than the leading version—for example, a Latin American version—one might discover that other kinds of figures (figures that may seem to stand outside the dominant story's frame) reappear—and thereby further complicate—any such reading of "the author." Although the chapters that follow aim to suggest how Spanish American narratives have been shaping their own authorial tale, the story that needs to be told here is the European/Anglo-American one. For that is the story that has imposed itself as the predominant way of thinking about the author in Western culture. Inevitably, it is also the story that frames the reading and writing of Spanish American fiction and the alternate stories it may (or may not) have to tell.

As it happens, the *auctor* (that is, the ancient author-authority) came to be conceived of as a human author (rather than as principally a figure of divine authority) only in the late Middle Ages. For medieval Biblical commentators, the *auctor's* individuality was constituted principally by "his individual literary activity and his individual moral activity" (Minnis 5).[36] However, opinions do vary about whether attention was paid to the author as an individual person, about whether the author's name was viewed as a mark of either individuality or immortality.

According to one view, although authors were understood to be human writers, their identities as biographically determined persons or as individual personalities carried little if any weight for the reading of medieval texts. For those texts were authorized through a chain of authority whose origin was viewed as either divine or human, depending on whether the author was Christian or pagan.[37] But ultimately the privilege or authority held by the "ancients," though considerable, did not go unchallenged by the "moderns." Indeed, the development of the concept of poetic license is a reminder of the complex relations of authority that governed the production of texts by medieval and Renaissance authors, who, following in the path of the ancients with whom the concept originates, gradually claimed for themselves increased individual authority.[38]

Although authors began to stake their own ground and to make gestures toward establishing some autonomy as individual writers, the authority of "modern" authors was tied up with their relation to authorized tradition.[39] Indeed, the Renaissance "awareness of history and human creativity" gave rise to significant debate about the value and meaning of texts and, consequently, about the authority of individual authors.[40] Thus develops the movement toward the secularization of literary texts and the authorization of authors as writers whose individual activity and originality creates or carries within itself its own authority.[41]

The question of the author's name or identity—both the matter of whether the identity of an author was important for the reading of texts and the issue of whether the author ought to identify himself or not, and what such mention or suppression of his own name might represent—seems also to have been tied to the issue of authority. It would appear that, like the poets of antiquity who both made mention of and concealed their own names, medieval writers' practices varied considerably and for a variety of reasons. Though "giving the author's name is first prohibited in Christian times" (writers are to guard against the sin of vanity), this prohibition does not seem to have ruled "always and everywhere" (Curtius 515).[42]

Regard for the author's name seems to have varied, and the degree to which anonymous texts or those identified by author were accepted or valued seems to have changed from the medieval to later periods. One view has it that, at least since the Middle Ages, determinations about the importance of an author's name could be related to the type of text or form of discourse under consideration. For example, it has been claimed that the author's name was of little or no significance for some texts (that is, "literary" works) but was crucial for others (that is, "scientific" works) during the medieval period. But around the seventeenth or eighteenth centuries this situation would seem to have reversed itself, and the author's identity may have come to give value to the former while no longer being required to establish the truth of the latter. From this perspective, the author-function would seem to have ceased to inform the one while taking what might seem to have been unprecedented importance for the other (Foucault, "What Is an Author?" 149).[43]

On the other hand, it could be argued that readers' interest in the biographies of the *auctores*, as well as the abundance of pseudo-authorial texts (texts attributed to but not in fact the work of their named *auctores*) in the Middle Ages, attest to the importance of the author's name for establishing a text's value.[44] Though it appears that it was not necessary to certify the authenticity of the name in relation to a particular text, the proliferation of such texts would indicate that the name of the author was of some, if not in some cases of considerable, consequence in the medieval era. Moreover, in some cultures (for example, France) authors of literary works seem to have begun to function as virtual "owners of the language" well before the postulated subsequent shift to authorial predominance, and to have monopolized forms of literary production through the end of the eighteenth century.[45]

Questions about author's lives, the relation of life to work, and the kind of authority attributable to an author's text prevailed (but in forms characteristic of their own epochs) well before the period when the author emerges as a personal, creative figure central to literary discussion. However, the more definitive establishment of the idea of the author as an individual creator, or the "individualization of creativity," in the eighteenth century finally brings "the name and personality of the author to the forefront" in the reception of works of art (Tomashevsky 48).[46]

Generally speaking, it appears that since around that time determinations about a work's meaning and value have been derived substantially from questions such as "from where does it come, who wrote it, when, and under what circumstances, or beginning with what design?" (Foucault, "What Is an Author?" 149). That is, knowledge about the author (as person, as creator) becomes crucial for understanding and interpreting a text; the author (as origin of meaning or source of expression) becomes pivotal for reading. As we know, this shift finds its most influential development in and is ultimately exemplified by the Romantic conception of the artist as the center of both the process through which works are produced and the means by which such works are to be judged. This is a shift in critical and cultural perspective that characterizes the expressive theory of art that comes to dominate thinking about literature in general and the place of the author in particular in the Romantic period (Abrams 22).

As we recall, the author or artist becomes the focus of attention for criticism of that era's literary production. For example, poetry is conceived of either as "the overflow, utterance or projection of the thought and feelings of the poet" or it "is defined in terms of the imaginative process which modifies and synthesizes the [poet's] images, thoughts, and feelings." That is, literature generally becomes "an index to [authorial] personality" (Abrams 22, 23). Moreover, when authors emerge as public figures in the eighteenth and nineteenth centuries, much interest is directed toward their personal identity, individuality, and life stories, which sometimes served their political enterprises or functioned as a means to uniting their diverse bodies of writing.[47]

Though the figure of the poet-hero may well have yielded to that of the professional writer in the late nineteenth century, and the author may have appeared to become a more distant and less personal figure, there have been significant and sometimes rapid shifts back and forth between these types of images and roles early in our own century (see, for example, Tomashevsky 53–55), as well as more recently. It may well be that our relative proximity to developments in twentieth-century fiction limits our ability to construct an adequately comprehensive overview of the more recent turns taken by "the author." One might, nonetheless, propose that the production characteristic of both modernist and postmodernist fiction (whether one views the latter as continuing or challenging the principles and practices of the former) has placed that critical figure in an ever more problematical position, and that alternate readings may well delineate it as an ever more perplexing figure.[48]

For example, one may read the poetics of modernist fiction as generally subverting the figure of the author as a unified, stable, or authoritative figure, if one takes that figure as equivalent to something like narrative voice, which many modernist texts fragment or disperse (see Hayman). Yet one might also argue that it is precisely from within such production that the twentieth-century figure of the "great modern writer" (for example, Proust, Joyce, Mann, or Woolf) becomes established or that the authors of such potentially subversive texts and "unique styles" (Jameson 112–13) found their own preeminent positions, and, consequently, forge the image of the modern author prevalent in Western culture.

Though one might read postmodernist fiction as further eroding the notion of the author as an authoritative source while also effecting an apparent return to representation and referentiality, to storytelling and the telling of history (see, for example, McHale 197–215; Hutcheon 105–23, 141–57), it seems that within some contexts of contemporary culture the figure of the author—that is, the real-world figure—has also acquired considerable authority. If one were to consider the recent phenomenon of the author as (media) personality, or superstar (see Franco "Memoria, narración y repetición," or "Narrador, autor, superestrella"; Rama 271–90; Viñas), or political (even presidential) figure (for example, Vaclav Havel or Vargas Llosa), it would become evident that the figure of the author makes quite a comeback. Indeed, the appearance of the author as a significant actor on the stage of contemporary culture may seem a return to another era's figure. The contemporary figures of the author—and especially those arising within the Spanish American context—may reveal the uncanny reclamation of a repressed figure, one whose problematical privilege and position may begin to be viewed more critically, especially in Spanish American fiction.

One is reminded, then, that there have been significant shifts in thinking about the author within the domains of both literary production and critical or theoretical speculation. Within the latter context, the review of modern critical theory above serves as a reminder about how the question of the author is dealt with in different ways (sometimes to propose corresponding, sometimes to present contradictory, notions) both in the successive and simultaneous developments that have so far shaped modern literary and critical theory. Within the literary framework, the poetics of fiction advanced by modern narrative seems both to challenge and to confirm thinking about the author that has been presupposed by the critical and theoretical models developed around it or by the cultural contexts in which narrative fiction and critical theory alike have become situated.

Thus, although critical notions about the author have moved away from the positions assumed by positivistic scholarship early in the century, the question of the author has remained—sometimes openly, sometimes under cover—within modern critical theory and practice. It has remained as a problematical question, much like the one posed in Borges's essay. The disparate responses to this question map out competing positions from which one might think about the author. In a sense, the question also becomes a question of critical and literary authority. For the question that gets asked in one way or another is not only "what do we, or ought we to, mean by the phrase 'the author'?" It is also "what kind of place or authority are we to grant to this person or figure, this concept or problem, for the reading of literary texts generally or for any text in particular?"

Some of these questions may, in addition, become entangled with questions of terminology. The critical vocabulary that appears to be available for the discussion of narrative fiction is problematical. But the perplexing features of this vocabulary are precisely what make it so instructive. For they reveal some of the practical difficulties of dealing with the concept of the author as one speculates about narrative poetics and the practice of literary criticism. While seeming to reinforce certain conceptual divisions, this vocabulary also reveals the complex and necessarily untidy state of thinking about the author. This vocabulary may well reflect some of the difficulties presented by contemporary narrative itself. Indeed, the poetics of the author characteristic of much of modern Spanish American fiction, for example, appears to exceed that vocabulary and suggests how such critical concepts and terminology, which attempt to account for what texts do, inevitably fall short of the literary practice about which they aim to talk.

Indeed, one might even say that the poetics of Spanish American fiction (and in this case, especially, the poetics of the author) goes beyond, if not also eclipses, a good many of the critical models and theoretical concepts proposed beyond its borders. In fact, I am sometimes tempted to argue that Spanish American fiction may be a good deal smarter (is, perhaps, even better "theory") than many of the literary concepts and critical theories advanced around it. This is one of the things that the readings of the texts that follow aim to demonstrate.

The question of vocabulary is a crucial one, especially as it often seems to confound as much as clarify the two principal concepts designated by the word author in modern critical discussion. We remember that the notion which has a long history and which may still appear to predominate among the various senses of the term is that of the author as a real person. The apparently more radical idea is that of the author as a textual figure. The same term has been used to designate either (or both) the empirical entity assumed to have written a text or the textual figure (that is, an abstraction or projection, a persona or personage) perceived or constructed through it. Though the place of the author-as-person may have become problematical within currents of modern critical theory, agreement about what is meant when one refers to the historical entity designated as an author would seem to be beyond major dispute.[49]

The use of the term author to designate not the person but an abstraction, textual figure, or authorial persona poses other problems. Indeed, the lack of any single term that might be opposed to the notion of the real author or author-person is a reminder that there is an array of terms and concepts that have become accepted for use in practical criticism. Such a lack perhaps points to the difficulties of fixing in language precisely what one means (or aims to mean) if, or when, one is not talking about the author-as-person. The proliferation of terms constitutes both a query and a set of provisional responses to questions about what it is that can be called an author if it is not the person responsible for a work's production, or perhaps also for its meaning. Difficulties arise here also because a good many terms designed to refer not to a person but to an abstraction nonetheless remain bound to the concept (that is, the author-as-person) from which this nonperson-author is to be distanced and distinguished.

For example, phrases such as "authorial image," "authorial voice," "authorial vision," "authorial presence," or "authorial personality," among others, hinge on synecdochical shifts that render visible, precisely in corporeal or psychological terms, the "personhood" of the figure that such phrases are also meant to circumvent for the practice of criticism. And, the deployment of the adjective "authorial" points out precisely to which "person" those parts pertain. Oddly, in privileging specific (and seemingly personal) characteristics, such phrases virtually reconstruct a figure upon whose inferred psychophysical existence the assertion of the author's inherently textual (rather than empirical) nature rests.

Thus, the terminology utilized to refer to and describe the author as a textual or discursive phenomenon is also anchored by references to apparently empirical, psychological, or existential attributes. However, some of these as well as other more general terms would draw attention to the apparent distance between themselves and the author-as-person. Among the potentially synonymous, or related, phrases available are, for instance, "authorial self," "authorial figure," "author-figure," "textualized author," "putative author," and "implied author." Though the referents for these terms, and others designed by critics to get around some of these terminological difficulties, can generally be distinguished from the empirical or biographical author, it is not always clear how they may (or may not) be distinguished from one another. And, as in the case of terms such as authorial image, authorial voice, or authorial vision, already noted, the compound labels inevitably situate their apparent referents in marked proximity to the figure of the empirical author, while also attempting to establish a considerable distance from such an entity.

For example, though well-known discussions of the implied author aim to differentiate this textual phenomenon from the author-as-real-person, its sense also remains bound to the more original and traditional figure. Though critics may find terms such as "second self," "persona," "mask," and "narrator" inadequate or inappropriate to represent the norms of "style," "tone," and "technique" for which the phrase implied author is chosen instead (Booth 73, 74–75), such a definition of what is essentially a textual effect ties that effect explicitly to the empirical author, who is seen as projecting a version or image of himself within his own text.[50] In addition, it could be argued that a phrase such as authorial voice both conjures up the image of the whole author, whose "voice" marks a virtual bodily presence within the text, and also reduces the author-person to an essential part or feature that finally stands for the whole.

However, one may be led to wonder about what precisely such a "voice" sounds like and how it might be "heard."[51] Likewise, one might wonder what such an authorial "image" looks like and how it might be "seen."[52] The voice that gets heard in or through a narrative text may be a voice that seems to speak directly (through what is literally stated by an authoritative narrator or character) or indirectly (through what is implied by or inferred from anecdotal, structural, or linguistic details). Such a voice seems to voice opinions, reveal attitudes, and take positions about issues explored within a particular text or about matters outside it. Similar claims could be made about the authorial image. The author is seen through what is said explicitly within or inferred from between the lines of the text, or through its structural organization and narrative techniques. And such textual evidence would often seem to lend support for talk about an authorial "personality" or "presence" within individual texts.

This recuperation of the author-as-person in critical tropes designed to move things to the realm of the purely verbal or textual may well be an indication of the hold that the figure of the empirical author, as well as some traditional concepts of authorship, have over modern readers. It may be most helpful, however, to view such notions not so much as entirely exclusive of or absolutely opposed to one another but rather as bound together in critical dialogue. Such dialogue, as suggested above, develops not only within the realm of critical or theoretical speculation about literary texts but also within the domain of literature itself. Moreover, such dialogue also conjoins those spheres of activity and speculation. The question of the author is a question that moves between, and keeps returning within, those seemingly distinct frames, as demonstrated by Spanish American fiction. Indeed, the poetics of fiction promoted by modern Spanish American narrative raises the question of the author in ways that both reaffirm and disavow the questions (and answers) set forth outside it.

To be sure, many developments in twentieth-century fiction generally (as suggested briefly above) seem to respond to this question through the production of texts that also appear to effect the author's disappearance or death. That is, it seems to be possible to talk about such a death or disappearance not only because some currents in critical theory have put "the author" into question and proposed models for reading texts as independent of the persons identified as their authors. This death or disappearance also seems to have been figured within works of fiction themselves—in works from which the figure of an authoritative author (often appearing, as it were, as the voice or eye empowering an omniscient narrator, that is, the author's traditional narrative surrogate) has been banished. For within such texts there seems to be no univocal or authoritative position from which the author-person's presence, ideas, or intentions might be inferred, or through which such a person or personality might be perceived.

Readers are likely to be familiar with such developments in the European and North American traditions. One thinks at least of Beckett, Calvino, Fowles, Grass, Joyce, Kundera, Robbe-Grillet, Sollers, and Woolf, among others, in the former context, and of Barth, Coover,

Faulkner, Hawkes, Nabokov, Pynchon, and Roth, for example, in the latter. And, some of the work of the best-known Spanish Americans—for example, Arenas, Borges, Cabrera Infante, Cortázar, Donoso, Fuentes, García Márquez, Puig, Sarduy, and Vargas Llosa—would seem in one way or another to exemplify, if not also radicalize, that trend within their own terrain. For example, one could consider, as will be done in some of the chapters that follow, some of the narrative strategies and thematic inquiries through which such texts dismantle the idea of a unitary discursive or scriptural subject that would govern their production or reception. One could find in their texts a good many experiments that seem either to presuppose or to produce such an authorial demise.

Yet, in their own inimitably adventurous fashion, Spanish American narratives also reveal that the question of the author remains, that both old and new questions about the concept and its figures can still be raised. For even in texts that foster its disappearance or death, the figure of the author may also be reclaimed. Spanish American fiction seems to divert one's gaze from this figure while (much like some of the texts of critical theory one might read around them) persistently drawing one's attention to it. And, as these texts turn one's reading to questions about the author, it seems that both the wrong and the right answers insinuate themselves as possible responses to them.

The poetics of the author proposed within contemporary Spanish American fiction might, in the end, be read as a poetics that resists one or another stable solution to a variety of questions that might be posed about the author. It challenges the possibility of answering in any unproblematical form the array of queries surrounding the author's many figures. Such resistance may turn one's reading around a dialogue of figures in a competition that cannot be settled. As suggested above, questions about the author seem to persist, in spite of the gestures aimed at confining them to one or another arena.

The readings that follow, then, are readings that in some way aim to restage this competition of figures and concepts as a dialogue among problematical critical notions and literary practices, and also to move, sometimes explicitly and sometimes implicitly, from the one to the other domain.[53] Perhaps the consideration of that virtual dialogue will have the possibility of informing not only the reading of texts from the Spanish American tradition but also the encounter with modern fiction as a whole.

2

In the Name of the Author

Reading Around Julio Cortázar's *Rayuela*

By virtue of the dramatic and apparently revolutionary turn it gives to Spanish American fiction, Julio Cortázar's *Rayuela* [*Hopscotch*] (1963) represents a critical moment in the development of contemporary Spanish American literature. Though one might now question whether this text is in fact as subversive as it seemed to earlier readers, it would be difficult to dispute *Rayuela*'s place within the modern Spanish American canon, or to challenge Cortázar's status within Spanish American literary culture.[1] I have chosen to begin with this title precisely because in *Rayuela*—a text noted for its radical questioning of some traditional notions about writing and reading narrative fiction—the author stands out as a concept to which Cortázar has paid considerable attention. The attention paid to that concept, and to different figures of the author, also appears to inform some of the unsettling directions taken by the novel as a whole.

The figure of the author appears to be a figure against which

Rayuela launches a deadly attack. At the same time, however, there is a vigorous defense mounted by various figures of the author in and around this novel. Rather than disappearing or dying altogether, the author remains in sight as a problematical figure one may be led to read now one way, now another. As one rereads *Rayuela*, then, one finds significant evidence of how contemporary Spanish American fiction begins to pose questions about the figure of the author and about the attribution of authorship. But one also finds evidence of how Cortázar's apparent ruminations about the author's authority leads as much to the affirmation as to the denegation of authorial privilege and position.

What I propose to do is read Cortázar's novel through the interrelation of authorial figures within it, and also through a sequence of interconnected and competing names (from outside as well as from within that text), which my reading will both construct and follow around it. *Rayuela* not only contains within its own pages but also draws into its orbit the names of familiar and foreign figures whose activity and identity inevitably return attention to the question of the author. In reading both the text to which the author's name is originally attached and others to which that name may be either overtly or obliquely connected, I also want to suggest how our own readings, as well as the texts upon which we focus, might address questions about the concept of the author. My reading of *Rayuela* may also appear to propose a program for reading "the author" that subsequent chapters will elaborate further. At the same time, however, it may also be that this reading of—and around—Cortázar's text merely performs the kind of reading that this complex concept and its competing figures requires, and which the readings of other texts pursue as well. Such a reading would anticipate, while also repeating, the meandering trajectory of the figures of the author to which *Rayuela* and, later, other Spanish American narratives draw attention.

Given *Rayuela*'s seminal position within the modern Spanish American canon, and also its initial position in this study, it seems somehow appropriate to begin to talk about this text by looking at one of its first (and famous) pages, where the question of the author begins to be raised by Cortázar. As we remember, in *Rayuela*'s famous "tablero de dirección" ["table of instructions"] (7/n.p.), the reader is told that Cortázar's novel is really two books ("A su manera este libro es muchos, pero sobre todo es dos libros" ["In its own way this book is many books, but above all it is two books"]; translation mine). The first of these books comprises the initial 56 of its 155 chapters (the other 99 are to be regarded as "prescindibles" ["expendable"]); the chapters of this book are to be read in the order in which they appear. The second book, on the other hand, is composed of all but one of the text's printed chapters and is to be read according to the numerical scheme provided on this page of instructions. (This scheme is what likens the second book or reading—perhaps even all of *Rayuela*—to the titular game of hopscotch; to read the novel according to that model would, in a sense, be to read it "à la rayuela."[2])

The now famous directive of the "tablero" not only defines the novel's possible modes of organization. It also identifies the reader as a "guest-author" who has the option to choose how the book will be read, how *Rayuela* will come into existence. (In some of the subsequent Sudamericana imprints of the original 1963 edition, moreover, that invitation was made explicit: "El lector queda invitado *a elegir* una de las dos posibilidades siguientes" ["The reader is invited *to choose* one of the following possibilities"; translation mine].[3]) The reading "à la rayuela" is proposed as a reading chosen, and thus authored, by the reader, whose primary role and privileged position are emphasized not only by this instructional preface but also by the literary theory explicitly proposed within *Rayuela*'s pages.[4] That theory, moreover, is presented as originating in a figure named "Morelli," a character-author whose poetics of the novel has generally been read as faithfully representing Cortázar's own position.[5] The tablero has usually been seen as the text through which the author-figure surrenders his place of preeminence in, as well as his authority over, the book that is read. It would appear that such a place and such authority are transferred directly to the reader through this opening text. The reader is virtually invited to choose the text he or she wishes to read, by eliminating or retaining the "expendable" chapters.

According to the tablero, then, the text read by *Rayuela*'s reader is a text over which the authorial subject figured by the introductory text (the figure that originally appears to be responsible for the novel) has no authority. However, this transfer of authority, one discovers, is quite problematical. Indeed, in the gesture by which an authorial figure seems to surrender his rights to the authorship of such a complex and self-conscious text as *Rayuela*, one can also read an affirmation of authorial privilege and position that is well suited for the novel in which it appears.

Given the tablero's position of anteriority and its instructional aims, it would appear as a text authored by a writer whose name is, or should be, Cortázar. This is the name of the empirical author whose virtual signature appears upon it. It is the name that identifies the author presumed to have written and signed the text and, as its original author and owner, to have staked a claim to it. The tablero's instructions, however, would seem to confound the author's place, if not the rights attached to his name, as it appears to open a path to the figure of another author.

The gesture by which the tablero's author-figure resituates the site of composition from one "side" of the text to the other (that is, from the place of the author to that of the novel's potential reader) is also a gesture that reasserts an original right of authorship. For it also asserts that the one who assigns that right to the reader authorizes himself (or is authorized by the place of authority he occupies) to make such an assignment, to propose how the novel might be read. Moreover, the freedom offered the reader-figure is the freedom to choose not among an unlimited number of texts (or readings) but between "two books" defined beforehand here in the tablero.

The choice put into operation will thus be a choice predefined and controlled—that is, already authored—by the figure who simultaneously proposes and implicitly proclaims his abdication of authority, his loss of control, over the novel. However, we recall that the table is a table (that is, a "board") of instructions, and that certain conditions would seem to obtain in a situation in which instructions are to be given. Obviously, one who gives instructions would appear to be situated in a position from which instructions or directions can in fact be given. Such a position may be a position that certifies prior mastery and, therefore, acknowledges the knowledge and privilege assumed to be held by the subject so situated in that position. But the position may itself also confer upon its occupant another (and perhaps new) kind of authority, an authority assumed not prior to but simultaneous with the positioning of that subject.[6]

In the tablero the authorial figure would seem both to surrender and to confer upon himself the authority (that is, the authorial function) that is apparently ceded to the reader. Thus the author-as-teacher/instructor affirms his own identity as author/master through a directive (the virtually pronounced invitation) that would put in the place of textual authority a figure (that is, the reader) who, nonetheless, still requires some kind of instruction. The reader may well be proposed as *Rayuela's* virtual author. However, the conferral of such an identity (and, moreover, the right to such a title or role) is postulated, it must be remembered, by a figure whose own authoritative image is reinscribed within the text at precisely the moment when his authorial position appears to be surrendered.[7]

The instruction table proposes, then, a theory of reading that is at the same time a theory of authorship. But such authorship is of a precarious sort, since the freedom granted the reader is a dubious freedom: the powers surrendered by the author, it seems, are the very powers that he also retains and keeps from his reader. Moreover, the place of the reader-as-author is explicitly legitimized by the figure whose apparent anteriority, and thus authority, would situate the reader as a belated author. That reader-author's late arrival places him in a somewhat equivocal position: he who comes after the text (in a position posterior to authorial activity) is authorized to move to a place somewhere ahead of it—to a position of anteriority from which one might author, as it were, Rayuela's reading.

One sees then that the reader, posited as a free agent, is the guest of a host whose apparent invitation sets up not so much a transfer of privilege and power as a dialectic of authority and authorship through which the authorial subject posited by the tablero assumes a somewhat deceptive position. One can, of course, read this relation between authorial and readerly figures as a partnership—a theoretical partnership that could be read as both foreshadowing and reiterating similar proposals from within and beyond Spanish American borders. That is, here in Rayuela of 1963 the proposal of this problematical relation between those figures precedes—anticipating in a decidedly critical fashion—modern critical theory's more recent notions about the figures of the reader and the author. (In some sense, one could argue that Cortázar's text, like a good many by Borges before him, is yet another of the precursors of, among others, the Barthes and Foucault essays discussed in chapter one. Borges is, of course, the Spanish American author to whom both European and North American critics and writers have often found it instructive to turn their gaze for considering these sorts of critical notions.[8])

This partnership prefigures (and, for some readers, might appear to put into practice) the theories of reading and authorship set forth in Rayuela's own pages.[9] Oddly, this partnership, which both affirms and disavows the notion of a singular and original author, is proposed by still another (and apparently secondary) authorial figure. This figure, who is encountered only fleetingly and, yet, everywhere in the novel, is the character-author named Morelli. It is he who proposes within its body a set of literary theories often identified with the practice of Cortázar's novel. But his is also a problematical role, which is likewise prefigured here in *Rayuela*'s tablero.

Though the name "Morelli" designates a fictional entity in the novel, his presence is established not by anything he says or does within its narrative chapters, but by what he has supposedly written and what gets repeated and discussed by some of *Rayuela*'s own characters. Readers familiar with Cortázar's novel will recall how its narrative structure and story situate Morelli in both marginal and central positions. As we remember, *Rayuela* is composed of three sections. Chapters 1–36, headed by the phrase "Del lado de allá" ["From the Other Side"], and chapters 37–56, headed by "Del lado de acá" ["From This Side"], comprise what has generally been called its narrative, which is set in Paris and Buenos Aires of the 1950s. The oscillating narration in first and third person gives an account of the metaphysical and erotic "searches" undertaken or lived by Horacio Oliveira, the protagonist, first in Paris ("Del lado de allá") and then in Buenos Aires ("Del lado de acá"). Chapters 57–155, headed by the phrase "De otros lados" ["From Other Sides" (translation mine)], beneath which one finds the significant (though also problematically parenthesized) disclaimer "Capítulos prescindibles" ["Expendable Chapters"], contain a heterogeneous group of texts. Some of them relate episodes in the story of Oliveira, some present Morelli's literary thoughts and theories, and others appear as fragments extracted from the writings of other authors and incorporated into Morelli's notebooks (and Cortázar's novel).[10]

Morelli is an author whose works have been read, revered, and recovered by Oliveira and his bohemian Parisian circle of friends. His name circulates within the text mainly as a sign of authorship. It virtually becomes a place where authorial activity is figured and through which the identity of the author may appear to be revealed, especially when this author is materialized as a personal figure in the story. But the mention of the name Morelli also places within the text a figure whose identity that name would suspend as much as solidify. In fact, Morelli materializes only briefly as a fictional character. Initially he is merely "un viejo" ["an old man"] injured in an accident witnessed by Oliveira (chapter 22); later he is identified as the person-author named Morelli, whom Oliveira and his friend Etienne go to visit in the hospital after his accident (chapter 154).[11] There, the coincidence of identities (that of the initially unidentified "viejo" and that of the living author formerly figured only through the writings that bear his name) is revealed simultaneously to the characters and the readers of *Rayuela*.

This discovery gives an illusory fullness to an authorial figure whose presence is otherwise signaled not so much through the materialization of a personal character within the fiction as through the figuration of a writing subject constituted through a collection of texts that are read in the novel. We remember that Morelli's literary theories are not set forth as a textually unified or integrated body of principles, through which an illusion of authorial unity and presence might be created. They are instead dispersed throughout the novel's "expendable" chapters, and therefore interspersed within part of its narrative. (In a reading "à la rayuela" the chapters containing Morelli's literary theories are grouped with the chapters relating the Parisian narrative. Other of Morelli's heterogeneous notes and textual clippings are intercalated throughout the entire narrative from their "exterior" site in "De otros lados.")

The scattered notes figure Morelli as a fragmented, if not altogether absent, author-theorist—as an author who has no single or stable place within the text. The presentation of the "viejo" under the name Morelli restores the image of the whole author, while producing a figure whose days appear to be numbered. Indeed, one might argue that the introduction of Morelli into the narrative as a character-person at the very moment when, it is suggested, he appears to be about to die, can be read as an appropriate, even though anticipatory, figuration of the "death of an author." (After leaving the hospital, Etienne says to Oliveira: "En el fondo es un encuentro póstumo, días más o menos" ["When you come right down to it, it was a posthumous meeting, a question of days"] [628/558].)[12] The absence already marked by the texts and theories he has supposedly composed, and which have been scattered throughout the novel (by another and apparently more primary author), are potentially literalized by a text that in so many other ways (as the tablero recalls) works to keep the figure of the author alive.

Indeed, Morelli the character-author, along with Morelli the name, seems to turn one's gaze to the scene of its imminent death and to expose both the appearance and disappearance of the name Cortázar. This last name is of course the name of the empirical author who has suggested the fictional character's impending death. It is also the name given to the textualized figure who survives the fiction of that fabricated author's demise. Morelli—whose role has been read as that of the literary "master absent from Hispanic culture in general" and here invented by Cortázar as a "mythical 'good-father' author" (Mac Adam, *Modern Latin American Narratives* 54), or as that of the "apocryphal author" or "tacit writer who works behind every major work" (Ortega 45), or as a "producto de las citas" ["product of citation"] and a "lugar de cruce de citas" ["point of citational crossings"] (Sarlo 943)—is brought to life, while also being readied for death, at the hands of the figure whose role as author, or father-figure, derives some of its authority from the demise of another figure (that is, Morelli) who may otherwise appear to usurp the author's place. The name of the one (Morelli) thus competes with the name of the other (Cortázar) for the place of authorial privilege in this text. The name of the one or the other becomes a place of competition between different figures of the author.

Yet the figure who is left to die is revived as a textual authority, within the other fictional characters' reading and discussion of his texts as well as through the mere mention of his name. For instance, in a well-known key chapter (chapter 99), Oliveira and his Parisian group engage in a detailed discussion of Morelli's theories, which they have read, it seems, from the very same texts presented to the readers of *Rayuela*. This discussion—which brings Morelli back to textual life perhaps more than his appearance as a "person" in the hospital— takes place in Morelli's apartment, to which Morelli himself has given them the key (chapter 154). There, in the home of this author who has been ejected from his own place by an accident authored by another, they find his notebooks—original texts from which, presumably, Morelli's contributions to Cortázar's novel have been made.

Morelli's place is filled with his readers' rephrasings of his ideas about literature and language. His writings, at once originals and copies and collected in notebooks he himself has supposedly composed, are thus not only fragmented and scattered in the "Capítulos prescindibles" and throughout the reading "à la rayuela." They are also mediated by a group of readers who, in their discussions, would revise as well as review the author's theories. These texts belong to an author whose expendable work, placed as Morelli's materials and the characters' key discussion of his theories are in *Rayuela*'s margins (that is, in its "capítulos prescindibles"), is, of course, essential for what appears to be Cortázar's revolutionary literary project. Thus the discovery of the old man's name is the recovery of the name of an original, but also unconventional, author whose position in *Rayuela* is at best equivocal.

Morelli's name is both at the center and on the edges of things in the novel. His name appears to mark the place of an original author but also to identify the work of an author whose writing repeats, and is thus contingent upon, the work of others. In that he would figure the activity of his own literary father (Cortázar), whose attempt to propose a new beginning for the work of modern writers is materialized by the author named Morelli, Morelli (as both name and fictional entity) figures the critical nature of *Rayuela's* confounding authorial practice and theory.[13]

Morelli is the author-reader and master-father invented by Cortázar, who is himself identifiable in such terms. That is, the name Cortázar would seem to designate a figure who is at once a belated reader of Morelli's work (as well as the work of other authors, who are also read by this fictional author) and a writer who makes that work appear to precede his own. The name of the one appears as both prior and posterior to that of the other; the name of the one is both subordinated to and supported by the name of the other. The author's place would seem to accommodate the figure of the one or the other author.

Rayuela has frequently been read as presenting Cortázar's own theories about language and literature in general and the novel in particular.[14] In such readings, the name Morelli would appear to cover the name Cortázar, the name of the biographical author whose ghostly presence in the figure of the textualized author is also called forth by that name (that is, "Cortázar"). However, the name Morelli can also be read as revealing, rather than concealing, the name of the other author. As noted above, it has been suggested that *Rayuela* may well be the novel on which Morelli himself is working within the fiction and in which he tries to work out, if not put into practice successfully, the literary theories proposed in its pages.

However, if one identifies Morelli as the "source" of *Rayuela* itself (that is, as the source of both its fictional narrative and its literary theories), one posits for him a position literally equal, if not also superior, to that of Cortázar. The position held by the author (that is, both the biographical figure and the textualized subject), who is referred to through the name Cortázar, then becomes a crowded place indeed—a place in which the name Morelli is superimposed on (while supplementing and replacing) that of both the empirical author and the authorial subject figured by *Rayuela.* The name Morelli is positioned in something of a metaphorical relation to the name Cortázar, which all but jumps out from behind the transparency of Morelli's figure. (Moreover, if one accepts Cortázar's own identification of this figure as a double for the novel's protagonist, Oliveira, whom some have read as the novel's first-person narrator-author and who would thereby serve as but another cover for Cortázar, such an identification would further destabilize the frame of authorship, and the apparent singularity of any authorial name or place, in this text.[15]) Each of these names remains identical to itself, but also becomes identified with the name of the other.

That the name Morelli is bound to the name Cortázar and that a good many readers have found it virtually impossible to talk about *Rayuela* without connecting the two is not surprising.[16] Some of these connections go so far as to join—sometimes graphically—the two. When these names are written together to form the name of another author (that is, "Cortázar-Morelli" or "Morelli-Cortázar"), the doubled or divided name reveals what the name of one—if not both—of these figures already displays. When the names Cortázar and Morelli are bound together, two significantly specular figures emerge in the place of a single author. (Indeed, if one were to read the hyphen between the two names quite literally, respecting its etymological, original meaning as a sign written below two consecutive letters to indicate that they belong to the same word, the two names would have to be read as one.)

In this reunion of original authors, however, each also becomes the offspring of the other, each appears as a figure of anteriority and belatedness with respect to the other. Moreover, the figure of the two composite authors (or the composite figure of a single author) is irreducible to either of its proper names—though one of them, one might argue, is supposed to refer to a primary author who begets or creates the novel.[17] Though, theoretically at least, Morelli may be seen to have a certain priority, from a perspective outside the text, his name bears no more than the appearance of a term that designates a character or copy. Yet it is precisely through such a secondary figure that the activity of the original author—and perhaps the problem of authorship itself—becomes inscribed with such vigor in *Rayuela*.

How, then, is one to read, or read through, the name of one or the other author? The name of the one not only leads to the name of the other; each seems ready to reveal and to hide the names of a variety of other authors. Indeed, the question of reading the author's name is rendered all the more significant here because, within the text of the novel, Morelli's name is a name that also marks the place where the work of other authors may be read. The "morelliana" (that is, the materials from Morelli's notebooks, presented throughout the expendable chapters), as we recall, incorporate fragments of writing attached to and signed with the names of other authors.[18] "Morelli" virtually hides those other names, while also becoming identified as but the name of the reader of those other authors, whose writings become identified with, even absorbed into, the figures of the author in Rayuela.

"Morelli" seems to fix in place (that is, within the text of Rayuela) the name of the author. But it also opens a space for the circulation of such a name and the figures (or names) of the author that seem to compete around it. The meaning of such a name would thus seem to arise from its relation to other such names and to the name Cortázar. However, one might argue that to get at the meaning of Morelli one ought to return to Cortázar, perhaps so as to consider other figures from which his own appearance or identity might seem to be derived or upon which he may have aimed to model his character.

Though one discovers that the name Morelli appears to have been chosen by Cortázar without any explicitly formulated authorial design, as one tries to situate and read its significance this name comes to resonate between one text, one author, and another.[19] Indeed, one of the possible choices of nominal precursors through which to read Cortázar's Morelli leads to a name that refigures and repeats itself, as it moves to other texts and authors, without abandoning Cortázar or Rayuela. Moreover, the name Morelli within one or another context finally suggests that the name of one author may necessarily lead to the name of another. The author's proper name, perhaps even an authorial signature, seems always ready to embody—while also being unable to contain completely—both a critique and a consolidation of authorial originality and authority.[20]

As we wander a bit with the name Morelli, hopscotching, as it were, to other names and signatures potentially hidden under as well as uncovered by it, we come across another problematical figure of the author—in fact, another figure named Morelli. Interestingly enough, it could appear that Cortázar's Morelli is prefigured by this other namesake who has become identified with the problem of authorship, and in whose name one might again raise the question of the author. The other Morelli to whom I refer is, of course, Giovanni Morelli (1816–91), the art historian known as the father of modern connoisseurship

and the originator of the "Morelli-method," once considered a revolutionary theory of artistic attribution.[21] Put forth in the late nineteenth
century, Morelli's theory presented a theory for establishing the authorship of the work of art; it proposed a method for distinguishing an
original painting from its copies. Purported to be a scientific method
of attribution, Morelli's method provided a potentially authoritative
return to the figure of the artistic author.[22]

Essentially, Morelli proposed that the artist's identity (and thus,
also, the work's authenticity—its status as an original) could be determined by examining the secondary or little noticed, and thus seemingly insignificant, details in a particular painting (for example, finger-
nails, hands, or ear lobes), instead of by reading its general patterns or
overall design. The proper application of the method would lead to
the restoration of the original artist's name in the case of incorrect
attribution, and to the certification of a signature's authenticity in the
case of unverified authorship. Morelli's theory was, in a way, a theory
of signatures, of how artists sign their works through seemingly insignificant details. Such details, he proposed, are the sites through which
a painting's true origins (that is, the singular identity of the original
artist) are revealed. For it is there, in the "insignificant detail" (which,
of course, is elevated to a position of the greatest significance by
Morelli's method), that the artist virtually gives himself away.[23]

This theory was not only a theory of what constitutes evidence of
originality and authenticity—that is, a theory of authorship. It was also
a theory of reading—a theory of how to read such evidence, how to
read through the work to its singular, original author. But the author of
this theory of artistic authorship was also a figure who played with the
authorship of his own theory. Indeed, he would appear to have defied
his readers to read the name of the author (that is, his own name)
correctly. For Morelli originally attempted to obscure the origins of his
theory by concealing his name beneath an alias, a false signature
which, nonetheless, also gave away its author's identity. When he first
published this work as a German translation of "original" Russian
writings (1870s–1880s), he used the name Ivan Lermolieff, which is, if
one reads it correctly, a partial anagram of Giovanni Morelli.[24] (Moreover, the name of the "translator" of Lermolieff's writing is Johannes
Schwarze—another alias of Morelli, who was fluent in German. This
name, as one might expect, is but another play on "Morelli": "Giovanni," "Johannes," "John"; "Morelli"/moro, "Schwarze," "Black".)

Morelli's name, as well as his identity as an author, is thus both veiled and revealed by a succession of signatures that reinscribe, while also appearing to erase, evidence of original authorial activity. Morelli's "translated" work is an original designed to pass itself off as an authentic copy. This copy is a counterfeit whose originality is retroactively authenticated through the revelation of its author's name, which remains attached to, if not also completely obscured by, the name of another. Morelli signs his own name by signing or using the names of others, other names ("Lermolieff," "Schwarze") that both cover and copy his own. In the case of the name Morelli, then, the author of a theory that proposed a method for uncovering the name, the identity, of the original artist signs his work with a name that both displaces and consolidates the place of its own author and origins.

One can read Morelli's name as situated within complex relations of affiliation not only with the other names he would author as substitutes for his own, but also with those of established figures in art history. The Morelli-method, it is said, was proposed (like any new theory or method, perhaps) as an unconventional, revolutionary turn against the conventional theory and practice of his own discipline. Moreover, it appears that Morelli was not unconcerned with the issue of priority or originality within the discipline of art history. It has been suggested that he was so concerned to establish his own originality and authority that he failed to attribute to one or more of his colleagues their rightful authorship of parts of his own "original" theory.[25]

Morelli's theory of artistic authorship was a theory that established his own place as the father, or author, of a new critical practice. It thus challenged the authority of the traditional figures whose places of paternal privilege he usurped, but from which he himself could also be displaced later.[26] Within the history of art history, then, the name Morelli, the name of the father of connoisseurship, has become the name of an equivocal figure of authority. The figure of Morelli thus attaches itself to the images of many other authors, and the name Morelli continues to raise a variety of questions about the attribution of authorship.

Indeed, in Morelli's name one can read not just the literally affiliated figures of his namesake (or vice versa). Morelli also figures as the virtual father of another self-consciously affiliated author whose name as the "father of psychoanalysis" has clearly eclipsed the importance of that of the art historian. I refer, of course, to Freud, who, it turns out, in his well-known reading of Michelangelo's Moses ("The Moses of Michelangelo"), cites directly the name Morelli and the method of attribution from which Morelli's fame was derived.[27] There, Freud draws attention not only to the similarity between Morelli's "method of inquiry" and the "technique of psychoanalysis." He also remarks upon the pseudonymous nature of Morelli's "original" signature and his own pleasure at learning of the Italian master's "concealed" but true identity (Freud 91–92).

Indeed, in his rereading of Michelangelo's Moses, Freud appears not only to draw openly on Morelli's method; he seems to copy surreptitiously the method for producing his signature as well. First, Freud's method for discerning how the Moses figure's pose should be read rests upon a reading of the insignificant details or clues to its composition. Freud's reading of those details leads back to the scene and psychological state immediately preceding the moment inscribed in the statue's pose to expose Michelangelo's supposedly intended original design. The homologous relation between the "insignificant detail" and an artistic origin (that is, either authorial identity or artistic psychology) in the methods of connoisseurship and psychoanalysis bring the figures of Morelli and Freud into virtual contact with one another. (This contact, as suggested below, may have proved characteristically problematical for the latter.)

Given the methodological similarities of the Morelli and Freud methods for reading artistic works, as well as Freud's acknowledgment of Morelli's prior influence, one might be tempted to call this method the Morelli-Freud, or the Freud-Morelli, method. From this perspective, the identification of the method with only the one or the other author (or perhaps even with the two of them as a composite author) might seem an inaccurate attribution of authorship or authority. (In fact, a very suggestive reading of Morelli, Freud, and Sherlock Holmes has juxtaposed their methods as evidence not of singular originality but, rather, of a shared epistemology—as evidence of the emergence of an epistemological paradigm [that of the "conjectural method"] at the end of the nineteenth century.[28])

The intimate connection between Morelli's and Freud's methods, it has been conjectured, may also explain the homologous relation of their (real or virtual) signatures. For, when originally published in Imago in 1914, Freud's essay on Michelangelo appeared as an anonymous— an unsigned—article (Freud 80). Speculation about Freud's desire for anonymity assumes, as one might expect, problems with the idea of authorial filiation. It has been speculated that his pose of anonymity may have merely been imitative of Morelli's "taste for concealed authorship" (Ginzburg 85); or it may have been a filial gesture of "unconscious rivalry with Morelli" (Wollheim 210); or it could be read as Freud's way of dismantling a "theological conception of art" through which one presumes that the discovery of the author's (that is, the father's) name constitutes accurate, and thus appropriate, access to the identity and meaning of the artistic work (Kofman 19–20).[29]

The explanation of this maneuver itself remains, of course, in the realm of conjecture, along with the answer to a question such as "who is the original or real author?" What one reads in this circulation of authorial names and signatures, as well as from the models of authorship those signatures and names (or their authors and referents) propose, are the alternately revealing and obfuscating effects that the appearance (or disappearance) of the name of the author may have. The name of the author—an apparently significant detail—also becomes a place of insignificance. But it is an insignificance that is nonetheless likely to be invested with a great deal of meaning. Indeed, the name becomes a place where significance and insignificance both meet and compete. In naming the author, as we are aware by now, one is likely to mean a number of things at once.

For example, we are yet pushed to ask, as we return again to *Rayuela*, what did Cortázar mean by the name Morelli? Is Cortázar's Morelli meant to figure the Morelli from art history, or does it refer perhaps to an author or character we have not yet considered (for example, most obviously, Borges's Morell, or Bioy Casares's Morel, or Wells's Moreau, or Poe's Morella, or, more obliquely, Macedonio Fernández; see notes 13, 19)? And, if it is meant to figure the art historian, for example, what, for Cortázar, would have been significant about such a figure? What would its meaning have been for him?

If one aims to discover the significance of this name, one takes up the text's (or the name's) invitation to read the name as meaningful rather than as arbitrary. One discovers that the name opens up a determined field of meanings but that the space of that field and its parameters are, as has been seen here, rather wide. The author's name seems to efface itself behind the names of its substitutes (that is, Morelli and his namesakes), but also seems to keep coming back from around or behind those other names. One discovers that the significance of this name would lie as much in its apparent arbitrariness as in its possible determined meanings. If, on the other hand, one does not presume that the name Morelli has some particular (and perhaps original) significance—that is, if one views the name or the figure of

Morelli as insignificant, the name Cortázar becomes a convenient but confounding nominal cover. The name of the author would thus signify an author distanced from original or final meaning. It would appear to figure an author of unfixed significance.

What is significant is that either reading allows one to move from "Cortázar" to "Morelli" (and even to "Freud" and others), and back again, as one attempts to read *Rayuela*, or the names it proposes, properly. The move between the names Morelli and Cortázar appears to be an unavoidable move; each name provokes a shift to the other. The shift from one way of reading their names to another, and therefore from one theory of authorship or reading to another, is critical in reading *Rayuela*. Indeed, reading (or, rather, rereading) *Rayuela* seems to mean precisely that—reading between competing models of reading the figure of the author.

If this reading suggests that Cortázar is, in some way, not the (only) name of the author of *Rayuela*, it is because the author's name may well become a sign of instability, a sign of secondariness and subordination as well as of originality and authority. Such a sense of things would of course run counter to traditional notions about what the name of the author signifies and where it ought to lead in reading literary texts. Moreover, as one reads further around *Rayuela*, the author's name retains its position of instability while also recovering considerable authority. Such a problematical position, which emerges initially from within *Rayuela*, is, interestingly enough, underscored as well by another text that may seem to establish definitively *Rayuela*'s authoritative and stable authorial beginnings. I refer to the 1983 *Cuaderno de bitácora de "Rayuela,"* published under the names of both Cortázar and Ana María Barrenechea, one of the author's best-known readers.

The logbook, which contains the author's original plans for his novel, purports to reauthor, in a way, the reading of *Rayuela*, the process of whose authorship by Cortázar the logbook would finally appear to reveal. But, appropriately enough, the juxtaposition of the names Cortázar and Barrenechea situates the two as complementary, if not also competing, author-figures. These figures meet and compete not only on the text's cover and title page, where they are explicitly united, but also throughout the book's pages, where they are implicitly joined in both Barrenechea's introductory study and Cortázar's personal notes. The name of the one may be read as vying with the name of the other for the primary position of authority in the *Cuaderno*, and by extension, perhaps, around *Rayuela*.

Published by Sudamericana exactly twenty years after *Rayuela*, the *Cuaderno de bitácora de "Rayuela"* is a heterogeneous text.[30] It combines the variegated writings of both Cortázar and Barrenechea. In introducing Cortázar's notebook pages, Barrenechea also introduces the problem of textual priority and authority, as she reviews, first, the tenets of genetic criticism she seeks to follow and, second, the relationship between Cortázar's notebook and his novel ("Estudio preliminar"). Within that preliminary essay, Barrenechea's introduction of Cortázar's original notebook pages takes a secondary position to the discussion of genetic criticism. This discussion legitimizes in general terms the attention given to "pre-textos" ["pre-texts"] such as Cortázar's logbook; it authorizes, in particular, her undertaking in the publication of the *Cuaderno* and her reading of its originary texts.

Barrenechea's presentation of the logbook grants a place of central importance to Cortázar's preliminary notes and aims to counter other readings that would subordinate the author's original ideas to the text that comes after them. Barrenechea confers upon the logbook an independent status and authority by which its comments are virtually elevated to a status equal to that of the novel that would otherwise supersede them. In the face of the authoritative, completed text that succeeds the originary notes, the "pre-textos" are restored by Barrenechea to their former position of authority. As set up by Barrenechea, the relation between the author's notes and the completed text both undermines and underwrites the privileged status of the one with respect to the other.

Barrenechea's reading of *Rayuela* through the logbook is presented as a rereading of the novel through the notes that reveal both the author's original dialogue with his fictional work and the process of writing and reading through which it was composed. Following Cortázar, Barrenechea proposes to read *Rayuela* as a dialogue between text and pre-texts. Through the reading now authorized by the logbook and the textual organization it allows Barrenechea to author, this dialogue also upends the apparently primary or secondary status of the one set of texts in relation to the other. Moreover, the configuration of the various pre-texts and her discussion of the relationships among them raise related questions of textual priority and privilege. They are questions that Barrenechea's reading seeks to address and that Cortázar, before her, considered.[31]

The origins of this book are to be found, it seems, in the writing of not one but (at least) two figures, whose names and work have been tied together for many years. Barrenechea, entrusted with the logbook of which she is made proprietor by its original author and owner, assumes theoretical, as well as editorial, responsibility for Cortázar's writings. The work of one figure becomes the support for the writing of another; the writing of the one becomes the pretext for the work of the other. Each is proprietor of the text to which his or her name is attached. Yet each name, bound to the name of the other, puts into question individual rights of ownership and authority. Such are the relationships that have been made problematical by these authors individually in other texts and, here, together in the *Cuaderno.*

Barrenechea's name has long been connected to that of Cortázar (her readings of *Rayuela* are seminal; she is regarded as one of Cortázar's most important readers). Here in the logbook that connection is literalized in an overt fashion. As noted above, the logbook was published under the virtual signatures of both Cortázar and Barrenechea, under the auspices of the author and one of his most accomplished readers. Barrenechea appears all at once as a reader who edits, a copier who compiles, and a commentator who authors the text of another author.

The responsibilities attached to the different roles assumed by Barrenechea (the roles of a modern *scriptor, editor, compilator,* and *commentator*) combine within the performance of a single figure. They consolidate her authority and situate her as a competitor of Cortázar, the original author, even though she seems to be a secondary figure. Indeed, under the guise of a copier-compiler-commentator-editor, Barrenechea assumes a central, authoritative role in the *Cuaderno.* As she reads she also rewrites and organizes, much like the author she takes as her critical object. As she restores Cortázar's notes, and thus his retroactively recognized original activity, to a privileged position for the reading of *Rayuela,* her own activity seems to become more, rather than less, like that of an author—perhaps like that of a modern *auctor.*

In fact, Barrenechea's name appears on the text as the signature of Cortázar's coauthor, rather than as the signature of an editor or compiler of Cortázar's texts. Her name is virtually signed with the name Cortázar and appears in the place reserved for the name of the primary, and original, author. In the *Cuaderno de bitácora de "Rayuela"* the name of the author thus appears as a doubled or divided name, one that shifts the responsibility of authorship from one to another of the figures to which it would refer. The juxtaposition of names puts the work of the two authors on an apparently equal footing while also seeming to allow for the priority of one (Cortázar) over the other (Barrenechea). The author named by this text, it is tempting to suggest, is a composite figure, a figure designed by the texts of one and another author: Cortázar-Barrenechea or Barrenechea-Cortázar.[32]

These names, and the figures they conjure up, are in one sense clearly distinguishable. The name of the author and the name of the critic refer to distinct subjects and discursive situations, and to different moments of signature. But in the publication of the *Cuaderno* and the reading produced by Barrenechea, who moves back and forth among Cortázar's texts as well as between her own comments and his writing, these names also come to identify the writing of the one with that of the other. Barrenechea, a formidable critic and trusted friend of the empirical author, inscribes her own critical presence within the texts of Cortázar. His writing is not only reshaped by her readings but also reorganized by her editing. The relation between their names suggests the uncertain state of authorship throughout the *Cuaderno de bitácora de "Rayuela."* As in the novel whose origins the *Cuaderno* purports to establish authoritatively and whose authorship it would doubly certify, the name of the author can be read here as a destabilizing sign rather than as an absolute marker of authorial singularity, priority, or originality.

In rereading *Rayuela* through the *Cuaderno*, then, one may place the author's name in a position that would allow for the attribution of the text's ownership either to its original author or to one of its readers. (The latter move is, as we recall, apparently proposed by the tablero.) However, the idea of unequivocal authority over or ownership of the text is also precisely what the activities of Cortázar's renowned critical reader attenuate. The author's name, which here shifts between naming the authorial subject at the moment of writing and identifying the texts to which that name has become attached and through which its meaning is partially established, is reauthored as well as reread by Barrenechea.

That Cortázar is a name of distinction his writing and Barrenechea's readings would confirm; that this name is the name of the author of *Rayuela* the text's authorial signature would underscore. But, that this name is the single name that authorizes *Rayuela* or one's reading of it, or that this name is the only name that creates a place for the author, is open to question. Indeed, our wandering to the figure of Barrenechea, whose name circulates with that of Cortázar around the text of *Rayuela*, would situate the name of the author in an unstable position. And the leap to the name Morelli (and from "Morelli" to "Freud," and back again to "Cortázar") would position the author's name so that it would be as ready to defend its authoritative place as to surrender that place to the authority of another author.

Such wanderings and leaps seem to mobilize each name, each place, of the author. Yet, this mobilization of the authorial proper name, and consequently the destabilization of the place given to the author, also reinvest such a name and such a place with considerable authority. The chain of names that leads away from Cortázar, and for which *Rayuela* unwittingly opens the way, also returns the author's name to a place of privilege. The shift from one name to the other may well intensify rather than attenuate the authority of such a name. The sharing of names of the author confers upon each of the author's figures a status that in one sense or another is both authoritative and authorial. As one reads, or reads around, *Rayuela*, then, the figure of the author seems to reclaim (if not retain) its own privilege under the names of a number of authors.

When one reads this text as originating with the writing of an authorial subject named Cortázar, or considers its connections to the work of a fictional author-figure named Morelli or his possible namesakes, or reads it as tied to the activities of a critic named Barrenechea, one is led around *Rayuela* and the questions it raises about the author's identity and activity. Such questions concern the meaning of the author's name or the nature of authorial rights and responsibilities, how authorial figures become endowed with authority, or how texts come to be read as authoritative, and so on. These are questions familiar and foreign to both modern criticism and to Spanish American fiction, where they continue to be debated rather than settled. The succeeding chapters will explore further how Spanish American narratives not only offer a variety of possible answers but also reframe and even complicate the way those questions get asked.

3

Gestures of Authorship
Lying to Tell the Truth in Elena Poniatowska's
Hasta no verte Jesús mío

How does one read a text that lies? How can one read a text that, somehow, persuades one to believe what it says, though one suspects that it doesn't really tell the whole truth? Documentary fiction—and especially the Spanish American "novela testimonial" (the testimonial novel)—raises these familiar questions.[1] They are questions that may well suggest themselves as one reads any work of fiction; they are also questions that, given some recent thinking about literature, one is likely to disregard. Oddly, the novela testimonial would suggest that one reconsider some of these queries, and see them perhaps as meaningful rather than as marginal issues toward which one's vision might yet be turned. Moreover, in raising the question of how texts tell the truth (or not), this current in contemporary Spanish American literature leads us to look once again at the figure of the author. And what one sees is a revitalized figure that yet claims a critical position of some significance.

Though this documentary trend has in some ways established its distance from texts thought to be typical of Spanish American new narrative, the novela testimonial also reveals that it has some surprising affinities with the seemingly more literary focus of boom and post-boom fiction, and with the kind of speculation that such writing has raised about traditional literary conventions and characters.[2] In particular, the testimonial novel seems to make it difficult, if not impossible, to talk about the author as either an original or privileged figure. Yet, it also reaffirms the importance of the author's role, as it redefines that role by resituating the author's investigative and editorial, textual and testimonial, responsibilities.

To talk about the testimonial novel, and the activity or identity of its authors, is to talk about a variety of testimonies that would aim to establish such a text's truth. That testimony is given not only within the novel itself, but also around it and in its borders. However, inasmuch as the novela testimonial seems to testify to the truth of what it tells through the language of literature, a good many questions may be raised about how such a text may become accepted (or not) as truthful, and about how the figure of the author associated with it may come to exercise any authority at all.

Elena Poniatowska's *Hasta no verte Jesús mío* [Until I See You Again My Lord; translation mine] (1969) addresses such questions not only through what its author says about and does with the documentary materials that comprise the text.[3] Its narrator-protagonist also problematizes such matters (unwittingly, it seems) within the narrative itself. Poniatowska's novel may well serve as an instructive example of how the route to a verifiable referent or to demonstrable veracity (apparently plotted out by the testimonial novel) is also a reflexive route that turns any reading away from as much as toward so-called reality.[4] It also suggests ways in which the figure of the author associated with such a work becomes visible (while also appearing to efface itself) as a figure of renewed authority.

That documentary or testimonial novels are inherently duplicitous, in the way that narrative literature is itself always double or divided, may well be evident. That such texts may somehow take note of their own discursive duplicity (in a sense, of their own lies) is perhaps less noticeable.[5] *Hasta no verte Jesús mío* implicitly raises the matter of its own doubled and divided status, its own propensity to lie in order to tell the truth, as forcefully as it seems to bypass such self-recognition through the testimonial narrative it unfolds. Indeed, this work openly introduces the question of the truth precisely at those moments when it insistently raises the specter of the lie.[6] It tells a number of things about the kind of text or the kind of author that seems to have to lie, as it were, to tell the truth—that is, about a text such as a novela testimonial or an author such as Elena Poniatowska.

Like other works that utilize the testimony of a single subject who may also represent a group of similarly situated individuals, Poniatowska's novel is narrated in the first person by the character whose life story it tells.[7] We recall that the narrator-protagonist is one Jesusa Palancares, a Mexican woman who was raised in poverty and who lived through and took part in the Mexican revolution. Moreover, Jesusa survived to old age by living a life whose patterns may be regarded as somewhat literary. That is, the autobiographical tale she tells comprises episodic employments and adventures one may be tempted to read in terms of (or even as having originated from) an established literary tradition—that of the picaresque.[8]

Though there may be points to be made about such literary resemblances, Poniatowska's novel also purports to be something else. In fact, her own testimony about the text's origins and production moves in two directions. On the one hand, Poniatowska emphasizes the literary aims and techniques employed to produce *Hasta no verte Jesús mío*. She explains briefly how the text was composed, how she suppressed or selected, combined or cut, materials from Jesusa's testimony so as to construct what she herself calls a novela testimonial. But she also insists that Jesusa (her "native informant") and her story are fundamentally the "real" thing.[9] As Poniatowska reveals the techniques by which she transformed the material gathered directly from the person she calls Jesusa, through tape recordings and notes, and as she talks about her own relation to the woman she presents also as a textual figure, she reaffirms the existence of an objective reality beyond the discourse that gives her text and its protagonist the appearance of truth (see "Jesusa Palancares" and "Testimonios").

Poniatowska's revelations about the novel's composition thus provide some ground for talking about the author's "artistic" intentions and the text's "literary" qualities.[10] But, given the attention paid to Jesusa as an empirical entity, as a person with whom the author developed a personal relationship (see especially "Jesusa Palancares"), Poniatowska's comments also aim to testify to the material reality that informs Jesusa's story and Poniatowska's presentation of it. Therefore, as the author's confessions insist upon the novel's origins in historical and biographical fact, in social and cultural history, in the life, memory, and discourse of its own narrator-protagonist, her readers are reminded of this text's problematical generic affinities and of the unstable boundaries of the novela testimonial more generally.[11] Such authorial comments would seem both to establish the origins of Poniatowska's text and to raise the question of whether the author's activity might be considered in some (if in any) way original.

One might argue that, although Jesusa's narration and the autobiography fashioned through it may seem to be assimilable to an established, familiar literary tradition such as the picaresque, the statements made by the author concerning the novel's genesis nonetheless emphasize that, on the contrary, Jesusa ought not to be taken only as a textual effect. That is, Jesusa's narrative, though shaped by Poniatowska, ought not to be read as a "lie." What one is supposed to read in *Hasta no verte Jesús mío*, then, is essentially the truth, not a verisimilar fiction.[12] Moreover, one is directed to consider the text itself as a testimonial to truth, even though, the author freely admits, such truth has been shaped by a good many lies inherent in the techniques of literature.

Oddly, this text one is to take as an accurate testimony, as a reliable and essentially truthful (not simply verisimilar) account of what its narrator has told the author and she presents to her reader in literary form, is a text that puts into question the possibility of fashioning such testimony. In *Hasta no verte Jesús mío* access to such truth, if not to reality, is proposed as problematical, if not also impossible, by Jesusa herself, the subject whose seemingly truthful discourse fills its pages. Indeed, the novel seems to block the path to certainty about the correspondence between what has been said and what has happened, between what is told and what is truthful.

There are a number of places where this matter of lying or telling the truth is introduced in the text. Its introduction is the responsibility of no less an authority on the story's truth than Jesusa, the narrating subject whose appearance as a character one is to take as faithfully resembling the person with whom Elena Poniatowska spoke as she gathered the material for her book. Appropriately (and, perhaps, intentionally) this question is first raised in the text's epigraph, attributed by the author to Jesusa, who, in one of their conversations, is quoted as envisaging a moment when the telling of her story to Poniatowska will already be in the past:

Gestures of Authorship **49**

Algún día que venga ya no me va a encontrar; se topará nomás con el puro viento. Llegará ese día y cuando llegue, no habrá ni quien le dé una razón. Y pensará que todo ha sido mentira. Es verdad, estamos aquí de a mentiras: lo que cuentan en el radio son mentiras, mentiras las que dicen los vecinos y mentira que me va a sentir. Si ya no le sirvo para nada, ¿qué carajos va a extrañar? Y en el taller tampoco ¿Quién quiere usted que me extrañe si ni adioses voy a mandar?

[One day when you come by you won't find me; you won't run into anything but the wind. That day will come and when it does there'll be no one here to give you any information. And you'll think that it's all been a lie. It's true, we're living in a fake world: what they tell on the radio are lies, lies what everyone around here says, and a lie that you'll miss me. If I'm not good for anything anymore, why the hell should you miss me? Or the people at work. Who do you think will miss me if I'm not going to say goodbye to anyone?] [8][13]

If Jesusa's words are read as merely a preliminary revelation of "character" through the idiosyncracies of discourse, the quotation becomes a predictive disclosure of the attitude, personality, and mode of expression that will individualize the protagonist throughout the text. But if her epigraph statement is read in relation to the text that follows it, the quotation highlights the text's status as a novela testimonial, which its narrative body might otherwise seem to conceal. It also begins to raise the question of truth in a rather telling fashion.

Jesusa's comments set up an oddly "literary" statement about the relation between the text that will be read and the tale she will be seen to have narrated, if not entirely authored. For it posits her absence as an inevitable ending for the dialogue between the invisible (but necessarily audible) author and the protagonist, between the documentary researcher and the native informant. It prefigures the disappearance of the character, whose responsibility for the text may come to be regarded as equal to, if not greater than, that of the author who also authorizes her appearance. Moreover, her statement prefigures the precarious placement of her own author-interlocutor, whose aims she would challenge but whose authority she would certify in the act of saying (or appearing to be permitted to say) anything at all.

Jesusa's epigraph statement also implicates Poniatowska in a virtual dialogue about telling lies. This dialogue runs throughout the testimonial novel and also seems to spill over into the author's statements about it.[14] Jesusa's intermittent insistence on the idea of telling the truth, which she repeatedly opposes to that of telling lies, draws attention to the question of how something told might be taken or not to be true, to how, or under what circumstances, telling or learning the truth is possible. Indeed, her statements become a problematical and reflexive introduction to—an oddly "theoretical" statement about—some of the constitutive features of the novela testimonial itself.

According to Poniatowska, the person she has identified as Jesusa has herself insisted vehemently that the text one reads (the text in which the narrator named Jesusa makes similar statements) is a sham, a lie. It has little to do with the truth she has told to the author, who presumably has also aimed to tell it to her readers. Poniatowska relates that, after *Hasta no verte Jesús mío* had been read to Jesusa, she declared to the author: "Usted inventa todo, son puras mentiras, no entendió nada, las cosas no son así" ["You invent everything, it's all lies, you didn't understand anything, that isn't the way things are"] ("Testimonios" 160).[15]

In fact, Poniatowska has had to lie to tell her interlocutor's story, which its readers may wish to regard as otherwise essentially true. For, it has recently been revealed that the name "Jesusa Palancares" is an authorial invention, an agreed-upon design to cover her informant's real identity. The name Jesusa Palancares displaces and hides, as it also takes the place of, the name "Josefina Bórquez." This newly revealed name is the real name of the woman whose story the novel tells. It is the name of the person with whom Poniatowska spoke over the course of several years and a good percentage of whose conversations she recorded and transcribed as well as shaped into the text that bears her own name.[16] Thus, in order to present this tale as a testimonial, Poniatowska has had to veil her subject's legitimate identity; she has been obliged not to tell the truth. This literary, nominal lie, then, is precisely what permits the telling of the story and empowers the presentation of the character (and the apparent truth about her) in the novel.

The disjunction between referent and proper name, which the empirical Jesusa (or, rather, Josefina) underscores indirectly with her statement of dissatisfaction, also figures a rupture between reality and the discourse presumed to resemble it. Jesusa's own performance would lead the reader, along with her, now to consider or now to conceal precisely such a rupture between the real and the true. Besides raising the question of authorship, as well as the whole issue of authority, for Jesusa's story, Jesusa's (or Josefina's) critical statement puts a wedge between the text (Josefina's story as arranged and authored by

Poniatowska under the name Jesusa) and the truth (Josefina's "real" life, told by her to Poniatowska, who has Jesusa merely repeat it—or not—for the reader).

Her view of the relation between the real, the true, and the act of telling seems to assume that an accurate, truthful presentation of things, an adequation of discourse (as either speech or writing) and the world, is possible, but that in this instance a disjunction has instead been produced by the text (or the author) she thought was aiming to solidify it. The tension within Jesusa's statements is a telling one. For it demonstrates how the novela testimonial (a genre whose truth-value many readers have come to accept as self-evident, given its apparently faithful resemblance to the real) may inadvertently suggest its own distance from the true as well as from the real. It shows how such a text may inevitably recognize its own verisimilar, and therefore textual, properties.

Jesusa (the "authentic" narrator who establishes herself also as a credible character) is the one who introduces these problematical matters within the novel. Jesusa's statements within the text of *Hasta no verte Jesús mío* draw distinctions between the telling of things (that is, the narrative as such) and the things themselves. Through these statements she also proposes to her interlocutor a view of the relation between reality and discourse that undercuts the apparent aims and essence of the text in which she makes those proposals. In fact, for Jesusa, reality finally amounts to subjective reality and the possibility of telling the truth (that is, the possibility of producing a discourse that corresponds to the real) becomes a subjective possibility. Access to the truth about things finally depends upon subjective experience; the truth can only be told or produced by a subject who is also the subject of the reality that such a discourse would be seen to resemble.[17] As one reads her text, one sees that Jesusa the narrator would present herself as telling the truth. But as one considers her "theories" about the truth and how it gets told, and also what Poniatowska says that Jesusa (or Josefina) has said about the novel, one may read Jesusa's narrative not as unquestionably true, but rather as convincingly verisimilar, as a persuasive lie.

Jesusa's notions about telling the truth go something like this. If one witnesses an event, if one is present to reality, one knows and may well present (or not) the truth about it.[18] Yet, the truth is only evident to the one who tells it, to the subject who can verify that the true is true precisely because it adequately resembles the real. Throughout the text, Jesusa makes comments about the inherently uncertain status of truth for stories told by others, and which cannot be verified by her own experience. These comments arise equally from her confrontations with everyday explanations of events or people's actions as from her encounter with popular sayings or beliefs. Indeed, rumors, popular stories, political or cultural myths, as well as personal reports of particular events, all become objects for her skeptical, and often corrective, criticism.

For instance, about a rumored familial intrigue (that is, that her brother was forced to marry his wife because his mother-in-law was Jesusa's father's lover), she says: "Quién sabe si sería cierto porque eso no lo vi" ["Who knows if that's true because I didn't see it"] (56); about the explanation of her brother's death provided by presumed witnesses, she declares: "Todo eso me lo contaron a mí, ahora quién sabe cuál será la mera verdad" ["They told me all of that, but who knows what the real truth is"] (62); and, about the popular belief that earthquakes are actually the movements of a large animal within the earth, she says: "Eso cuentan, pero no me haga caso, váyase a saber la verdad" ["That's what they say, but don't pay any attention to me, who knows what the truth is"] (39).[19]

Jesusa repeatedly questions, if not entirely discredits, the discourse, the narratives of other subjects precisely because she, as listener to their tales, is not in a position to verify that what is told actually corresponds to the real and that it is therefore true. She (and, consequently, her narrative) is, from her perspective of course, exempt from that judgment. No such skepticism surfaces within her own tale of what she claims to have experienced or witnessed herself. In fact, as one reads the text, and Jesusa becomes more familiar, her narrative more plausible, it would appear that though others may lie she always tells the truth.[20]

There is a particularly telling instance in which Jesusa reveals distinctions of this sort. And, because of its suggestions about how a lie may disguise itself, about how the telling of the effect of such a disguise may figure the discursive or textual nature of the true, it is also a significant moment for the novel as a whole. Jesusa's account of her forays into the center of military activity during the Mexican revolution, disguised in men's clothing, draws a distinction between an accurate testimony and a suspect narrative in rather suggestive terms:

Casi no iban mujeres en campaña; a mí me llevaba Pedro [her husband] sin orden del general Espinosa y Córdoba; por eso me vestía de hombre para

que se hicieran de la vista gorda. Me tapaba la cabeza con el paliacate y el sombrero. Por lo regular, unas iban como yo, porque sus maridos las obligaban, otra porque le hacían al hombre, pero la mayoría de las mujeres se quedaban atrás con la impedimenta. Doy razón de varias partes porque si me hubiera quedado en la estación, allí no veo nada ni oigo nada. La verdad, es bonito porque siquiera no es cuento. Uno vio.
[Women almost never went along on the campaigns, but Pedro took me without getting permission from General Espinosa y Córdoba and therefore I had to dress as a man so they'd pretend not to notice me. I covered my head bandana style and with a hat. Generally, some women went like I did, because their husbands made them go, another because she acted like a man, but most of the women stayed behind with the provisions. I give my report from various places, because if I had stayed in the station, I couldn't see or hear anything from there. Truthfully, it's nice because at least it isn't a story. One saw.] [109–10]

The effect of Jesusa's disguise is to produce in those who see her the acceptance of her appearance as real. Yet, her disguise, which is at once a simulation (she pretends to be what she is not, a man) and a dissimulation (she pretends not to be what she is, a woman), has the effect of making her disappear to those who would see her as she can—or ought to—be seen. Disguised, Jesusa may be taken for the real; however, she here reveals herself as but a verisimilar appearance. That she can successfully disguise herself depends, however, as much on the willful blindness of those who could see her for what she is as on her own ability to disguise the truth about her appearance.

One sees that, in pretending not to see, or in turning a blind eye to, her, Jesusa's witnesses are themselves seen as allowing her to disappear, along with her disguise. She would appear as a veritable man precisely by being allowed to disappear as a disguised woman. Jesusa thus makes an equivocal appearance on the field; this is a field one can of course read as both the military space into which she appears to place herself and the textual stage upon which she is presented. It is precisely this appearance of resembling the real that gives Jesusa, as participant-witness, an apparent access to reality, and that later makes it possible for her to claim that she is telling the truth. Her telling of that truth, however, becomes subject to the distinctions she herself proposes. It also remains open to the judgment of other witnesses (or readers) who might (or might not) be able to turn a blind eye either to her discourse or to her disguise.

Indeed, the implicit hierarchical relation between her own narrative and what she calls "cuento" rests on distinctions that the text of *Hasta no verte Jesús mío* also renounces, and which Poniatowska's readers, like those of Jesusa, might (or might not) be willing, or able, to see. Though Jesusa's story advances mainly by recounting events that she herself appears to have seen and heard, it also incorporates presentations of dialogue and descriptions of action in which she has not participated or at which she has not been present (for example, Jesusa's recounting of the exchanges between her husband Pedro and Refugio, a young boy he once befriended [118–19], or her versions of her ancestors' history or immediate family's story as imagined by her or retold to her by her father [220–24]). Clearly, some of her narrative does not qualify to be taken as true.

One can see, then, that the test of truth that Jesusa implicitly proposes for the tales she hears becomes a test that her own text also fails. If one applies to Jesusa the conditions of truth she applies to others, her story emerges as unverifiable, as another example perhaps of the "mentiras" she herself ridicules throughout the novel. Her implicit claim to the authority to tell her story (after all, she was participant and witness throughout) and to contradict the stories of other tellers, to whose tales she counterposes her own, is also a self-authorizing claim. This simulation of authority becomes one of the necessary fictions of the novel, wherein Jesusa's story would finally produce a persuasive, verisimilar effect rather than a certifiable resemblance to the real.

Readers may be led to accept Jesusa's narrative as generally, if not completely, truthful precisely because it seems so verisimilar. The effect of verisimilitude would here (and perhaps characteristically in the novela testimonial) have the effect of masking itself (as does Jesusa in the passage about her disguise, cited above) so as to lead the reader to take the text as a presentation of the truth.[21] But, as that effect becomes visible, it also becomes possible to see that Jesusa's narrative places the reader in the very position from which, her own comments recall, the path to certainty, the route to truth, becomes problematical. Indeed, it is the very place from which one might be pushed, just like Jesusa, to say "váyase a saber la verdad" ["who knows what the truth is"].

This undecidable situation, one could argue, is a situation that obtains in the novela testimonial generally. For the genre is predicated upon the kind of lie, the type of disguise, inherent in the play of names and the performance of lying or truthful figures that shape Poniatowska's text. The testimonial novel inevitably shifts its focus between the subjects that seem to frame and the subjects seemingly framed by it. It also seems to make any such framing a shifting, unstable line of demarcation between the truth and the lie, between one kind of subject or discourse and another.

Jesusa's concern with the truth implies a dialogue (if not an outright polemic) about that issue. As she focuses on the topic she also calls attention to the effects produced by both her own discourse and the text attributed to the novel's author. Jesusa's statements bring under scrutiny the subjects presumed to be responsible for such statements' intentional (or unintentional) design. The question of truth as raised by Jesusa thus implicates the different subjects and sites of authorship that seem to authorize the textual or discursive activity out of which *Hasta no verte Jesús mío* arises to present its testimony.

What is also particularly telling in the cited passage about Jesusa's battlefield appearance is that both her access to and subsequent recounting of events appear through a set of disguises, through devices of verisimilitude. These disguises allow her to present another face, a believable identity, which, in turn, allows her both to see and to be seen, to tell and to be told in the novel. Moreover, such a play of identity may be inherent in the apparent truthfulness that the novela testimonial seems to exhibit, as well as in the authorial performance that supports it. Poniatowska's testimonial novel thus both disguises and displays its relation to the real and the true. It makes visible and at the same time conceals the effects of verisimilitude through which the truth, as it were, about Jesusa's story seems to be either veiled or revealed.

Jesusa's disguise as a man, as a figure of disguised difference, also figures the conditions of possibility for such a display in Poniatowska's novel. Her self-presentation as a disguised figure also implicates the conditions under which either the novel's author or its narrator-protagonist is able to present the story or produce the text. As she unwittingly figures the authorial duplicity that underlies her appearance as a teller of truths, Jesusa manages to disguise with verisimilar effects the very lie upon which the telling and writing of her story depend. Indeed, as we have already seen, though *Hasta no verte Jesús mío* would seem to demonstrate the possibilities for presenting the truth about Jesusa (or, rather, about Josefina), it also testifies to the limits of the discourse through which such truth would seem to appear.

Jesusa's insistence on the matter of truth assumes, from another perspective, that there exists an authoritative subject from or through whom such truth can be emitted, or who might attest to the truthful status of individual statements or whole stories. We know that Jesusa is empowered to speak by the author of the text in which her story appears. However, like other testimonial novel narrators, she performs as a self-authorizing subject within her own narration. Though her performance also depends on other figures around her, Jesusa's voice may nonetheless be heard as independent and masterful. It resounds as apparently adequate to the tale and the "truth" she would tell.

Jesusa fashions herself as a figure of more or less authority within her narrative not only through the way she is presented as telling her life story but also through her depiction as a figure who has insistently challenged, even while also having had to accept and abide by, the authority of others. Jesusa becomes a figure of resistance as she presents her corrective readings of the public tales or private opinions she is compelled to counter, and as she represents herself as an actor in events through which she can be seen to play a variety of unconventional roles.[22]

Jesusa's opinions and actions situate her as ever at odds with, and sometimes openly critical of, the major institutions and political or popular myths of Mexican culture (the family, the military, the church; the Mexican revolution and its heroes). Rather visible are her vehement attacks on some of the strategies and end results of the revolution, and on the legendary status achieved by some of its leaders. Jesusa's counterstatements to and criticisms of the stories that have come to stand for the truth about Mexico's well-known military and political figures present her as a subject engaged in a virtual polemic with popular discourse, and thus potentially with history as well. They also reveal how she authors for herself a role as a purveyor of truths, and especially as an authority on the history and myths that, according to her testimony, have been fabricated out of lies.

Her general characterizations of the injustices and inefficacy of the revolution are aimed as much at its participants as at its overall results (see 94, 126, 134, 137). Her revelations of the truth, as it were, about its leaders take aim both at the fabricators of untrue stories and at their fabrications, which seem to have passed from the text of popular discourse to that of official history. She aims to correct as well as to criticize the legends and lies that, having been told and retold, have been propagated as fact. Jesusa's denunciation of the telling of untruths about well-known figures, or her criticism of the disguising of facts about particular incidents, has a certain force within the novel's text. However, it must finally be read as having a questionable relation to the real (that is, as a statement whose truth-value cannot be determined, though it has a convincing, because verisimilar, appearance in her narrative). The forcefulness of Jesusa's convictions, the certainty her voice projects (but which some of her confessions nonetheless disprove) may well provide the ground from which her appearance as an authoritative figure arises.

For example, her revelations about Pancho Villa, the revolutionary leader for whom she confesses a particular hatred ("Yo si a alguno odio más, es a Villa" ["If there's anyone I hate the most, it's Villa" [95]), are pronounced also as invectives against untruth. In fact, Jesusa's truths are as often as not just the contradictions to lies. In Jesusa's discourse the truth is proposed as the negation of a lie, and not only as an assertion of a truth. She presents her version of the truth so as to debunk and displace the "mentiras" through which the glorified, but false, image of Villa, for example, is perpetuated. And her counterstatements take aim both at falsified figures (for example, Villa) and at those who tell the legendary lies—that is, at the falsifiers of the "truths" that Jesusa is compelled to contradict.[23] Those who falsify do so not only by telling untruths but also by failing to tell all that could be told. Moreover, Jesusa insists that the falsification of the truth can be found even in newspaper and radio reports—precisely in those forms of discourse that would appear to present and preserve the truth for modern culture.[24] (They are, it might also be remarked, the same forms of discourse with which Poniatowska has worked so extensively, and thus Jesusa's—or Josefina's—expressed distrust of and disappointment with the author, already noted above, may seem a logical extension of the statements within the novel.) In many of her negative assertions regarding such falsification, however, Jesusa does not actually offer a statement that can be taken as a complete and truthful account (that is, a discourse that can be taken as corresponding to the real). She merely makes declarations of her own doubts or beliefs (for example, 96).

Nonetheless, Jesusa always seems to speak as an authority. But her voice has no real ground to stand on except the virtual ground she, as self-appointed arbiter of truth, constructs for herself from her own marginal position. Jesusa is a figure of counterauthority, and, like that of a good many other testimonial subjects, her voice comes from below, as it were, to overturn some of the stories about which, her narration would propose, it is precisely the marginal subject who knows, and can thus tell, who is lying and who is telling the truth. And although, as we have seen, her discourse would have to be characterized as capable of producing an effect of verisimilitude rather than of truth, Jesusa's narrative succeeds nonetheless in concealing the shaky supports of its narrator's (and perhaps also its author's) testimonial performance.

This voice from below would not only give another version of things. It would also upend the relations of authority within which its subject seems to be situated. Jesusa's verbal or physical challenges, her ideological or inspirational positions, may well seem unconventional, as well as idiosyncratic, perhaps because her marginal status (she is a woman at the lower end of the socioeconomic order) would seem to provide her with no place of authority from which to speak. But Jesusa's authoritative appearance derives not only from her pronouncements about lying or telling the truth within her narration. It also emerges from the narrative in which, as a character, she assumes positions or plays roles of authority, or resists yielding to the power of others. In fact, Jesusa often challenges paternal or spousal privilege (for example, 52–53, 83–84, 99, 109); she makes self-authorizing declarations of independence (for example, 152–53, 267); she assumes various roles of domestic or military responsibility and power (for example, 48–49, 129–30, 174–75, 213, 288): such are the gestures, the attitudes and actions through which Jesusa becomes the most visible, if not the most viable, figure of testimonial authority in *Hasta no verte Jesús mío*.

Jesusa's story, which surfaces from the margins of social, political, and cultural history, is also a story about being marginal. Such is the situation characteristic of many of the figures who would speak in the *novela testimonial* generally.[25] Indeed, the authority of the subject in such a text derives precisely (though paradoxically) from the denial of his or her authority elsewhere. This figure of marginality, then, becomes a figure of textual as well as testimonial authority, much like the authorial figure that also authorizes Jesusa's performance in the novel. But Jesusa, the textualization of the person called Josefina, is a figure that remains subject to the authorizing gestures of another figure (that is, the author), whose position she supplants as she gives her testimony. Although the figure of the novel's author may well recede behind the text of Jesusa's narrative, Poniatowska, nevertheless, reclaims an authoritative (and properly authorial) position around it.[26]

One could talk about *Hasta no verte Jesús mío* as the work of not one but of two authors—as a "compositely authored work"[27]—inasmuch as the novela testimonial puts into question the activity of its named author (in this case Poniatowska) as an activity of original authorship. (That is, the author does not herself originate or found the story told in her novel, and is therefore, in some sense, not an *auctor*.) But, since the reading of Poniatowska's testimonial novel is, perforce, tied up with the reading of other of the author's texts around it (that is, the authorial documents or testimonies), her position as authoritative figure (as much as her appearance as author of the text) is reasserted by the different testimonies that are incorporated into, or are attached to, her novel.

Oddly, authors of testimonial novels seem to be called upon, either by private or public demand, to give further testimony about the materials that have shaped the texts that bear their names, texts that presumably tell a self-evident truth.[28] By more or less revealing the process by which the documentary materials have been copied, compiled, edited, and arranged, Poniatowska's statements do a number of things. They redirect attention to the author as a person engaged in an activity that is both more and less than that of a traditional author. They establish Poniatowska as a secondary and editorial figure, as an author who would speak through the voice of another. Yet, given that she also confesses to being responsible for the novel's overall composition and even for the invention of some of its discursive features, her testimony also seems to establish her role as originator, in addition to confirming her status as textual authority. Moreover, Poniatowska's statements become reminders of the testimonial novel's (and also its author's) responsibility to try to tell the truth. For the author's apparently extraliterary testimony, as much as (or perhaps more than) the novel itself, aims to authenticate what is told, principally by telling more about where its stories and subjects come from.

That the author speaks at all about the origins of his or her work might in itself be taken as evidence that such explanations are necessary. It might be taken as proof that someone else needs to speak or that something else needs to be said about what otherwise appears to stand truthfully on its own. Indeed, Poniatowska's statements about the novel appear as a necessary supplement to the testimony offered by its main text, which also spills beyond its original borders when some of its passages are repeated within her auxiliary comments. Yet, the status of this authorial testimony may be as equivocal as that of the text whose truth it would appear to reassert; the position of this author may be as problematical as that of the narrator whose tale she supports.

The one and the other kind of testimony—the one projected in the voice of the author, the other pronounced by the voice of her interlocutor—would suggest that the truth-value of each is to be taken as readily perceivable. But each would also reveal that the truth of the one may be visible only from the telling of the other. This reciprocal authorization of testimonies takes Poniatowska, as much as the apparently self-sufficient Jesusa, from a seemingly invisible and secondary position to a position of discursive privilege and textual authority. In fact, the two figures may be seen in competition with one another, a competition from around which the figure of the author also emerges with renewed, rather than reduced, vigor.

Poniatowska speaks about the origins of *Hasta no verte Jesús mío* as a virtual response to the queries that might be posed by her readers and as a direct reply to the questions that have been put by her interviewers.[29] Her testimony about the process through which she came to write the novel supplies the facts regarding her encounters with Jesusa (or Josefina) and the techniques she deployed to compose the work.[30] Her testimony can be read not only as a virtual response to the text of the novel itself, but also as a way of replying and paying homage to the subject in whom her opportunity for authorship originates, and through whose discourse she herself also speaks. Moreover, her testimony is cast in confessional terms. Poniatowska emphasizes her personal debt to the woman to whose life her novel is meant to bear witness and with whom she claims to have identified herself; she describes the personal experiences as well as authorial decisions that determined the production of its testimonial tale.[31]

Poniatowska's discourse purports to tell the truth about the truth apparently told to her by her informant. Yet that it may persuade her readers of its adequacy to such a truth is due as much, if not more, to its adherence to the conventions of authorial explanation or testimony as to its presumed resemblance to the real. Like the story told by Jesusa, the confessions of Poniatowska would present themselves under the guise of the true precisely because they are constituted through a discourse whose verisimilar appearance is sufficiently effective to persuade readers of its own authority and veracity.[32]

That Poniatowska's statements may tell less (or even more) than the whole story is perhaps, like the testimony of Jesusa, of less consequence for her authorial performance than that she makes any state-ment at all. Indeed, it may well be that the conventions of producing testimonial literature virtually dictate that the author must assume additional responsibilities and authority for texts that purport to be based on, if not to tell exactly, the truth. In such cases, it is the respon-sibility of the author to supply additional testimony, to provide supple-mentary and original statements that would further certify the status of a text whose nature is also presumed to be self-evident. The respon-sibilities of the author of a testimonial novel may thus appear to be at the same time restricted and all-encompassing. They are the respon-sibilities of a figure who seems to have relinquished his or her role as authentic originator but also to have retained (or reclaimed) consider-able authority and responsibility characteristic of more traditional authors.

Given the kinds of responsibility subsumed by the activities of the author of a testimonial novel, such a text seems to bestow upon that figure responsibilities that might be associated with very different, though related, figures. As a matter of fact, the function of the author of testimonial fiction may be viewed principally as that of a researcher, organizer, or arranger of personal testimony and/or historical docu-ments—that is, as a "gestor."[33] Such an identification would appear to position the author as a secondary, mediating figure, as a figure of considerably reduced authority.[34] It would virtually situate that figure in the position of a modern *scriptor, compilator,* or *editor.* Yet, the addi-tional, and apparently authoritative, documents or statements (that is, the testimony) offered around the novela testimonial, as well as the special kind of responsibility attributable to the figure of the gestor, would also establish such a figure in a significant, and essentially privileged, position—a position one might be tempted to identify with that of a modern *auctor.*

Indeed, the role of the testimonial author would fulfill the respon-sibilities of both the one and the other figure. The gestor, it could be argued, asserts as much as repeats the assertions of others, and thus, according to one view, could be understood to do precisely what an *auctor* is responsible for doing.[35] The gestor would himself or herself appear not as the personal origin of the story to which the testimonial novel testifies but, rather, as the professional compiler of the text of another, who is presented as the original subject of the text's asser-tions. However, it is also in the nature of the gestor's role to assert as well as repeat or report the apparent truth told by another. Though assertions made by the author-as-gestor around such a text may appear as secondary statements, they also have a crucial role to play: they function as essential critical complements without which one might not be willing to read the text as telling the truth.

The figure of the gestor confounds as much as clarifies the relations of textual authority, and perhaps even the rights of authorship, that would appear to obtain in the novela testimonial. The gestor, a kind of *auctor* in disguise, is a figure through which the author gestures toward the authority of another subject while also consolidating his or her own authorial position. The confession of a secondary discursive function becomes a gesture that finally underwrites, as much as it might first seem to undermine, the activity and identity of the author. Though such gestures may well proclaim the depersonalization of authorial activity, they also shift authority from one image or role of the author to another, and back again.[36]

If viewed as the gestor of *Hasta no verte Jesús mío*, then, Poniatowska, much like the subject with whom she might be seen to compete for testimonial, and consequently textual, authority (that is, Jesusa or Josefina), would reclaim her position as authoritative author by virtually coming from behind the apparently more authentic subject whose position her authorial gestures also support. Though Poniatowska's role in and around *Hasta no verte Jesús mío*—that is, the role of a gestor—may figure a critical break between originality and authority, it also reveals how, in the novela testimonial, the one finally appears to inhere in and acquire added meaning through the other.

The gestures of the gestor recuperate the author's privileged place, if not also his or her marks of personality, which otherwise might be regarded as having disappeared. Poniatowska's performance becomes a reminder of her equivocal identity as a gestor as it reveals how the gestures of such a figure move things in several directions at once. Poniatowska's testimonials (her novel, her personal testimony) recover as much as reject the gestures of authorship associated with other, perhaps more traditional, figures of the author. The figure of the gestor, then, may well revitalize, in a somewhat altered form, an authoritative figure presumed to have disappeared with the "death of the author."

The gestures of authorship inherent in Poniatowska's roles take the figure of the author to a place in which it seems to have appeared before and yet in which it seems to be seen for the first time. The testimonial novel, therefore, also gives testimony to the authority assumed by contemporary figures of the author as much as it seems to testify to that figure's demise. *Hasta no verte Jesús mío* would thus appear ready to tell something more about itself, about some of the issues raised by the genre to which it pertains, and about the critical figures through which all kinds of texts get read, even when one might be inclined to believe that, as a novela testimonial, it has already told everything there is to tell.

4

On Shifting Ground
Authoring Mystery and Mastery in
Carlos Fuentes's *Terra nostra*

To position the titular phrase "*Terra nostra*" as I have in this chapter's title is to suggest a conventional relation between author and text. Indeed, the iconic relationship suggested by this genitive construction (as opposed to the *by* or *of* construction that would put greater distance between the author's name and the title of his text) makes more or less visible how authors and texts traditionally have been linked. It also suggests that, whether our critical vocabulary situates author and text in greater or lesser verbal proximity to one another, the inevitable reliance on such possessive constructions to identify either one or the other entity preserves a relationship that much of contemporary criticism aims to set aside. For even when the author's name is taken to refer to the figure produced by a text (or by a group of texts) rather than to the author-as-person, such a positioning of names and titles suggests that the one somehow circumscribes or subsumes the other. To situate the proper name of the author as the noun that governs the genitive "*Terra nostra*" thus seems to posit a relation of ownership and subordination, mastery and containment, between Fuentes and this novel.

Such phrasing seems to privilege a relation that Fuentes's text, as we shall see, also upends. Yet *Terra nostra's* [*Terra Nostra*] (1975) ruminations about the author's authority develop this relation as a problematical affiliation that empowers now one, now another figure of the author.[1] The possessor figure (the one also produced by my title) is a figure whose authority *Terra nostra* would undermine. But it is also the figure from which Fuentes's consideration of authorial privilege derives its power.

I have elected to retain this critical phrase (both here and in other chapters) not only because it virtually materializes a model of author-text relations that maintains considerable force even in those texts that position the figure of the author in an unconventional fashion. It reappears here also because it compels us to look at the author as a possessive figure that still eludes possession by available critical formulas.[2] For the name "Fuentes" would slide among a number of possible referents, and "*Terra nostra*" would identify a text whose title already problematizes the limits of its own borders and body.[3]

Terra nostra situates the figure of the author in equivocal positions; its text incorporates figures of the author that seem to be positioned both inside and outside its borders. Fuentes's novel also figures the limits of any author's power to contain his own text, or the text's ability to contain its author's image(s). Rather than obliterate the figure of the masterful or authoritative author, however, *Terra nostra* situates its authors (that is, the character that will be read as an author-figure, the figure of the author constructed by the text, and the empirical author) as powerful, paradoxical figures. Fuentes's novel reestablishes that the disembodied textual figures of the author may also be figures of authority; the textual image of the author may also be that of a masterful and authoritative figure. *Terra nostra* problematizes the hierarchical relation implicit in the possessor-possessed construction employed in my chapter title. But as it does so it further provides a recognizable ground on which to anchor the illusion of such a relation between its disparate possessive figures.

The question of the author, or of the author's authority, is raised as part of Fuentes's exploration of the problematics of absolute authority within Hispanic civilization. The Spanish monarchy and its emblematic sovereign, Philip II, serve as principal metaphors for the political privileges or powers, and also the textual authority, which *Terra nostra* interrogates. Fuentes's novel, an enigmatic text that develops around a variety of mysteries and mystery texts, aims to consider the enigmatic quality of the monarchy's enduring hegemony, which the empirical author regards as "based on death. . . . on *nada*."[4] As we know, the Spanish kings prevailed for centuries, despite political errors, military defeats, and economic losses. The discovery, conquest, and founding of Spanish America allowed their reign to expand and endure. The kings survived to rule in America if not in Europe, even while dwelling on death and the past (as Fuentes emphasizes). The end of dominance in the Old World coincided with the beginning of sovereignty in the New.

Terra nostra focuses on the period of this important shift. Fuentes attempts to elucidate the nature of political and cultural relationships between Spain and Spanish America (Mexico in particular) as they were formed in the sixteenth and seventeenth centuries. Although the text focuses on a specific king who is a composite monarchal figure and whose exercise of power and obsession with death figure the paradox of authority its author investigates, it also examines the origin and structure of power in the Hispanic world as a whole. However, the novel appears to focus on the cultural consequences of such structures for Spanish America in particular.[5] Fuentes sketches the intricate connections between the Spanish monarchy and its New World subjects. His text reveals (sometimes unwittingly and potentially to its own virtual undoing) the constitutive relational networks through which power is exercised and authority is assumed in historical circumstances and literary fictions.[6] In *Terra nostra*, a specific historical situation becomes a paradigm of the mythical and political models which that situation also repeats.[7] Fuentes's theoretical meditation on and fictive representation of the Hispanic context implicate different models of political and textual authority in *Terra nostra*. The novel replicates within its thematic development and narrative structure the textual realities and systems of authority to which its own fictional tale and authorial figures are ineluctably bound.

Mystery and mystery texts are important structuring principles of *Terra nostra*. Its mysteries lie in both its fictional story and its narrative structure. Through diverse narrative forms, *Terra nostra* presents a nonlinear arrangement of events that unfold in Rome at the time of Tiberius Caesar, in sixteenth-century Spain, in Mexico just before its discovery by the Spaniards, and in Paris at the end of the twentieth century. In both the Old World and the New a battle is waged for eternal possession of power. In the Roman world the emperor Tiberius is killed by the reincarnation of Agrippa, the person he himself had killed in order to ascend to a position of power. In the sixteenth century, the imaginary yet real struggle between Felipe (also called El Señor) and those he believes threaten his power appears to be part of the fulfillment of a curse pronounced at the time of Tiberius's death.

As a safeguard against any future exercise of power equal to that of the emperor, the curse or myth was formulated as follows: "Resucite un día Agrippa Póstumo, multiplicado por tres, de vientres de lobas, para contemplar la dispersión del imperio de Roma; y de los tres hijos de Agrippa, nazcan más tarde otros nueve; y de los nueve, veintisiete, y de los veintisiete, setenta y uno, hasta que la unidad se disgregue en millones de individualidades, y siendo todos César, nadie lo sea, y este poder que ahora es nuestro, no pueda volver a ser" ["Let Agrippa Postumus, multiplied by three, one day be revived from the bellies of she-wolves, so he may contemplate the dispersion of the Empire of Rome; and from the three sons of Agrippa may another nine be born, and from the nine, twenty-seven, and from the twenty-seven, eighty-one, until unity be dispersed into millions of individuals, and as each will be Caesar, none will be he, and this power that now is ours will never again exist"] (702/697).

In the New World, that battle, soon to be fought by Spaniards and indigenous peoples, is cast as an eternal and mythological conflict between life and death. Quetzalcóatl (the Plumed Serpent) and Espejo Humeante (the Smoking Mirror) wage a futile battle for sovereignty. But these conflicts are without resolution, without an original or final explanation: they are the mysteries of civilization upon which civilization itself is founded.[8] In Terra nostra Hispanic culture is viewed in terms of universal myth and history, for which it becomes a privileged model. The temporal and spatial specificities of the novel, however, emphasize that, although the text allows extrapolation to wider arenas, Fuentes is primarily concerned with the cultural and political realities of the Hispanic world. In fact, much of the novel is set within the space of the Escorial, the famous Spanish structure that has become an emblem of the empire's successes and failures. Built near Madrid in the sixteenth century as an edifice of multiple identities, the Escorial encloses within its walls a church, a palace, and a monastery.

Fuentes's Escorial is primarily a metaphor for the Spanish monarchy's morbid preoccupation.[9] Both museum and mausoleum, its main function is to preserve the past. As founder of the structure he inhabits, Felipe, one of the historical figures fictionalized in the novel, plays a central role.[10] He both cultivates and resists death, and he attempts to ground his power and authority in that contradiction. The Escorial, an emblem of the novel as project and projected idea, is a monument to that venture. Fuentes's Escorial reaffirms while enduring beyond death itself: as the Spanish monarchy's castle and crypt, it is figured as a cemetery for both the living and the dead. Yet this self-divided, morbid site is also the seat of imperial authority. From inside this paradoxical space (almost, as it were, from inside the grave) the novel's Felipe attempts to exercise absolute authority and to wield eternal power.

The mysteries of the novel's fictions are matched and, indeed, further empowered by the complexities of its narrative strategies. In *Terra nostra* anecdotal enigmas are supported by narrative mysteries: the power of mystery itself would appear to sustain Fuentes's readers through the 783 pages of the novel. The mysteries that circulate in *Terra nostra*'s fiction, like those of detective fiction, are orchestrated around scenes of death. The narrative traces a route from one such setting to another: besides the Escorial, the principal sites of action include sacrificial temples and an apocalyptic city. While no initiating criminal scene is presented for investigation, Fuentes does weave into his text the notion of an original murder that gives rise to (Hispanic) civilization and the exercise of power within it (see note 8). Thus, the mysteries of power and death are connected in several registers of the text at once.

Terra nostra's structural enigmas and thematic mysteries regulate, as they also limit, the reader's access to the novel. Reading becomes a reading of parallel puzzles; the search for meaning is also a search for what might explain the difficulty of the search itself. The main thematic problem (the nature of authority, the mystery of power) is developed by a narrative that creates more puzzles than it solves. The reader cannot establish a hierarchy of discourse in *Terra nostra*, clearly identify many of its narrators and characters, nor accept some of the answers the novel appears to provide. But Fuentes, not unlike a careful author of mystery fiction, leads his readers to believe that all the answers to the novel's enigmas will emerge. The author presumed to orchestrate the text even employs the manuscript-in-the-bottle device as a promise of such a resolution. This cliché of mystery fiction reinforces the likelihood that the reader will believe in an ultimate and single truth, both thematic and structural, that awaits discovery at the end of the novel.

This truth turns out to be a fiction in which the reader, like El Señor, may be led to believe, mainly because the author seems to have virtually asserted that such a truth exists, even if it is never actually revealed. The reader must read—again like El Señor, whose reading of secret manuscripts the individual reader would duplicate—in order to acquire the knowledge that will allow mastery of the text of *Terra nostra*. The author's exercise of authorial power is derived from the expectation of the reader's desire for, and eventual belief in, a univocal, authoritative reading of the novel.[11] Though *Terra nostra* is apparently written to counter such a reading, it must, of course, also support and be supported by it at the same time.

Terra nostra appears to resist readerly efforts to solve its mysteries. While many of its secrets are revealed by the novel's end, the solutions to other puzzles remain beyond its reader's grasp. The mysteries that persist in the text seem to contaminate and undermine even the answers revealed by it. It is suggested, moreover, that the veiling or unveiling of such solutions is the natural prerogative of figures of authority, and specifically of authors. Indeed, authorial privilege is openly invoked to explain and even justify the perpetuation of narrative enigmas. For example, Fray Julián, one of the novel's (and Fuentes's) characters, declares: "todo ser tiene el derecho de llevarse un secreto a la tumba; todo narrador se reserva la facultad de no aclarar los misterios, para que no dejen de serlo; al que no le guste, que reclame su dinero" ["every being has the right to carry a secret to the tomb; every narrator reserves to himself the privilege of not clarifying mysteries, so that they remain mysteries; and who is not pleased, let him demand his money"] (660/655).

Though this "manifesto" of narrator's rights opens on a democratic note ("every being has the right"), it mainly serves as a defense of an authoritarian theory, if not also practice, of authorship. Such theory and apparent practice both support, as much as they also subvert, absolute authorial authority in *Terra nostra*. This challenge to the desire and demand for knowledge by the reader (or, more accurately, by the narratee-as-reader) is a challenge to those who would resist the secrets kept by a narrator and the power exercised by an author. It thus responds to pressure from a partner and becomes a sign of resistance to mastery by an adversary. But *Terra nostra* shows that such a contest between characters or readers and authors is problematical. The absolute authority of, or proof of victory by, one over the other figure is put into question by *Terra nostra*, even as its author appears to assert otherwise. Fuentes's novel may well betray the absence of authority (especially absolute authority) that its narrative strategies and stories seem designed to overcome.[12] The absolute authority seemingly wielded by its historical and textual author-figures is staged as part of a complex play for power and position among adversaries who are also accomplices of some consequence. This play may well reveal itself to be a powerful fiction on which the weight of *Terra nostra* (perhaps the last of a dying breed of novels) uneasily rests.[13]

Let us consider first the novel's narrative strategies and how they empower while, oddly, also dividing fictions of authority and authorship in Fuentes's novel. *Terra nostra*'s narrative web engages the reader in an effort to unravel and reorder its multiple threads at the same time that it thwarts such an undertaking. It is difficult to establish the temporal and spatial distances among many of the settings within which narration occurs, as well as the differences among the stories that are told and the narrators that tell them. *Terra nostra* is structured such that several stories are at once inside, outside, before, after, and simultaneous with one another. Moreover, their narrators seem to duplicate one another vertiginously: they relate and repeat discursive dialogues and interior monologues that are themselves repetitions, revisions, or new versions of what has, or seems to have, been said already.

In *Terra nostra* telling becomes a repetitious retelling, and narrators proliferate endlessly. But narrators in Fuentes's novel are inevitably characters in their own stories or in those of other narrators. A number of problems are also posed by characters in *Terra nostra*, where "character" refuses to function consistently as a referent for the proper name assigned it. Indeed, proper names (which according to convention function as signs for fictional characters) are given both to clarify and to confuse; they make identification simultaneously possible and impossible. It is difficult to know whether the repetition of a name signals the reappearance of an individual and identical character or whether a change in name marks a shift in its fictional referent. For example, it is often easy to confuse, and thus to deny a difference between, the two figures called "El Señor" or the two called "La Señora."[14]

The enigma of identification develops around a variety of characters. However it is most problematical (and important) in the case of the three identical youths who mysteriously appear and reappear throughout the novel.[15] These three, apparently also reincarnations of Agrippa Póstumo, named in the curse cited above, are also many. Each, accompanied by an enigmatic green bottle containing a manuscript, seems to maintain but also to change his identity—to be and not to be himself. Although distinguishable, as a group or individually, from the other characters, these three youths cannot easily be differentiated from one another. The marks that identify them (the six toes on each foot, the cross on the flesh of each back) are also those that confound identification. Differentiation would here mean individualization: in order to distinguish one from the other one would have to be able to particularize so as to identify them. However, the information that permits such an identification, it is suggested, is held within each of the mysterious green bottles and in the texts enclosed by them.

The reader is told that the three bottles are given to the youths by a gypsy who tells them not to open the vessels "o se quedarán sin suerte, azar o destino, han estado embotellados largo tiempo, uno llega del pasado: el destino, otro del presente: el azar, otro del futuro: la suerte, éste es el regalo del mago tuerto" ["or you will have neither fate, chance, nor destiny, they have been sealed for many ages, one comes from the past, destiny; another from the present, chance; the other from the future, fate; this is the gift of the one-eyed magus"] (557–58/551). The magus mentioned here is presented as both author of the manuscripts and protagonist of the tales they tell; his status is thus as perplexing as the texts for which he is supposedly responsible. This author is presented as a paper figure and his authority, contained in the writings from which his figure is produced, would appear as shaky as the surface on which it stands (558/552).

As we shall see later, the description of the magus might also be read as a projection of Fuentes (at once real and implied author, personal as well as textual author-figure) within the novel's own pages. Indeed, the magus's "literary" project resembles the aims stated by the empirical author of *Terra nostra*. The gypsy defines the creative process of the former as follows: "Se remontó al origen, condenado a escribir sus propias aventuras una y otra vez, creer que ha terminado el libro sólo para empezarlo de vuelta, relatarlo todo desde otro punto de vista, de acuerdo con una posibilidad imprevista, en otros tiempos, en otros espacios, aspirando desde siempre y para siempre a lo imposible: una narración perfectamente simultánea" ["He returned to the origin, condemned to write of his own adventures again and again, to believe that he had finished his book only to begin again, to relate it all from a different point of view, according to unforeseen possibilities, in other time[s], in other spaces, aspiring from the beginning and to the end of time the impossible: a perfectly simultaneous narration"] (558/552).

This "impossible" text is a text reserved, it seems, not only for a reading by its own author but also for decipherment by three other privileged, and thus potentially powerful, readers: the three youths. The narrative suggests that they are the only readers to be allowed access to the manuscripts, the only figures privy to the information they contain. But the three young men neither act nor speak as if they had acquired such knowledge. Indeed, they appear to have either forgotten or repressed it, as each obsessively repeats the same single question, a question of identity the manuscripts are supposed to have resolved: "¿Quién soy yo?" ["Who am I?"] (see, for example, 69/64, 277–78/270–72, 401/395, 414/407). And this question is echoed (and mirrored) by other questions of identity—"¿quién eres tú?" ["Who are you?"] and "¿cómo te llamas?" ["What is your name?"]—directed to the three young men by other characters in the novel (see especially the section entitled "¿Quién eres?" ["Who Are You?"] [63–69/58–63]). Thus, the problem of identification of these three key characters-turned-readers is sustained throughout the novel. The text of truth through which that problem would be dissolved is never revealed, never presented for the novel's reader to read. It appears to be reserved as a secret to be kept by the text and its author, whose unquestionable authority, the novel's characters would remind the reader, is figured as an absolute prerogative.

The problem of identifying narrators is analogous to that of individualizing characters in Terra nostra. Such an identification would depend on the stable differentiation of the temporal and spatial frames of narration for each narrating subject. To identify, by giving a single proper name that would individualize, the source of a "voice" or to designate the antecedent of an "I" would also be to clarify the identity of the subject in control of the narrative produced through each act of narration. The identification of individual subjects would, of course, lead to the differentiation among the instances of discourse in which each subject is produced and would clarify the knowledge each narrator appears to possess.

Such differentiation would amount to establishing not only a hierarchy of knowledge but also a hierarchy of discourse, a narrative hierarchy for the whole of *Terra nostra* itself. At the top of that hierarchy would be situated, presumably, the subject (a "voice," an "eye") that appears to know or see more than everyone else, a subject whose voice might reveal all it knows or whose eye might display all it sees. This privileged narrator would also be the principal subject of authority in the narrative, over which, by virtue of the superior position and knowledge held, she or he would appear to exercise complete control of the text and its multiple narratives. However, *Terra nostra* does not allow the reader to construct this narrative hierarchy. It makes it difficult, if not impossible, to acquire sufficient knowledge about the novel's narrative situations and subjects so as to master its narrative order.

Fuentes's novel is not unique in this respect, as readers are well aware. Contemporary fiction, especially Spanish American narrative, has already taught its readers much about the complex possibilities of modern texts and has revealed the distances between theories about narrative and narrative practice itself. The significant problems of *Terra nostra* are connected to what might be called narratological issues, but they are not delimited by those questions. The narrative complexities are important because they are related to the elaboration of a thematics of power and authority, which also structures the relationships among the characters in the novel.

Mystery functions at one and the same time at the levels of anecdote and structure. As such it links these different registers, for the problem faced by the fictional characters and the reader is something like "the problem of a problem." The novel as a whole is therefore buttressed by interdependent mysteries that are parts of a larger problem of mystery. The strategic arrangements of *Terra nostra* not only produce that enigmatic appearance. They may lead, or seduce, its readers into believing that they will find the solutions and ground— the *terra firma*—from which the novel's story and structure can be viewed and comprehended. Fuentes's novel plays on readerly desire for mastery of the text as it also creates, through the narrative mysteries on which it rests, the illusion of coherent solutions over which mastery might be achieved.

The narrative both suggests and subverts the possibility of such mastery. As we turn to some textual details, we may perhaps see, if not the whole picture, something of the frame for that possibility. *Terra nostra* begins and ends its many stories with what may appear to be a frame setting, since the time and place within which the action of the first and last pages occurs are almost identical. The narration of all the novel's stories seems to begin in an apocalyptic Paris on July 14, 1999, and to end there on December 31 of the same year. When the reader finishes the novel and finally begins to see it as a whole, she or he may, for a moment, also read this return to Paris of 1999 as the resurgence of a narrative position from which all the others can be comprehended.[16] The novel moves from that July 14 setting back into the world of sixteenth-century Spain and El Señor, then farther back to a mythic, pre-Columbian era in Mexico, only to return to sixteenth-century Spain and, finally, in the last chapter ("La última ciudad" ["The Last City"] 764–83/760–78), to Paris of 1999.

In spite of the jump of five and one-half months that signals the temporal distance between the first and last chapters, the return to Paris marks the reappearance of a familiar setting. But a discursive gap between the two chapters underscores a crucial difference. The novel begins with an omniscient third-person narration that seems to ground partially all the narrations that follow. The unnamed narrator of that chapter appears as the novel's potentially authoritative subject who sees, knows, and tells more than any other subject of narration. However, somewhere in the course of the succeeding chapters that privileged narrator or voice of authority—the figure of an authorial surrogate—is lost. The return to the Paris of 1999 at the end of the text does not mark the continuation of the omniscient third-person narration of chapter one. The last chapter is in the second, not in the first person; its narrator is not located above, as it were, but rather on the same level as the other person named in the narrative.

The difference between these modes of narration, and thus the significant movement from one to the other in the chapters mentioned, is revealed in the differences among the subjects and objects of both narration and focalization.[17] In the first chapter the invisible narrator (the one who speaks) is also the principal subject of focalization (the one who sees), while the character named Polo Febo (Pollo Phoibee) functions as the main object of both narration (the one who is spoken about) and focalization (the one who is seen). Even though Polo himself becomes a focalizor, whose perceptions are viewed by another and reported to the reader, he remains in a position subordinate to that of the more external and original narrator-focalizor, from whose position as subject he is clearly distanced.[18]

In the last chapter, however, the difference between subject and object is called into question; their hierarchical relation is undone. At the end of the novel the invisible narrator addresses himself to the object of narration, Polo, who appears to be at the same time both the one who sees and the one who is seen. That is, the invisible narrator, who presumably sees Polo, sees almost entirely through the eyes of Polo, who thus becomes the dominant subject of focalization. Most important, however, is that what is seen by Polo is Polo himself, or Polo seeing and thinking about himself—both in the present and in the future—since these are the verbal tenses that dominate the last chapter. The temporal and spatial distances between the subject and the object of focalization are virtually impossible to diagram, except as mutually self-negating intervals or gaps by which the one displaces the other.

This oscillation of subject and object is precisely what characterizes the structure of second-person narration and the authorial manipulation of that mode in this text. Second-person narration emphasizes the intersubjectivity inherent in discourse, the potential for each object of discourse to become a subject and each subject to be an object. The speaker who says "you" is always potentially a "you" named by an interlocutor, in the same way that a "you" who begins to speak becomes an "I" in, and a subject of, the produced discourse. In *Terra nostra*'s final chapter, then, the one who speaks is always potentially the object of the discourse of the one to whom he speaks. Thus the identities of the narrator and Polo, translated into the pronouns "yo" ["I"] and "tú" ["you"], continually move toward and displace one another vertiginously in these last pages.[19] Just as the gap between the subject and the object of focalization cannot be seen conclusively, the narrator's voice cannot be stabilized in a position outside or above that of its object nor can it be assigned a stable pronominal tag.[20] By definition, this narrator cannot, in fact, be located "outside" the dialogue with the "you" it names or "before" or "after" the discursive situation in which he is situated.

This shift in grammatical person from the first to the last chapter of *Terra nostra* signals the parallel shifts in the mode of narration and focalization that serve to subjectivize the text as a whole. This shift subverts the notion of an objective discourse. It thwarts the possibility of stabilizing the seemingly authoritative narrating voice or seeing eye in an omniscient, superior position. The hierarchies apparently established in the first chapter are thus virtually denied—rather than reaffirmed—in the last.

Fuentes multiplies the complications produced by the final chapter's narrative technique by casting its protagonist as a reader and possibly also an author. It is only at the end of this chapter that the name of the character addressed as "tú" is revealed to be Polo Febo (777/773), the protagonist already named in the first chapter, "Carne, esferas, ojos grises junto al Sena" ["Flesh, Spheres, Gray Eyes beside the Seine"] (13–35/9–31).[21] Until that moment of nomination, Polo's identity is unclear—not just because he has not been identified with a proper name but because he resembles, even seems to reincarnate, one of the three youths who escaped the Escorial some three centuries before and also to suggest indirectly Agrippa as well. Mysteriously enough, he is also presented as the reader and possible author of some manuscripts that he found inside three green bottles, now located in his Paris garret (768–70/764, 772–73/768–69, 778/774).

Polo is identified as a reader and an author of a text that may be identical to the one in which he is also a character. The words addressed to him also seem to be the words he himself utters. Polo the author is at the same time Polo the reader, who is inscribed within the pages that are read. The identification of Polo Febo as a reader-author addressed by the pronoun "tú" places the character in a position that is also assumed by Terra nostra's own reader. Through the character named Polo the roles of reader and author converge: reading the pronoun "tú" addressed to Polo Febo, the novel's reader may also "hear" it as addressed to himself or herself. Even though linguistically the two figures are distinguishable, the one is excluded in a first moment but then maps itself onto the other. (The discursive interchange, signaled by the presence of the second-person pronoun, would also exclude from itself the presence or sign of the [real] reader, who has become a "he" or "she" outside this dialogue but may yet project himself or herself into it by identifying with one or the other subject or object of the represented discourse.) The superposition of possible antecedents for that pronoun suggests, and virtually creates, the identification of the extratextual realm with the intratextual reality presented by the novel. Such a superimposition virtually collapses discursive stratification and undermines the separation of realities that would permit the isolation of a frame setting as well as the differentiation of textual roles and fictional identities.[22]

Both the structural denial of a discursive hierarchy and the reflexive conflation of the spheres of fictive representation and extratextual reality work against the notion of absolute authority or stable authorship in Terra nostra. It is not only that the reader cannot identify a single subject of sufficient knowledge and authority suitable for the position at the top of the textual hierarchy. Fuentes's novel also offers a proliferation of possible authors whose explicit declarations of their own authority appear, in the moments they are voiced, to constitute the final word on the question of authorial knowledge and narrative privilege. All those who appear to know more than any other narrating subject cancel each other out as final authorities for the text, just as those who are finally revealed to know considerably less than one or another rival narrator-author undercut the authoritative position of their competitors.

Of the narrators whose stories are presented as authoritative and whose voices momentarily appear as having authorial status, three overtly claim their own privileged position in *Terra nostra*. For example, Celestina, a self-conscious narrator who begins one of her stories at the end of the first chapter, not only presents herself as the most knowledgeable of narrators but also identifies her story as *the* story to be told (257/251).[23] Though in his "Confesiones de un confesor" ["Confessions of a Confessor"] Fray Julián, another self-privileged narrator, later concedes momentarily that his knowledge is incomplete (660–61/656), he forcefully asserts the ultimate veracity of his tale above all the others told in the novel (657/652). And when Fray Julián finishes his story yet another authoritative narrator, the Cronista (Chronicler), takes over and assures his reader that it is he who authors "esta crónica fiel de los últimos años del reinado y la vida del Señor don Felipe" ["this chronicle faithful to the last years of his reign, and the life of Don Felipe, El Señor"] (674/669). The plurality of privileged narrators, as much as the proliferation of partially knowledgeable voices, belies the existence of an original or absolutely authoritative source of truth or of a figure originally or finally identifiable as the author. It also serves to deny a univocal or privileged reading of the text. This is a curious, though powerful, denial in *Terra nostra*—one that, in order to make itself powerful, must constantly pose as having no power at all.

The quest for knowledge is a quest for an individual and authoritative text that would either resolve the questions whose answers are sought or constitute in and of itself a coherent and uncontradictory master-version of all the stories and storytellers encountered in the novel. This is a communal quest, one inscribed within the fictional realm beyond which the reader is situated and engendered in the textual sphere within which reading is anchored. The reader of *Terra nostra* figures the readers inside its fiction, and the principal reader within that fiction figures the readers outside it.

Indeed, El Señor, the key reader within the novel's narrative, is engaged in a hermeneutical activity virtually identical to that which shapes the reader's relation to Fuentes's text. The three mysterious youths are as much of an enigma for this fictional, though also authorial, figure as they are for the novel's own reader. As a reader-figure, El Señor searches for information that would reveal the origins of the three men. He seeks a text that tells the truth—the unique, authoritative story. He literally reads the available texts so as to identify that privileged text and to acquire the knowledge contained by the manuscripts enclosed within each of the green bottles.

The manuscript sealed in a bottle is a familiar device of mystery fiction and has a double function. It is both a mystery and a solution; it both suggests and solves a problem. While the text remains hidden, it retains its identity as a puzzling and secret text designed to arouse curiosity and create suspense. Only when the manuscript has been read does it eradicate the mystery of its own contents by providing the solution to its secrets. When such a manuscript functions as a pivotal text, the revelation of its contents often resolves the structuring mystery of the work within which it appears. On reading a text (such as *Terra nostra*) that employs this device, the reader may well expect that the manuscript in the bottle will function simultaneously as a figure of mystery and as a sign of a solution.

In *Terra nostra* the green bottles, along with the manuscripts hidden within them, pose as repositories of knowledge, partly because of their conventional identity and the expectations that readers are likely to hold about such conventions. However, as noted above, they are likely to be assigned such a role not only because of their conventional status but also because of the connections made within the fiction (that is, the gypsy's comments, cited above). The reader may well come to believe, much like El Señor, that the bottles do indeed contain authoritative texts, which, when read, will finally disclose the truth about the youths' origins and history. In order to master the text as a whole, the reader must first, or simultaneously, obtain mastery over its mysterious parts—over the separate and secret manuscripts that apparently serve as keys to its design. Knowledge of the youths' true identities would lead to, or simultaneously reveal, the identity of the narrator(s) and character(s) also in possession of the novel's truth.

Such knowledge would therefore also call forth a figure of textual authority, perhaps even the figure of the author, as the emblem of such knowledge. The solution to this fictional or thematic problem thus appears to be linked to, even identical with, the key to the mystery of its narrative design.

El Señor wants, and indeed needs, to master (so as to become master over) the manuscripts he desires and demands to read, and which, once he has read them, he also desires to erase or rewrite. According to his reading, his power as a monarch, his authority as a unique and sovereign ruler, rests upon his ability to acquire those texts, so as to possess and then read them. For the knowledge about the youths' real names and identity—their origins—can only be acquired through a reading of these texts. It is that knowledge that will identify for this potential master-reader those who may well threaten his absolute authority. Here the desire to exercise power, to wield authority coincides with and is mapped upon the desire to read: knowledge, power, and authority become inseparable.[24] This knowledge originally is, but also becomes, the ground on which El Señor's power seems to rest as well as the foundation from which his authority arises.

El Señor believes that reality itself is not only defined by but also contained within that which is written; the text is constituted through a writing whose inscription marks an authoritative and permanent life for what he calls reality. He says: "nada existe realmente si no es consignado al papel, las piedras mismas de este palacio humo son mientras no se escribe su historia" ["nothing truly exists if it not be consigned to paper, the very stones of this palace are but smoke if their story not be written"] (111/106); "lo escrito permanece, lo escrito es verdad en sí porque no se le puede someter a la prueba de la verdad ni a comprobación alguna, ésta es la realidad plena de lo escrito" ["what is written remains, what is written is true in itself, for it cannot be subjected to the test of truth, or to any proof at all; that is the full reality of what is written"] (193/188); and "únicamente lo escrito es real" ["only what is written is real"] (677/672).[25]

This faith in the written word, in the text as sacred revelation of truth as well as constitution of reality, appears to empower El Señor's own exercise of power. However, this figure of authority conceives of power in general, and thus of his own in particular, as something like an object, something that can be circumscribed or isolated in a particular place—for example, in a building (El Escorial) or in a text (the mysterious manuscripts—or even *Terra nostra*). The text generates and becomes both the source and ultimate emblem of power and authority: "El poder se funda en el texto. La legitimidad única es reflejo de la posesión del texto único" ["Power is founded upon the text. The only legitimacy is the reflection of one's possession of the unique text"] (611/605). However, to believe in such an absolute definition of power—or, rather, to believe in power itself as potentially absolute—is to believe in a fiction. El Señor appears to misread how power works, for he seems to be blinded by his own desire to possess it. He thus misses its relational nature.[26] This is precisely the situation that obtains within both the fictional and textual realities of *Terra nostra*.

El Señor's attempt to circumscribe reality is also an effort to concretize power so as to possess it absolutely and eternally (to take it with him to the grave like a secret and sacred object). But his attempt is unsuccessful, and the Escorial becomes an emblem of both his enterprise and its defeat.[27] This edifice is a monument to El Señor's belief in, and desire for, absolute authority; but at the same time it figures the dispersion of his authority and power. The building is a concrete, singular place and yet it is many places at once (we recall that it functions as a palace and monastery, museum and mausoleum). Like a fortress, it is constructed to endure through time, yet its strength is not so great as its author-inhabitant would imagine it. El Señor attempts to enclose and maintain within that structure the power he thinks he commands, the authority he believes he wields. The edifice would therefore become the space within which his power-as-thing would be located if power were concretizable and if El Señor wielded as much authority as he imagines or desires. However, the Escorial, constructed as a monument to authority and a symbol of power, is in the end an emblem of powerlessness, a figure of problematical authority, much like El Señor himself.

The Escorial is the space within which El Señor would enclose himself completely, wall himself up and seal himself off from the outside world. His main project, in fact, seems to be to achieve this isolation through acts of self-enclosure. His desire to block out the passage of time and the movement of history from the space within which he exists is a refusal to see beyond his own immediate space, his own text. Indeed, El Señor tries to author and authorize a text of reality that would refuse temporality, textuality, and history.

Such a textual reality would, theoretically at least, empower him. Such a text (or world) would reveal its secrets only to him, the original, singular, and authoritative author whose knowledge no reader or character could acquire, and whose absolute authority and privilege no other subject could hope to obtain or equal. But, in order to become the authoritative founder of such a text, El Señor must first become a master-reader. He must master a set of texts on which his authority also seems to depend. Oddly, his desire to possess a power that is absolute and to exercise an authority that cannot be challenged is what assures that this desire cannot be fulfilled. El Señor's acquisitive strategy is precisely what keeps him from achieving his goal and from seeing that it is unachievable.

El Señor virtually buries himself within the Escorial, becoming a corpse whose hermetically sealed place matches that of the necropolis he constructs to house the past and present members of his family. This self-burial is part of his attempt to dominate and give order to reality by reducing it to a manageable set of elements whose restricted order suggests something like a self-sufficient text. When El Señor tries to impose his own order, he is attempting to constitute a reality for which he would serve as the sole author and authority. This authorial movement, however, is a contradictory one. In some sense, El Señor does not really want to be an author, though he does want to exercise absolute authority over a text that he also tries to create. We remember that the traditional role of the author—or the traditional conception of that role—not only presupposes the exercise of control over a (literal or figurative) text or the possession of superior knowledge. It also presupposes the fulfillment of a paternal role (the author engenders offspring whose existence as filial subjects would establish a paternal identity for their progenitor). El Señor's goal, however, is to undo the possibility of being a father, literally to negate his identity as a father-figure in one realm so as to consolidate his paternal privileges in another.[28]

According to his implicit theory of authorship, which would propose the author as supreme and paternal, El Señor is unable to become the author he desires to be. For the only way he can achieve the position of power and the authority he plots to attain is to deny or dispel all evidence of paternity. If El Señor had no heirs (that is, no sons) he would become the last figure of monarchal succession, the last king or emperor—and, paradoxically, the final father-figure. By denying his own potency, he would constitute (or so he imagines) an eternal position of power. This is precisely what El Señor appears to try to do in *Terra nostra*. He not only aims to decipher the identities of the three youths, who may well be his kin and who would have the right to succeed, and thus disempower, him. He also plots to capture and control them. The urgency of his investigative readings becomes evident when it is revealed that, according to Ludovico (the character who has, in fact, played the role of father to the three) and Celestina (the mother of two of them), it is likely that the three are either his brothers or his sons (596/590).

Knowing of Tiberius's prophecy, El Señor reacts with alarm when first informed of the existence of the youths marked with six toes and a cross. But he thinks of them only symbolically as his sons: "¿el signo de los usurpadores, los esclavos rebeldes, he engendrado a los esclavos y a los rebeldes que habrán de usurpar mi reino, mis hijos parricidas, el trono levantado sobre la sangre del padre?" ["Is this the sign of the usurpers, rebellious slaves, have I engendered slaves and rebels who will usurp my kingdom?, parricidal sons?, a throne raised upon the blood of their father?"] (666/661). Once they have been identified as potential heirs to the throne, obviously they become potential threats to El Señor's position of authority and privilege. The mystery of their identities exercises a power over El Señor, who is virtually powerless without the information presumed to be inscribed within their manuscripts, information which may or may not, of course, actually undermine the monarch's position.

If the information disproves the youths' identity as his heirs, El Señor supposedly can continue to wield power and exercise authority. If it verifies their royal filiation, he must attempt to constrain so as to control, or to destroy so as to defeat, them. In any case, El Señor's power, if not his authority, rests upon what the manuscripts reveal to him, and, according to the theory of power he himself has proposed and in which he believes, he must follow what they virtually tell him to do. He will be empowered by the information they contain. He will be rendered powerful by the knowledge they impart to him and vested with absolute authority by virtue of his unequivocally unique position. But to make those texts yield their information (their power), which would further authorize his exercise of authority, El Señor must first master them. El Señor thus grants power to that which already has power over him but which will finally return it to him (see El Señor's words on 611/605, quoted above).

Although El Señor (and perhaps the reader of *Terra nostra*) wants to read all three manuscripts, he is unable to do so. As noted above, the contents of only two of the green bottles are revealed to the monarch.

Indeed, when he dies he remains obsessed with the mystery contained in the third, and in a last will and testament commands: "Encontrad la tercera botella, eran tres, sólo encontré dos, sólo leí dos, buscad la tercera botella, debo leer el último manuscrito, debo conocer los últimos secretos" ["Find the third bottle, there were three, I found only two, I read only two, seek the third bottle, I must read the last manuscript, I must know the last secrets"] (753/748).[29] That ultimate text and its secret contents contaminate El Señor, even after his death. For as the Cronista observes while gazing on his corpse— "Pobre Señor. . . . [E]n su frente leo la palabra: Misterio" ["Poor Señor. . . . upon his forehead I read the word: Mystery"] (757/753)— within the fiction El Señor is transformed by his own obsession and quest into yet another mystery to be read (and perhaps deciphered) by the reader of, if not other characters in, *Terra nostra*.

The complete text that might have been formed by the conjunction of the separate but related manuscripts eludes El Señor. He has the possibility of mastering only two of them; the third, and consequently the total text, remains unread and undeciphered, out of his control. In a similar fashion, two of the three youths escape from the enclosure of the Escorial, denying El Señor's ability to cloister or control them. The fortified edifice reveals its weakness, for it fails as a fortress when it allows the youths to slip through its walls without El Señor's knowledge, much as it ultimately fails as a fortification against time and death for its own author. The Escorial, literally and metaphorically, is not entirely able to hold all that its author(s) would wish to enclose within it.

As the youths and their manuscripts slip out of the reach of El Señor the notion of a completely coherent or truthful reading of the text also slips away. The end of the novel does not signal the resolution of the thematic and narrative problems that emerge within the text. Indeed, readers are left in a somewhat powerless position as their expectations for the solutions to the novel's mysteries are finally frustrated. Mystery always exercises some kind of power over those who search for its solution.

In *Terra nostra* the author's strategy is to increase the potential force of the text's enigmas by suggesting that they are decipherable. The author would appear to manipulate the reader, to convince the reader that there exists an ultimate truth that he, as author, possesses and will reveal by the end of the text. In the end, however, the novel's author appears to retain or refuse to reveal (perhaps even to invent) such a truth. As author of *Terra nostra*, Fuentes creates, and even presents himself as, an author-figure who appears to be and who yet undermines his own appearance as an authoritative author. This figure is a subject who plays, while also playing at being unable to play, the privileged role of the author who would command the truth but be unable (or choose not) to tell it.

Fuentes's apparent authorial power play replicates the thematic paradox explored in *Terra nostra*. The power the author presumes to exercise throughout its weighty pages is sustained by a fiction of truth, which may lure readers on when they might not otherwise continue with the novel. It could be argued that this fiction, generated by the various techniques briefly sketched here, is necessary because it gives life to a text that is otherwise obsessed with death. From Paris as apocalyptic site to the Escorial and Aztec temples as necroplises, *Terra nostra* moves from one funereal spot to another. Yet the death that pervades the novel is also precisely what its author appears to try to circumvent.

Terra nostra is, to say the least, an ambitious work. Its scope and length suggest Fuentes's attempt to write a "total" and yet self-perpetuating novel.[30] Indeed, it is arranged so that its own end, its own death, can be neither located nor imagined. (Paris is the site of death on which life appears to be engendered anew in the final pages of the novel. While making love, Polo Febo and Celestina are transformed into a hermaphrodite from whom a new being and beginning will be generated [781–83/777–78].[31]) The sheer length of the text and the techniques deployed to circumvent a decodable end become strategies that keep the reader reading and the text "alive." Thus is the text perpetuated and its death deferred. Of course, in a literal sense, its end does come and the maneuvers used to ward off that last page are defeated. The author eventually must give up the text to silence and hand it over to the reader.

Yet the question of which figure may be read as the text's possessor, or how any figure may become identified in such a role, persists at the end of, if not also beyond, the text of *Terra nostra*. The masterful author figured by the text, as well as the author known by the name Fuentes, would seem concerned to defer, if not to defeat, the reader's appropriation and possession of the novel. Those figures would seem poised to forestall, if not also to foreclose, the author's loss of the text as an object over whose possession there might still be some debate.

Fuentes, the author, fashions a text that empowers a masterful author-possessor figure whose possession of the novel, like El Señor's possession of the secret texts, would be put into question, in spite of that figure's apparently masterful performance. The authorial subject dominates his readers by thwarting their ability to solve the novel's mysteries and master its text so as to transform it into an uncontradictory whole. This authorial power play within the text may be read as part of a broader authorial project, defined by Fuentes himself. Much like the magus, who is identified as author of the stories told in the secret manuscripts (see above), or El Señor, who attempts to author the story of history itself, Fuentes defines *Terra nostra* as "una aspiración a la simultaneidad" ["an aspiration to simultaneity"] through which he, as master of the text, would overcome the "determinismo del acto de leer y de escribir" ["determinism of the acts of reading and writing"] (Fuentes interview with Coddou 9).

By definition, this project is impossible. We remember that language marks time, and that reading and writing are temporally organized activities, facts Fuentes also recognizes (Fuentes interview with Coddou 9). Since the linearity and forward movement of language on the written page can be negated only illusorily, Fuentes appears to design an elaborate scheme to suppress that fact within *Terra nostra*. The authorial project—a project designed, it seems, to reclaim authorial authority, while also aiming to erode it—is therefore both an attack on and a defense against the nature of literature. In this battle the author invokes a personalized adversary over whom a certain victory seems to be possible. Readers, always in the position of the ones who know less, are virtually powerless before the complexities of *Terra nostra*. They submit to that position in the act of becoming readers, but they are kept there by an author determined to avert his opponents' potential mastery of the text. The possibility of readerly control may well be what provokes the engaging display of authorial power, which is then also a "counter-exercise of power."[32]

Though these authorial manipulations are indeed powerful, they may also be read as the signs of the limits of authorial power, perhaps even of an inherent powerlessness. For the figures of Fuentes and El Señor appear to be caught by similar paradoxes. El Señor persists in trying to control that which must ultimately elude his grasp; he tries to deny death and to resist the loss of eternal power and absolute authority, neither of which he ever really wields. Aware of his own mortality, he works to conceal his imminent death beneath complex and lengthy disquisitions that serve only to fill up time, never to deter it. His effort to exercise control and create a univocal, linear reality is powerless before the circular and repetitive movement of history. The more he attempts to dominate the world, the more he assures his own defeat.

Likewise, Fuentes may well betray his project while striving to create a simultaneous and multiple text that would contradict El Señor's linear and univocal reality. The tactics by which various mysteries are created in *Terra nostra* also bolster the weighty explorations of questions about history, myth, and literature that circulate in the novel. This strategy emphasizes linear solutions and, in a sense, gives Fuentes's figure its power, for the novel otherwise might collapse from the weight of its own theoretical discussions. But Fuentes tries to sustain the discursive weight of the novel by invoking the same literary limitation it apparently rejects. While the author attempts to construct a nonlinear, simultaneous narration and narrative, the only support sufficiently forceful to keep it moving (and, perhaps more important, to justify it) is the repeated insistence on its potential linearity. The fiction of linearity is indeed a significant fact in *Terra nostra*; it cannot be easily dismissed.

The maneuvers by which the author seems to exercise power over his readers, while attempting to negate the real movement of reading and writing, are those that also betray such an authorial presence or project. That betrayal, and consequently the defeat of the author's stated enterprise, are potentially kept from view by the repeated assertions of authorial control, and by the virtual presence of an authoritative author. To read *Terra nostra* critically, then, may well be to see in those demonstrations of power also the limits of power they belie. The assertion of such absolute authority may instead be a response to the realization that such authority, as well as such power, is but a fiction, though a very powerful fiction indeed. Fuentes's insistence on *Terra nostra*'s potential strength—its apparent ability to overcome the limits of literature—may in the end prove the inevitability of those very bounds.

Nevertheless, that the limits of *Terra nostra*'s powers or of its author's authority may well be demonstrated by Fuentes's novel does not necessarily mean that the figures of the author produced by that text are ultimately subordinate, secondary, or inconsequential figures. On the contrary, as we have seen, *Terra nostra* reclaims substantial figures of the author, though its narrative structure and story would also dispossess any one figure of absolute authority. Its ground becomes, in a way, the shifting ground on which a competition between the author-as-possessor and the author-as-possessed figure is plotted and played out. Attached to the title *"Terra nostra"* in this chapter, then, the name Fuentes draws both a figure of authorial resistance and a figure of authorial surrender. Those figures persist as competitors locked in an ineradicable struggle over textual possession and power.

5

The Dis-Appearance of a Popular Author
Stealing Around Style with Manuel Puig's *Pubis angelical*

Authorial claims, or disclaimers, about literary influences, aims, and effects have an equivocal status for the reading of fiction. Readers have learned to be wary of taking the authorial word as the first, the last, or the authoritative word on reading. However, it may not always be clear how such words are to be placed in relation to the texts around which they circulate. When the word of the author concerning a work of fiction's aims, techniques, or meaning is granted a critical role it may have more of a rhetorical or strategic importance than exegetical or interpretive significance. Indeed, some contemporary criticism has found it instructive to read what authors say in relation to what they write if for no other purpose than to demonstrate that what authors do in their work does not necessarily coincide with what they say about it.

Talk about texts or about texts and their authors thus fashions different positions for the statements made by authors and the comments produced by critics. The word of the one may arise either to counter or to confirm what the other says, to accept or to reject the other's authority.[1] Moreover, the issues of concern to the one may become associated with the interests of the other. The one figure may be seen to build on—to borrow or to steal from—the word of the other; the one may be seen to teach or to be taught by his or her literary or critical interlocutor.[2] The status of authors' words around their texts may thus reduplicate that of the writing for which they are otherwise principally known. The word of the author presents itself as original and authoritative, but also as a word that emanates from and depends on its dialogue with the words of others.[3]

The recuperation of the figure of the author from statements surrounding literary texts may well be as problematical as its recovery within them, especially when the author implicitly or explicitly addresses the question of who may have the last and authoritative word. When that question is raised by an author whose own work flaunts its debt to the words of others, and who himself talks about how he has worked with and reworked others' styles, the question becomes even more perplexing. But, oddly, such an author may either retain or reclaim a place of preeminence for himself (and also for the figures of the author produced within his texts) precisely by pretending to keep himself out of sight, behind the styles and statements of others. Though such a figure seems to disappear into such borrowed or stolen statements and styles, he may nevertheless establish his own privilege and authority through them.

The case of Manuel Puig is exemplary in this regard. The initial reception of his work in France hailed what it took to be an intended connection between modern literary theory and practice, which certain of his first readers believed they could detect in his earliest novel. Some statements Puig made concerning that reception provide a suggestive entry into his own dis-appearance as an authoritative figure.[4] The case of Puig's various responses, moreover, discloses how an author may become engaged with—and even assert while seeming to disavow—the critical ideas, cultural concepts, and theoretical terminology characteristic of his own times.

As Puig tells it, when his work (that is, his first novel—La traición de Rita Hayworth [Betrayed by Rita Hayworth] [1968]) was first read by French critics, it was acclaimed for representing the recently theorized disappearance of the author. This disappearance, it was suggested to him, was one that he, the text's author, had both planned and promoted. Though ignorant, he claims, of what the critical phrase meant, and certainly not responsible for intending any fictional elaboration of such a theory, Puig readily agreed to this characterization. He claims he was grateful for the praise and recognition of, as well as general interest in, his work.[5] In recounting not only the anecdote about the characterization of his early fiction as illustrative of the author's disappearance but also how he came to write his first novel, Puig seems to disregard, if not also discredit, the theory that others would see it as exemplifying.[6] In making fun, as he did, of the attribution of theoretical aims or critical intentions to an author so unschooled, as it were, in the ways and words of literary criticism and theory, Puig's anecdotal disclaimer both supports and subordinates the critical enterprise with which his writing has become identified.

Indeed, Puig's declared ignorance of the theoretical significance of the "disappearance of the author," and his apparently innocent production of texts that, nonetheless, may have seemed to put into practice such theories, suggest a number of things. First, they reinforce, from an authorial perspective, conclusions drawn by much of, if not most, modern criticism about the relation between authorial aims and output (that is, to read the latter as determined authoritatively by the former is, to say the least, a problematical exercise). They also underscore the space between the writing of narrative fiction and the theorizing about it. Puig's authorial disclaimer differentiates and distances the one activity from the other, the one form of discourse from the other. But, given the inherently critical nature of Puig's writing, which itself questions the relation between apparently opposing theories or practices virtually everywhere, the idea of such distance or difference may well be difficult to sustain around Puig's work.[7]

Not surprisingly, Puig's disclaimer of authorial intention, and his implicit denial of any knowledge of the theory he was supposed to have been aiming to elaborate in fictional form, take us to the question of the author, to which his novels propose some intriguing responses. Indeed, Puig's work, which for some readers would exemplify modern French notions about the author while also presenting the case of an authorial entity apparently unaware of any such ideas, appears both at odds and in harmony with conventional conceptions of the author. Puig's writing overall figures an unconventional, unanchored, and unlocatable author, but also reclaims inordinate authority for its author. In each of his novels, the author is effaced from the text as a traditional figure, yet his image or voice is also inscribed in authoritative, if not authoritarian, positions between their lines.[8]

Puig's novels seem to speak for an author who is rooted in contemporary culture, and who seems to speak from the position of a subject produced within specific professional and personal conditions.[9] These contextual factors situate the author-person in a somewhat ambivalent position, which he may (or may not) share with other Spanish American writers. Unlike a good many of those authors, Puig would present himself as theoretically innocent (indeed, even ignorant). While other authors may appear to fashion into fictional form certain critical issues that occupy their attention in other nonfictional writings, or to incorporate into the novel form essayistic ruminations about literary principles or tradition, Puig is one of those writers who seems to simply "do" (rather than "talk about") literature. However, his writing would recall the problematical nature of such a dichotomy, and the deceptive turn taken by this author's words around such an apparently clear opposition.[10]

In telling his story in retrospect, Puig casts himself as an uninstructed writer who knows little about the categories and issues of interest to literary critics. (Of course, as the narrator of that story, his knowledge is considerably greater than that of the authorial character into which he transforms himself through that telling.) In his writing as well as in his comments about his work, however, the figure of the author as innocent character also seems to reveal the face of the author as informed interlocutor. His work suggests that the figure of the unschooled author is at the same time an instructive figure, one that seems as ready to give as to take instruction. The question of precisely what it is that gets taught by Puig's writing and where exactly either the author-as-student or the author-as-teacher may be situated (in what position; on which side of a discussion or debate) is not all that easy to unravel.

In reading Puig's fiction, and perhaps in looking at some of his comments about one or other of his texts, the reader is confronted with the provocative dis-appearance of the author, within both personal statements and professional style. In particular, Puig's fifth novel, *Pubis angelical* [*Pubis Angelical*] (1979), leads one to consider the popular author's dis-appearance as it addresses topics with which Puig's name has become associated since he began writing narrative fiction and about which he has often talked in a variety of interviews and personal

Reclaiming the Author

appearances.[11] Like other of Puig's novels, *Pubis angelical* seems to eradicate traditional authorial indicators with the forms of discourse and narration through which its story (or stories, as we shall see) is told. But it also figures authorial interests and aims; it also elaborates a ground from which the signs of authorial activity and authority might emerge. It is thus both an idiosyncratic text (one that produces an authorial figure that becomes identified with either the person or the writing associated with the name "Puig") and an exemplary work (one that reestablishes that authorial figures appear in, as they are produced in one or another way by, narrative fiction generally).

Pubis angelical is organized into two parts of eight chapters each. It both juxtaposes and interweaves three lines of narrative whose interconnections can be read, it seems, one way or another. The principal narrative is set in 1975 in Mexico City, where the protagonist, Ana (also referred to as Anita), an Argentine woman nearing her thirtieth birthday, is hospitalized. The 1975 setting remains fixed in Ana's hospital room, where, while recovering from cancer surgery, she alternately talks with each of two friends who visit her, and also writes in her diary. The novel's text not only shifts between those dialogues and her diary entries within the sections advancing the 1975 narrative. It also alternates between that contemporary story and two other tales, which may well be different parts of a single narrative. The "other" story shifts from a 1930s/1940s setting reminiscent of Hollywood movie fantasies, in which it also seems to refictionalize a part of the life of a well-known Hollywood figure (that is, Hedy Lamarr), to a twenty-first-century science fiction scenario.[12]

Ana's story, which is composed of first-person diary texts written by the protagonist and immediate direct dialogues into which she enters with her feminist and political activist friends who visit her, engages issues current in contemporary culture. The dialogues thematize the problematic state of Argentine politics in the 1970s (for example, 114–24/94–103), issues raised by contemporary feminist theory and practice (for example, 19–21/12–13), and theories advanced by modern psychoanalysis (for example, 169–72/145–48).[13] The diary texts serve as confessional self-examinations and private ruminations about related (even identical) topics of intimate concern to Ana (for example, 190–97/163–69). Though these dialogues and diary entries alternate with each other and with the other narrative lines advanced alongside them, they are presented chronologically and as occurring over a two- or three-week period in October 1975.[14]

Dis-Appearance of a Popular Author   93

The text alternates between this narrative frame—the "realistic" story that anchors the novel as a whole—and the Hollywood movie/ science fiction narrative, presented through omniscient third-person narration.[15] Though Ana's contemporary story would seem to frame the other fictions that are developed alternately alongside it, it is also framed partially by them. For the text opens not with Ana's tale but with the narrative set in the 1930s and 1940s. This story, partly staged in Hollywood, evolves as a movie melodrama-romance of that same era, as it focuses on the figure of "la mujer más bella del mundo" ["the most beautiful woman in the world"] who is also identified as "el Ama" ["the Mistress"] (the counterpart to her industrialist husband, "el Amo" ["the Master"]) while located in Vienna, where her story opens, and mainly as "la actriz" ["the actress"] once she moves to Hollywood.[16] The end of this Hollywood movie story, however, gives way to the beginning of the science fiction tale, whose protagonist is a young woman identified as W218; her life in the "era polar" ["polar era"] during the twenty-first century is plotted through chapter sixteen. However, like the Hollywood-style tale before it, it too alternates with the episodes that advance the fiction centered on Ana in the hospital.

(The tales are set in distinct calendar eras, but their duration is difficult, if not impossible, to determine. As noted above, Ana's story, which is staged throughout the novel's text, develops over a period of two or three weeks, and its precise endpoint cannot be definitively fixed. The story of "la mujer más bella del mundo"/"el Ama"/"la actriz" begins in Vienna in 1936 and moves into the early 1940s [perhaps to 1943, as the reference to her completed seven-year Hollywood contract suggests (127/105)]. Information about the exact date on which the protagonist dies [and thus the duration of the immediate tale that is told] is not supplied by the narrator. And W218's tale, situated in some post-atomic, twenty-first-century year referred to as "Glaciario Año 15" ["Glacial Year 15"] [203/174], transpires over the course of several months during that future year.)

Pubis angelical is the conjunction of these stories, the juxtaposition and intermingling of narrative details from different, but apparently connected, fictional realms. And it is a problematical conjunction. Most obviously, the formal techniques of narration may have a considerably disruptive effect on the reading process. The forward movement of each story is interrupted by the insertion of a fragment or episode from another narrative frame that advances through analogous and parallel disruptions and movements. Each narrative progresses partly by interrupting the progress of the others, and each is cut up and cut off by another narrative, which is itself both curtailed and moved forward by another. Each alternately seems to deter and be deterred by one form of narration or the other, and each story advances by curtailing the advancement of other stories.[17]

However, the problematical nature of this conjunction of disparate narrative frames and lines of action may have less to do with the diversity of narrative techniques used within the text (such diversity is also characteristic of Puig's earlier novels), or with the disjunctions of story and plot or the differences of narrative duration, than with the problem of establishing the significant connections, if any, among them. That some sort of connection is to be made seems quite possible, if not altogether probable. The repetition of identical or markedly similar thematic concerns and anecdotal details within the separated stories would seem to establish not only a connection among the tales as a whole but also an identification among their protagonists.

For example, the possible identification of Ana, "la mujer más bella del mundo"/"el Ama"/"la actriz," and/or W218 is suggested by similarities in their appearance (these also suggest a resemblance to the Hollywood star Hedy Lamarr [for example, 33/24, 210/180]), and by references to similar experiences, dreams, or thoughts (for example, 11/5, 17/10, 41/31, 59/47–48, 107/88, 148/125, 102/84, 139–40/ 116–17). Moreover, Ana's own suggestion that, in writing her diary, she may well be trying to make contact with "mi anterior encarnación . . . una mujer que tuvo su apogeo en los años 20, digamos" ["my previous incarnation . . . a woman who was in her peak in the Twenties, let's say"] (26/17) does not exactly coincide with the figure of "la mujer más bella del mundo" nor with that of Hedy Lamarr (the height of the movie star's success comes in the later decade). But the other corresponding details may nonetheless seem to identify these figures with one another. Or, one might also consider the popular narrative models (that is, the episodes reminiscent of 1930s or 1940s Hollywood melodramas and romantic films) that not only inform the stories of "la mujer más bella del mundo" and W218 but also potentially shape Ana's life (for example, Pozzi's plot to have Ana lure her former lover Alejandro to Mexico so that he can be captured, held, and exchanged for political prisoners in Argentina; see 219–23/188–91).[18]

The juxtaposition of separate, but seemingly interconnectable, narrative frames and figures suggests that there is some way of reading these stories as one, some way of interpreting what they mean individually and together. The question of the relationship among these stories, and especially among their protagonists, is also a question of meaning—what each story signifies for the others, how each story is defined (or not) by other parts of the novel, what the novel as a whole seems to say or do. As such questions are considered, the question of the author is inevitably raised. For the enigmatic quality of the stories' relationships in *Pubis angelical* may suggest that there is some meaningful plan, some authorial strategy, that would explain connections otherwise encountered as difficult, if not impossible, to read.

As one attempts to establish the connections among the narratives—that is, as one attempts to figure out what those stories are about individually and together—one may unwittingly assume an intended authorial design. One may retroactively construct a set of (perhaps only provisional) answers as the original solutions to the puzzling nature of the novel's narrative. To consider such questions is to open the way for the reappearance of the author. As one attempts to figure out what is going on in the text one may be led to figure into it a place for a governing subject, even when the author may seem to have disappeared somewhere behind the scenes. Framed by Puig's own statements about the novel, *Pubis angelical* may tempt its readers to do just that.

One may wonder what would happen if one's reading were to turn in the direction of some of those statements. One wonders whether one would virtually see (or hear) an unquestionably authoritative figure, whether the author's figure would emerge as that of an authority, or as some other kind of figure. Admittedly, such a turn toward Puig's statements about the novel may constitute a recuperative gesture. Of necessity, such a gesture would reclaim authority for the figure of the author outside the text, if not for the authorial surrogate projected by it, whether that be Ana inside the novel or a larger figure situated around it. However, as happens in his novels, Puig's statements cast the author as a subject divided between different positions and proposals. When Puig talks about how one is to make sense of these three narrative settings he both provides an apparently authoritative pronouncement about their relation to one another and puts on equivocal footing the explanation that he, as the author of the fictions, advances. His authoritative explanation turns itself into a tentative interpretation, a provisional reading, which his own readers may (or may not) decide to follow.

Puig's explanation of the novel's narrative structure and stories is as follows: "La novela se divide en dos partes: una en la que cuento toda la vida consciente de la protagonista . . . , y allí pongo lo que ella habla, lo que escribe en su diario íntimo, es decir todo aquello que ella puede controlar, lo que está en su conciencia, los contenidos conscientes. Por otro lado, como una historia paralela que cuento, está lo que yo supongo que son sus fantasías más secretas, fantasías que ni siquiera ella se atreve a enfrentar, a asumir" ["The novel is divided into two parts: one in which I tell the story of the protagonist's conscious life . . . , and there I include what she says, what she writes in her personal diary, that is, everything she is able to control, what is in her conscious, its conscious contents. On the other hand, in something like a parallel story I tell, there are what I presume are her most secret fantasies, fantasies that she doesn't even dare to confront or assume" (Puig interview with Corbatta 617–18).[19]

That the story of Ana is manifestly distinct from that of "la mujer más bella del mundo" and/or W218 is obvious from the anecdotal materials (that is, temporal and spatial details, events) comprising each. That the latter two stories are in fact one narrative, or that they individually or together are related to Ana's story as Puig proposes, is not definitively established either by the text one reads nor, as can be noted, by Puig's own statement. Indeed, the authorial statement cited above proposes a division that is to be understood in terms of the opposition between the conscious and the unconscious, between what is under or out of control, according to Puig. But what does it mean to be in or out of control here? One wonders in what sense the protagonist or the author might control the opposition or the separate spheres to which the material of the one or the other is supposed to pertain. One wonders whether the figure of the author might appear or disappear as a figure of control above or behind the fictional character over whom he claims to exercise such powers.

What one encounters in the dialogue and diary sections is, however, not a subject entirely in control of things. Rather, the text presents a fictional subject who repeatedly confronts the limitations of any such effort (and especially her own) to stabilize facts, locate the truth, or understand either the way things are or the way they ought to be. Moreover, this figure's world is one into which there intrude fragments, details, images that supposedly derive from the material over which she apparently does not exercise any such control (that is, material from the "unconscious," images from the narratives that are superficially excluded from her own immediate fiction). And, what she presumably controls can neither control nor contain its own borders, nor what appears to erupt into it.

Puig's statement also acknowledges, even if only provisionally, the instability of those boundaries, the rough edges where one story meets, opposes, and virtually intrudes upon another. Indeed, the momentary recourse to a term of uncertainty within his explanation of the text's structure and sense (that is, "supongo" ["I suppose," "I assume"]) destabilizes both the interpretation he would propose (and a good many readers might wish to follow) and the authority presumed to inhere in the author's reading of things.[20] Curiously, this slippage from assertion to speculation in the authorial statement also figures the movement that characterizes the discourse of the novel's protagonist. Indeed, given Ana's certainty about being uncertain about how to interpret things, as well as her final discovery of her own contradictory stances, she seems to figure the stance of the authorial figure that emerges from Puig's explanatory statements around the novel as well as from the narrative developed within it.

The contradictions that inform Ana's discourse and also the seemingly startling self-conscious discovery of some of those contradictions (232/199) mark a significant moment in her constitution as a subject in the text. Her direct dialogues and diary texts produce a subject that becomes visible within situations of dialogue (virtual dialogue with herself and active conversation with others) that take the form of debate and discussion. Both Ana's diary and dialogues configure a shifting subject, and an entity at odds with, while in pursuit of, stable solutions to the complex interpersonal and political relations in which Ana finds herself. Indeed, it would appear that her desire for knowledge about, or for an understanding of, those relations is precisely what leads her to realize the partial truths, the inadequate interpretations that she, and others, are apt to produce around them.

The impulse to knowledge seems to be precisely what leads Ana to recognize that the route to that end is a problematical one to follow. Near the end of the novel, in fact, one sees her explicit and self-conscious recognition of the difficulties, if not impossibilities, of matching theory to practice or of grasping a theory that might adequately and consistently explain reality (in this case, the relation between cultural production and political systems, the possible correlation between cultural taste and political practice). Her arrival at a logical impasse serves to discredit, since it allows her to disavow and disown, previous positions and conclusions she had taken so much time to develop, and about which she once seemed to be so certain.

When Ana encounters a case that disproves, and thus destroys, her theory, she concludes that "todo lo que he anotado en este cuaderno esta tarde, no tiene el menor sentido. Tengo que admitir que no entiendo nada de lo que pasa, ni a mí ni a los demás. Pero no pretendo nada, no pretendo entender nada" ["everything I've written in this notebook this afternoon doesn't make the least bit of sense. I must admit that I don't understand anything about what's going on, neither with me nor with anyone else. But I don't pretend anything, I don't pretend to understand anything" (translation mine)] (232/199).

The section at the end of which Ana makes this statement is typical of others in which she both tries to analyze relationships and individuals who have played an important role in her life (for example, her husband Fito), and to extrapolate from such analyses a general theory about interpersonal relations, politics, and culture. In this particular instance, which occurs in chapter thirteen, she writes about what she plans to do after her release from the hospital, and then slips into ruminations about the differences between the emotional life of men and that of women, as well as about men's or women's relation to power. By calling up cultural stereotypes and characterizing men and women through sexist clichés—which she appears to take seriously—Ana opposes the world of men (activities of violence, attraction to sports and war) to that of women (attitudes of sensitivity, interest in dance, music, and art). And, she concludes that "[s]i los hombres tuviesen más música adentro del corazón, más Mozart, el mundo sería diferente" ["If men had more music in their hearts, more Mozart, the world would be different"] (231/199).

However, this theoretical conclusion to her cursory analysis of sexual difference, with its reductively simplistic response to the complex structures of global politics, disintegrates in the face of the evidence offered by the case of right-wing Alejandro, with whom she was briefly involved while still in Argentina and whom Pozzi tries unsuccessfully to convince her to lure to Mexico.[21] The exception to, and thus, she concludes, the final destruction of, her theory is noted in the "pero" ["but"] that introduces the counterexample of Alejandro: "Pero Alejandro jamás ve fútbol, y odia el box, y todo lo que sea deporte violento. Uno de sus proyectos en el gobierno era proponer la abolición de las carreras de autos. Y adora la música. . . . Y sin embargo es lo que es" ["But Alejandro never watches football, and hates boxing and everything that has to do with violent sports. One of his projects in the government was to propose the abolition of auto racing. And he adores music. . . . And in spite of this he is what he is"] (232/199).

Two points are of particular interest here. First, the conjunction "pero" ["but"], through which Ana's analysis shifts from the general rule to the particular exception that virtually destroys her theory, is a pivotal term that turns Ana from one side of her own reasoning to the other, from one kind of certainty or uncertainty to another. And this turn is itself turned around by the concluding conjunction ("sin embargo" ["in spite of" or "nonetheless"]) that leads Ana to once again contradict her own formulation. These turns around certainty and uncertainty seem to lead to a final stance of ignorance or innocence in Ana, who is both uncertain about what to be certain about and certain about what she is uncertain about. Each stance becomes more problematical as it unwittingly turns back upon and appears to reverse itself as well as the subject figured by it.

The other point of consequence has to do with the attempt to propose a general theory of social or gender difference and to relate any such theory to general formulations about cultural formation or political practice. Clearly, the intersection of such interests and problems is a salient feature of Puig's novel. Ana's self-conscious ruminations (many of which are echoed by those of the other two female protagonists, as noted above) serve to thematize the issues with which this novel also deals and around which Puig's writing has repeatedly revolved.[22] The issues under investigation for Ana are at once private and public, sentimental and intellectual. The insistent and explicit manner in which they are addressed by the novel's main characters situates them as topics of considerable importance for the text as a whole. One might also argue that they have a great deal of significance for the author, whose writing addresses those topics through characters such as Ana.

The novel's trajectory of dialogues and diary texts, along with the Hollywood movie and science fiction tales' quest patterns, also situate Ana as something of a didactic figure. That is, Ana's exchanges with virtual or real interlocutors with whom she engages in difficult discussions and self-examinations become scenes of instruction, frames for teaching and testing one or another idea to, or with, one or another partner. Such exchanges would suggest that much gets taught and learned here, but they also demonstrate that the role of teacher or student is not anchored absolutely or permanently in any individual character or subject.

It is precisely an interest in knowing more about, and thus understanding, how personal relations develop and how political situations and cultural realities connect up with one another that characterizes Ana's discursive activity and her presentation as the novel's principal subject. Her conversations and diary entries cast her as a figure tied to the question of knowledge. She is a figure whose desire to know things so as to understand and present them to others, and whose interest in informing others about them (or keeping such information from her interlocutors), in some way directs all that she says and does (see, for example, 18–22/10–14, 114–24/94–103).

Moreover, Ana's posture as a figure of knowledge may appear to repeat or reinscribe within the fiction the figure of a textualized author, whose manipulative as well as investigative gestures readers of Puig will recognize from his other novels. For Ana's position is also that of a subject whose desire to tell what she knows occasions a reticence, if not refusal, to reveal what could, it seems, be told or taught. This position is implicitly balanced with—it responds to as it is prodded by—that of an intelligent interlocutor (in the case of the authorial figure, that of an interested reader) who seeks to know, to learn what the other would reveal. Such an interlocutor would thereby become situated in a position of discursive (or textual) dependency.[23]

On the other hand, in her diary texts, where she turns her discourse back on herself in an effort to understand any number of private and public matters (such as the question involving Alejandro, cited above), she figures as an uninformed, but curious, subject in search of an elusive truth or understanding. She becomes but the student whose effort to learn or propose a truth only ends in the recognition of the contradictions, the impasse, to which the desire to know leads. As suggested, Ana is a figure both in and out of control; she is a masterful and a confused subject. Moreover, this fictional character appears to be controlled by an authorial subject whose own control of things might be assumed to be absolute, but whose performance might nevertheless reveal its own equivocations.[24]

It could be argued that Ana's posture (that of a figure of the will to knowledge[25]) figures an authorial disposition toward teaching and being taught more or less masterfully. Although she would seem willingly to place herself in the position of student, she is also cast in the role of teacher—one who teaches herself, it seems, as much as she may teach others. Indeed, in her conversations with Pozzi and with Beatriz—characters presented as more knowledgeable about the "serious" topics (that is, political and social history, psychoanalysis and feminism) she would also discuss—Ana appears to instruct even those who presume to act as her instructors.

For example, Ana's and Pozzi's conversation about Argentine politics (especially Peronism), which emerges from her request for explanations from (that is, her apparent desire to be taught by) him, ends with her forceful criticism of his position and of the tactics of the political group he supports. That is, it ends with her assumption of the role of knowledgeable critic or even prosecutor (121–24/100–103). And, though Beatriz would assume not only the role of feminist authority but perhaps also that of virtual (psycho)analyst (she refers to Ana's situation or "case" [59/47], which she is trying to understand or analyze), Ana seems to position herself as a subject of knowledge (even if only about herself, her own story) by whom her interlocutor will be informed if not also instructed (for example, 18–22/10–14).

The impulse toward instruction, so explicitly staged in this novel, might lead one to wonder whether Pubis angelical might not be read as some kind of modern thesis novel. However, with its narrative and discursive diversity, and its preoccupation with "trivial" as well as "serious" topics, Pubis angelical would appear to remove itself from the sphere of strategies and senses affiliated with that literary model. One might, nonetheless, read Puig's novels as exposing and espousing certain ideas about politics, art, and culture, and by doing so to have proclaimed his authoritative stand about a variety of significant issues.[26] Or, one might read his novels as staging a contest of different positions, as a kind of battleground on which different theses are entertained and tested but from which none emerges victorious.

In the first reading, the figure of Puig would be positioned as a somewhat authoritarian figure, as that of an author aiming to impose certain positions and opinions.[27] Indeed, the associations made with Puig's name as that of an author who has challenged the established literary order in the name of the popular situate him as an authority on, if not also an authoritarian practitioner of, subversion. However, the word of this subversive figure would not be heard directly; it would be heard instead through the words of others (for example, the novel's fictional figures). The author's word would be seen to disguise itself as the word of another, the better to resist readerly resistance to authorial (and potentially authoritarian) proposals. In the other reading, Puig's writing would be taken to counter the idea of an authoritative last word, to betray the notion of a privileged authorial pronouncement about its own didactic, if not dogmatic, authority. The author's word could be seen as but one word among many, or as the word of a subject whose own position keeps shifting.

Read one way or the other, *Pubis angelical* seems ready to both disguise and disclose the word of the author, to figure the author as a dis-appearing figure. As noted above, the traditional figure of the author (that is, the author as figured by traditional narrative) disappears behind the characters' discussions and debates (beneath their questioning and teaching each other about recent Argentine political history, or modern culture, or interpersonal relations) and beneath the conjunction of different stories. The disappearance of an authoritative narrating voice or narrator through whom the entirety of the text might be presented to the reader unhinges narration from a univocal subject onto whose image that of the author might be mapped or in whose words those of the author might be heard.

Moreover, in *Pubis angelical* one may recognize a figure one has seen or heard before (that is, in other of Puig's texts), or one may see or hear for the first time (that is, in this novel) an authorial subject who seems to take up particular and popular causes in idiosyncratic ways. The author-figure, which may be read as inscribed within this text or as produced between this one and others of Puig, is an idiosyncratic figure whose word it would seem difficult to confuse with the word of other authors. The author of *Pubis angelical* comes to the surface, as it were, as a singular figure. But this figure's distinctive style is, oddly enough, predicated on the stealing of the styles and words of others. This style virtually demands to be identified with the name Puig, the name of an author whose style (like that of any author, of course) is not to be subsumed by any single linguistic or anecdotal feature, by any individual technical or structural strategy.

There are, however, such features and strategies that have become associated with Puig's writing, and with the subject who appears to have signed *Pubis angelical*. The name Puig also names discursive and thematic (if not also narrative and generic) features that have come to be identified as the virtual property of the author who writes under that name. For example, when one thinks of Puig's writing one thinks of the themes and forms of detective or serial fiction, popular songs, soap operas, and Hollywood movies, as well as of the languages of fashion magazines, psychoanalysis, and melodrama, among others—

all juxtaposed and combined to shape Puig's literary signature. The figure to which one would give the name Puig thus surfaces through certain topics, talk, and techniques that have been regarded as characteristic of his writing—as constitutive of his style.[28] But Puig's work becomes a reminder of the difficulties of subsuming under a term such as "style" (or even a seemingly more precise term such as "idiolect") all the features that would be taken to identify or figure this (or any) author. Such features are nonetheless those through which Puig becomes visible and audible. They are the characteristics through which the authorial figure seems to recuperate and reconstitute itself as a significant figure, and to make an appearance in one form while disappearing in another.

One kind of disappearance of the author thus seems to occasion a different kind of authorial appearance within or around a particular novel. The absence of an authoritative narrator who would propose a tale or authorize a unifying perspective on it signals a dispersion of subjects of authority and sites of authorship throughout the text. However, this dismantling of the site of narration as a univocal and unitary source may merely remove the figure of the author as narrative authority to another site, beyond the frame of the traditionally privileged narrator, who has often served, or at least been read, as an authorial surrogate. The author of *Pubis angelical* becomes the organizer of the voices of others, behind whose figures he disappears but through whose discourse and disposition he also makes an identifiable appearance. Such an author appears as an editorial figure, who empowers anonymous, though also recognizable, discourses, which, in turn, identify the author's work.

Puig's writing, therefore, might be viewed at once as an exemplary demonstration and also as different from the example of what his early French readers saw him as doing. His work as a whole, and also some of his words spoken around his writing, call attention to two different notions of disappearance, and to the consequences of reading the one for the other. If, as suggested above, the so-called disappearance of the author is understood as the disappearance of a unitary site of narration or thematic speculation that might suggest the empirical author's presence or aims, then Puig's writing could be read as such an example. However, *Pubis angelical*, among other of Puig's works, moves things in other directions as well, as it stages the author's appearance as a singular and recognizable, though perhaps unstable, figure. Thus, in

Puig's writing the author may well disappear as one kind of figure but necessarily reappears as another.

Given the choices made concerning the issues addressed within the fiction and the popular stories told (especially the Hollywood movie and science fiction tales), the figure of the author proposed by this text is not only a figure developed by the features of narrative structure that inscribe an authorial subject in any text one reads. It is also a figure of ideas and attitudes, opinions, and positions implied by or inferred from *Pubis angelical* as a whole.[29]

As is typical of much of Puig's work, *Pubis angelical* promotes the author as an original manipulator of popular forms and styles, behind which the figure of the author may seem to vanish. Indeed, Puig has been celebrated for his elaborations on and control of popular culture—the languages, genres, and stories that characterize any number of popular forms. As emphasized above, *Pubis angelical* works with popular paradigms drawn from 1930s and 1940s Hollywood melodrama and romance, and also from the genre of science fiction. Moreover, it incorporates recognizable scripts from contemporary culture (for example, Lacanian psychoanalysis, feminist theory), sometimes objectifying them in the course of the characters' externalized dialogues or internalized discussions, and sometimes rendering them as explanatory referents represented by the position or posture of one or another fictional figure.

To a certain extent, then, Puig performs as a copier, as well as an editor, of the scripts of others (perhaps, one might even say, as a kind of *scriptor*). He presents himself as a virtual compiler who combines and correlates discourses that originate with no individual subject, and as a commentator who presents anew controversial topics and talk, apparently without taking his own identifiable or stable position about them. The dis-appearance of the author in *Pubis angelical* might therefore be thought of as a dis-appearance of individual style. Puig disappears as an author also because he works through a mode of writing that is grounded in the virtual stealing of the styles of others. But that style of stealing constitutes the very style designated by the name Puig and through which this author also appears. Puig's writing reveals its own recognizable signature in the style of stealing it develops and with which it is identified.[30]

Oddly, though his work derives from the cultural models that belong not to any individual author but rather to contemporary culture itself, those models have nonetheless come to mark Puig's position as a writer of original texts. They have situated him as an author responsible for an enterprise that would critically frame cultural forms considered to be subliterary or discursive models traditionally situated outside "high" art but resituated by his writing. Indeed, the status of the "low" models whose style is stolen by Puig is modified such that those models adhere also to principles identified with the "high." And the "high" is in turn somewhat transformed by the contact with what initially seems to be "low."[31] The ownership of such models is effectively (though in some sense illegitimately) transferred to Puig, under whose name they are read and reauthorized.

Popular models that originally belong to no individual, since they are the product of no single author, have become so identified with Puig that his name has become the name of an author to whom such models (which are in a sense originally authorless) revert through a virtual and retroactive attribution of authority and ownership. This author of the popular has become popular precisely for this enterprise, which would also give those forms new life and authority. Puig's project would thereby also reclaim a place for the author as an originator, even though what is taken to be original about this author's activity seems to lie in the copying or rewriting of the words and styles of others.

Puig's style, his signature as it were, is thus to be recognized in a writing that would implicate the styles and signatures of others. And in Pubis angelical, for example, that writing leads back and forth between the idea of a style that is unique and personal—the mark of a person, even a body, from which that style would seem to emanate[32]—and the idea of a style that cannot be attached to, or used to identify, any individual entity or subject. Moreover, Puig's writing becomes an uncertain matter because it seems to turn, or to allow one to turn one's reading, between two related but opposing textual strategies or discursive systems—between parody and stylization. That is, if one reads the story of Ana/"la mujer más bella del mundo"/W218 as an unstable play between parody and stylization, or their combination, the question of style (and the matter of authorial identification or position it might propose) becomes uncertain. Given the disparate authorial positions presupposed by either of those forms of discourse, or those styles, the questions surrounding the figure of the author produced by Puig's writing persist. In stealing the styles of others and in turning those styles into objects for stylization and/or parody, Puig also maps out a space—an equivocal but nonetheless enduring space—within which the author's figure may appear.

Since Puig works with a variety of forms of popular culture and language, his writing follows any number of generic and discursive conventions characteristic of models not originally his own. But as his work appropriates and transforms the models and materials of others it also makes them appear to be entirely and uniquely his. Puig's writing would thus identify itself with, and the author's image would attach itself to, a notion of style that shifts things from the idiosyncratic to the generic, from the individual to the conventional, and back again. Indeed, authorial style, as seen through the writing of Puig, is precisely that somewhat contradictory and implausible space where the generic and the idiosyncratic, the conventional and the individual, meet.[33]

With its exemplary objectification (through parody or stylization) of different discursive, thematic, and generic models, *Pubis angelical* appears to exaggerate the question of style precisely because it seems to display so openly the currents with which Puig's writing generally has become affiliated.[34] That is, Puig's style could be read as a stylizing—that is, as a conventionalizing—of the popular styles and conventions (modes of speech, types of stories and characters, written forms) appropriated from outside the text but recognizable within it. Style as such a conventionalization of what is already conventional would thus become a style that denies its own individuality. But at the same time it would also constitute its own idiosyncratic and identifiable manner and material, from which the author's figure might still emerge as a figure of individual identity.

Indeed, in Puig's work, what is recognizable or characteristic also appears as a confluence of individual, though also conventional, factors and features (that is, linguistic, structural, and thematic), or even as a confluence of notions of style. Such a confluence is precisely what seems to construct or disclose what one may take to be Puig's appearance as an authorial subject. For if one were to think of Puig's style as that which appears to characterize, and thus individualize, his writing in general or any one text in particular, one would have to consider the figure of the author as both the figure of an individual who inscribes himself in personal terms and the figure of a subject constructed by the popular cultural currents with which his texts have become associated.[35] That is, the question of style gets raised partly as a question of discursive or generic convention and partly as a question of individual performance.

Thus, if one reads the generic and discursive referents (for example, Hollywood romance and melodrama, science fiction fantasy, feminist theory, Peronist politics, dialogue of psychoanalysis) in *Pubis angelical* as objectified such that they are either reduced to the status of clichés, revealed as inherently trivial, or transformed into the banal,[36] the matter of locating a place, as it were, within which an authorial style could be clearly identified (or recognized) becomes problematical. For, if one reads the manipulation of those models also as the restaging of the commonplace, such a reading would see in them only the reiterated empty forms, themes, and languages that would both suggest that they originate only from a popular and common ground and recall that their author cannot be distinguished as an individual.

One may recognize that the stories of "el ama/la actriz" and W218, as sentimentalized stories of melodramatic ecstasy and tragedy, and the story of Ana, as a tale of personal quest and discovery, fashion what seem to be new narratives that would mark the work of an author whose writing might be taken to be original. But they also revert in such recognizable form to stories already told, images already seen, and languages already heard that their appearance acquires a decidedly secondary, derivative, and unoriginal status. If one reads Puig's signature principally in that reinscription, *Pubis angelical* could be read as a text that exemplifies a deterritorialization of authorship, a text that shortcircuits the notion of style as a mark of authorial individuality.[37]

However, even though Puig's writing entails a certain repetition (through imitation or emulation that may be regarded as having different aims or effects, depending on how it gets read), *Pubis angelical* is nevertheless an individual utterance. As such, it also differentiates itself from its models.[38] And, inasmuch as the aims and effects of the intertextual dialogues inherent in Puig's writing resist stable or univocal identification while his texts also suggest the figure of an author who manipulates everything from behind the scenes, Puig's image—or that of the author-figure produced by a novel such as *Pubis angelical*—both asserts the possibility of an author's final word and destabilizes the site from which any such word might seem to be emitted.

For here the author's word, and perhaps his style, becomes situated as a word that responds (sometimes directly, sometimes indirectly) to the words of others. As such it is both an independent word that would appear to have some kind of final say over things, and a word that, precisely because it is situated in dialogue with different forms of discourse and with the words of other (identified or anonymous) subjects, is neither entirely independent nor final. Thus, the words spoken around the author's text by the empirical figure of the author (words such as those heard, as it were, at the beginning of this chapter) or even by a fictional figure (such as Ana) within it, become words that would allow the author to appear and disappear as an individual, identifiable, and idiosyncratic figure.

Puig, the popular author, disappears as a stabilizable voice or face, but reappears as an ineluctable, though elusive, style—a style that also puts in dialogue the authorial figure to which one might wish to attribute authoritative statements about his work and the figure of the author that would slip away between one and another position within or around his own text. Perhaps "Puig" is nothing more than the name of an author whose writing would repeatedly return to the impasse inherent in reading the figure of the author as one or another image or voice, or in trying to imagine any final word about or by such a figure. "Puig" is but a style that shifts and steals, while also staking its own ground, around the styles of popular culture. In *Pubis angelical*, however, those styles also become the style of a single author.

To talk about Puig's style, or about "the author" as a question of style, may well mean to talk about the ways in which individual texts or individual authors shift one's ideas about style itself. Such talk may generate some kind of reconsideration of the critical metaphors that get used to discuss whatever it is that characterizes—and thus individualizes or identifies—the work of a particular author.[39] In a sense, then, the work of Puig would suggest that models and theories of style may well shift, or need to be shifted, along with texts that might be apprehended through such a notion. The figure of the author, as a figure of style, shifts while also giving support to those notions, even when the idea of style would predicate the impossibility of stylistic originality or individuality.[40]

To talk about Puig as a style is to talk about style as an instrument of inscription and about style as person. Even more, it is to talk about the choice of particular genres or forms of discourse; it is to consider the idiosyncratic mark stamped on or over generic and discursive law. As suggested, *Pubis angelical* also constructs its own style, or that of Puig, as a style assembled from the choices made and the combinations produced among the received—or stolen—models and ideas of others. The author's image or voice—and thus his style—may appear to emerge from what could be considered an identifiable field of thematics or language. Nonetheless, style may not be that easy to locate. It is also what appears around the text, what emanates from the dialogue of contradictory, but distinctive, discursive, thematic, or compositional features.[41]

The dis-appearance of the popular author from within *Pubis angelical*, and also around it, is both an idiosyncratic and a conventional development. Puig's dis-appearance is like that of no other author. Yet his figure exemplifies the trends that may be taken to be characteristic of contemporary fiction, and especially of Spanish American narrative. The question of the author as posed by Puig becomes fundamentally unpredictable and impractical—but still unavoidable—in his novels, where the author has yet to make a definitive or final dis-appearance.

6

Writing Disguises

Turning Around the Author with José Donoso's

El jardín de al lado

If the question "Who is speaking?" may have all but disappeared as a dominant concern for many critics and readers, it still appears as an intriguing query for some writers of fiction. José Donoso is one of those writers. His *El jardín de al lado* [*The Garden Next Door*; translation mine] (1981) plays with that question, and fashions a response which suggests that the answer may still have some significance.[1] The answer provided by Donoso's novel, like the question that frames it, is proposed obliquely by a text that would restrict as well as reaffirm the possibility of identifying an author. The revelation of authorial identity at the novel's end, where this unvoiced query appears to be answered, fashions both a conventional and an unconventional authorial figure. The response formulated by the surprising final disclosure of the author's apparent identity suggests a reconsideration of the consequences of asking (or answering) anything about the author.

Whether abstracted directly from a represented fiction in which authorship is thematized, or inferred from the kinds of roles assumed by fictional characters or textualized authors, in works such as El jardín de al lado the author-figure straddles the boundaries of positions that would situate the author either as an old or a new figure. Indeed, the authors revealed in El jardín de al lado are both fictive and textualized figures, whose performance would dismantle the idea of the author as a fixed or definitively authoritative origin. At the same time these figures seem to recuperate the author's appearance as a person and to point beyond the text to other figures surrounding them.

This novel both erodes and enforces the authority exercised by its authors, by the author-figures one reads as situated both around and within its borders. Moreover, El jardín de al lado binds textuality and power in striking ways. The formal problems of this text are intertwined with political struggles within it. These struggles are set among several author-figures whose competition for control of the text and over one another remains unsettled at the novel's end. Indeed, when the end is reached the complex signs of this conflict become increasingly visible. There, the text also presents evidence of an unsuspected correspondence between the tactics deployed as part of one authorial strategy and those that inform another.

El jardín de al lado closes with a strategic and surprising play of authority. It ends with a maneuver designed to reveal the text's structuring fiction and to unveil its author's identity. This calculated operation also discloses its own design for covering up several figures and places of privilege that support it. Indeed, this text recalls that authority is not to be located entirely in the person or place from which it appears to originate or be exercised.[2] It suggests that an author may be neither here nor there, but always elsewhere. El jardín de al lado, composed of six chapters, not only asks the central question about the author posed above. In the confounding narrative shift from its penultimate to its final chapter, the novel also raises questions about authorship more generally, and about textual authority in particular.

As one reads the novel's last chapter the reader discovers a significant inversion of the authorial position supporting the text. A radical reversal is seen in the identity of the subject who appears to occupy the place of the author. For it is discovered that one narrator (Julio Méndez, the novel's protagonist) has been exchanged for another (his wife Gloria) virtually in front of the reader's eyes. However, this exchange (and consequently the differences between these two subjects of narration) is artfully hidden from view, between the two final chapters where it occurs. The crucial difference that so radically marks the narrative, or the answer to the question that would reveal such a difference, is at first difficult, if not almost impossible, to see or hear.

Donoso's novel appears to close itself off through a play of substitution that opens a path to the figure of the author—a figure at once fictional and real, textual and personal. The unsolicited and unforeseen answer that it is Gloria who has authored the preceding narrative forces the reader to ask retrospectively about the author's identity. The novel opens itself to such interrogation precisely in the place where everything seems to be closing down. A retrospective inquiry of this kind continues to cast doubts on the powers of the text and the authority of its author-figures. Let us turn toward the narrative itself so as to begin to clarify how this authorial plot works.

In the first five chapters of El jardín de al lado one reads the narrative of Julio Méndez, a Chilean writer who has been living in exile in Spain for approximately seven years with his wife Gloria, a part-time translator and feminist writer. This part of the novel (its "body") concerns the summer of 1980 when Julio and Gloria, having agreed to house-sit for Pancho (an artist friend), leave their own place in Sitges and install themselves for three months in Pancho's elegant Madrid apartment overlooking a luxuriant garden—one of the gardens to which the novel's title refers.[3] Julio's story moves from the day Pancho's call to come to Madrid is received—around the end of May (chapter one)— to the end of August, when, having spent the entire summer in the city, the couple take a brief trip to Morocco before their return to Sitges (chapter five).[4] Julio's narrative comes to an end in the middle of this trip outside Spain, and at the end of the novel's penultimate chapter.

The move to chapter six gradually reveals that the identity of the antecedent for the pronoun "yo" ["I"] marking the novel's narrating subject has changed. Even though the narrative context and characters coincide exactly with those of the preceding chapters, the fictive origin of the narration that advances and then concludes that same story has been altered. Moreover, when it is revealed that it is now Gloria, and no longer Julio, who narrates this last chapter, the reader becomes virtual witness to the unmasking of at least two important identities.

Indeed, as the initial narrative disguise is dropped, the "face" that appears seems to be that of the text's author. Gloria establishes that role as belonging to her when she unveils her secret identity—her identity as the real writer in whom Julio's narrative has actually originated. Gloria appears to narrate and write the final chapter back in Sitges, after lunching with Núria Monclús, the literary agent with whom she has just discussed the rest of her novel. (In fact, her novel, as Núria's comments will later suggest, appears to be the five chapters Donoso's reader will have just finished reading.) Gloria picks up the narrative when she returns home, after the trip to Morocco.[5]

When Julio stops Gloria starts; Gloria begins where Julio ends telling their story. Although Julio's tale seems to be continued by Gloria, there is a crucial difference represented by her narrative. It is precisely this difference that the text at first hides from view but later flaunts in the final chapter. That there is such an important difference between their narratives Gloria herself, the still-unidentified narrator, underscores in a cryptic but finally meaningful manner early in her chapter. She says: "Estoy escribiendo esto a muchos kilómetros y a muchos meses de distancia de esa noche en el Hotel El Minzah [where they stay in Tangiers and where Julio's narration leaves everyone at the end of chapter five], después de la cual todo ha cambiado, y se ha vuelto, por decirlo de algún modo, al revés" ["I am writing this many kilometers and months away from that night in the Hotel El Minzah, after which everything has changed and, to put it one way, has been reversed"] (248).

Because of the strategic cover provided by the pronoun "yo" ["I"], the reader cannot "see" Gloria's move either to her role as narrator or to her position as author.[6] It is only when the narrative presents contextual signs of a difference in gender ("Me recojo *hecha* un ovillo junto al fuego, y Clotilde [the cat] se acomoda tibia en *mi falda* mientras copio estas páginas" ["I curl up next to the fire, and Clotilde makes herself comfortable on my skirt while I copy these pages"] [249; emphasis added]) that the critical change in authority for the text at hand becomes visible. The textual reversal is effected and the "truth" of the narrative is finally disclosed by Gloria, who seems to be the only subject positioned to reveal the difference.

To disguise this difference—indeed, to cover it up entirely—is to impede the identification of the text's apparent author and to defer discovery of the novel's structuring fiction. Gloria's plot to hide her identity and her plan for revealing her authorial powers are so very striking precisely because their appearance is delayed. The novel's possibilities for exercising some kind of power outside its borders are contingent upon the possibility of creating a new imbalance of power within them. The surprising final maneuver seems to throw off balance, if not also keep in motion, both the authorial figures within the fiction and the readers who must move with them outside it. Indeed, some of the power of Donoso's novel derives from this unexpected (but also already prepared for or predicted) subversion of an apparently stable and established order.

The final upset is an assertion of a new and evidently final truth about authorial identity and authority. However, it also undermines the possibility of asserting anything final about them. When Gloria is revealed as the text's author and final authority, her appearance undercuts seemingly stable assumptions, apparently established certainties about who is speaking, about who is the "real" authorial subject of this text. This revelation makes it difficult to place what the reader may have been led to perceive as a stable source of authority. It reveals that what has appeared to be a fixed and visible source of the narrative is now to be seen as a mobile and disguised origin. On the one hand, the text appears to identify the subject (that is, the authorial figure named Gloria) who would appear as a final figure of authority. But on the other, it would present that figure as an author who still competes with other potentially authoritative figures for that position of preeminence.

When the reader discovers that it is Gloria's text (still lacking its own final chapter, as one learns in the sixth and last of Donoso's novel) that seems to have been presented in the body of El jardín de al lado, it also appears that ownership of and authority over that text have been transferred from Julio to his wife. Thus any authoritative statement about the novel would finally appear to emanate from Gloria, in whom narrative and textual authority are conclusively, even if surprisingly, consolidated. However, Gloria's final appearance disguises, even as it discloses, the gestures of the other figures of authority that support her performance.

The switch from Julio to Gloria marks a radical shift in, and an apparent reversal of, the gender of authority for El jardín de al lado. It is a provocative shift upon which the novel's critical potential seems to rest, and of which its own subjects appear to be aware. In fact, the novel's final maneuver constitutes a self-conscious tour de force through which the narrative relations, as well as structuring design, of Donoso's text are redefined and the subjects who determine its closing moves repositioned.[7]

The narrative shift that reopens the question of the author in the novel is a move by which an apparent object of narration accedes to, if not also reclaims, the position of subject. More important, this position is not just any position, but that of the author. It is suggested later that Gloria has actually occupied that position silently and invisibly throughout the text. This maneuver transforms her into a linguistic "person" and a thematic power at the same time that it marks her husband's loss of narrative ground and discursive place. The image of one author virtually usurps the position of another: a seemingly secondary subject of authority replaces another whose primary position appears to have been authorized (but then denied) by the very subject who both follows and precedes him as the narrative text's original author and final authority.

In virtually silencing Julio (after presumably first having given him his power to narrate and to appear as an author), Gloria forces her husband into the only place left open for him. This is the very place that Gloria herself has just vacated: the place of the narrative object, the position of the linguistic "nonperson," which the pronoun "ella" ["she"] first marks for Gloria and the "él" ["he"] finally designates for Julio.[8] However, this switch takes place between chapters five and six, where it literally cannot be seen. When the last chapter is finally read, the reader perceives the effects of an authorial maneuver, which has the power to turn the narrative and discursive tables on both the fictive authors within the text and the readers outside it. Only "after the fact" does the resulting inversion of Julio's and Gloria's positions reveal the strategic importance of the whole operation for the novel's thematic as well as narrative designs.

In fact, to read the final chapter is to see the apparent outcome of several contests involving these two narrators, these potential or "real" authors, who are also partners in parallel plays for authority within the novel's story. In both the thematic and textual relations of significance the woman who first seems to occupy a less important position is transformed into, as she is also revealed to have been, the "real" power behind the man who has formerly seemed to control the text, and also her. As he moves from the position of subject to that of object of the narration, this apparently dominant male figure seems to have to surrender his privileged place to the woman beneath whom he is ultimately resituated.

The text's pronominal plays suggest that the place of the author is extremely problematic. They also uncover some of the ups and downs of authority in El jardín de al lado, which can be read as a network of cover-ups or subterfuges that alternately support and suppress the powers of the novel's disparate authorial subjects. For Gloria reveals that it is not so much that things have really changed when she finally speaks for herself (that is, in her own name and voice, through her own "I"), but that the "truth" once hidden can finally be "seen" and "heard." As author—as originator and provider of the facts, as master and manipulator of the text's fictions—she acts to uncover the truth behind the lies that are the very ground upon which her own text is built and around which her work as an author revolves.[9] In this final chapter Gloria discloses the kind of cover-up that sustains not only her text but also Donoso's novel. This narrating author reveals that she has been working undercover: she has been writing under or behind the "I," beneath or below the disguise, of another subject. That subject is the male figure who seems to keep her from her rightful place but nevertheless make it possible for her to write.

As the subject who appears to occupy a primary position, Julio is the authority to whom Gloria willingly surrenders her role as narrator, only to reappropriate it at the novel's end. To read Julio's chapters is also to see, however, that the truth about their ultimate positions (that is, the fact of Gloria's authorial support beneath Julio's narration) is already visible within his narrative. Even though the novel's final effects (its powers, so to speak) are generated by a strategy of surprise, the text also lays the groundwork for, and necessarily prefigures, this unsettling movement of authority. Julio himself actually prepares (the reader) for the shift in roles, the change from one order ("the old") to another ("the new").

Paradoxically, Julio also functions as a privileged figure who is fated to reveal the contingent nature of his authority and identity as an author. In the novel's first five chapters, that point is made retrospectively, not only in the revelation of Julio's lack of final authority for the text of the novel but also in the various oscillations that inform his marital, familial, and literary positions within the fiction. In fact, throughout those chapters the privilege seemingly conferred by his identity as husband, father, and author within a traditional framework (that is, within those orders or systems in which certain rights or powers automatically accrue to husbands, fathers, and authors) are already called into question by Julio himself.

Julio's authorial, paternal, and spousal powers are intermittently undercut through his descriptions of the inversions and negations of authority played out by him with his literary agent, his son, and his wife. As an author, Julio is controlled by Núria Monclús, the literary agent whose "telaraña" ["spiderweb"] awaits him, whose decisions have already caused him to cast himself as "culpable," "vulnerable," "débil," and "humillado" ["guilty," "vulnerable," "weak," and "humiliated"] (30, 114, 178), and whose powers are described as those of a "verdugo" ["executioner"] who seems to hold his life (that is, his success or failure) in her hands (212, 225).[10] On the other hand, Julio's son Pato sees his father as a "tirano" ["tyrant"] and "dictador" ["dictator"] (60, 77), though it is Pato, according to Julio, who really tyrannizes his own father (226).

As Gloria's husband, Julio is at once the object of her vigilance over and interrogations about the writing of his novel (110–11, 114), the victim of her (actual or potential) criticisms of his text (225), and the confessing subject for the confessor who is both his "conciencia" ["conscience"] and "enemiga" ["enemy"] (239–40). Together they represent what Julio's friend Carlos asserts about every married couple: "En una pareja no hay un solo verdugo y una sola víctima, ambos son verdugos y víctimas" ["In any married couple, there is never only one victimizer and one victim, both are victimizers and victims"] (202). Thus, Julio's narrative underscores his struggle to verify and maintain his precarious position. He cannot but confess, then, his consciousness of his own powerlessness before, even victimization at the hands of, certain (female) figures. These are the figures whom he would also seem to control and for whom he would have the right to serve as master, according to the established rules and roles that would empower him as well as other (male) figures.

By virtue of his performance as narrator throughout much of the text, Julio also projects an image of authority within the novel's body. Although his comments would frequently undermine that image, his performance as the narrating subject in the first five chapters is a sign of the privilege he holds within Gloria's (or, perhaps, Donoso's) text. However, such a privilege is also granted to him by the other author(s). Julio appears as an authoritative figure not only because he seems to be the primary narrating subject of a principal portion of the novel and, therefore, the subject whose consciousness informs so much of it, the one whose perspective dominates the text. His image of authority also derives from his apparent role as an author.

Indeed, the text leads one to consider whether Julio might not be the novel's author as well as its narrator, whether his role is not in fact dual (if not also duplicitous or disguised). Taken together, the following self-conscious moments in Julio's narration work to suggest his authorship of the novel's text: his references to the language of his narration (for example, 103, 164); his emphasis on the place and time of narration as "aquí" ["here"] and "ahora" ["now"] (for example, 65, 71, 73, 114, 165, 203); his seemingly self-referential mention of "esta novela" ["this novel"] and "mi novela" ["my novel"] (166, 211); and his private meditations on the problems of writing, sometimes linked with descriptions of the first and second versions of his novel, whose thematics seem to coincide with those of the text presented to Donoso's reader (for example, 22, 27, 31–34, 50–53, 71, 146–47, 159, 180). However, as soon as the novel offers evidence to support such a reading, the text discredits Julio's possible claim to authorship.

The novel's penultimate chapter (the last chapter of Julio's narration) brings the violent economy of the competition for textual and marital authority to the surface of the narrative. It prepares for the shift in positions that is to be revealed by Gloria in chapter six. In fact, Donoso's novel makes it virtually impossible to separate the textual and marital frames of conflict within its pages. The problems that shape the protagonists' relationship within both of those spheres revolve around the question of who is the real author and authority, who is the subject who can and will have the last word about or around the other. When either of the narrators assumes that role she or he is also identified as an author who has won a textual struggle that parallels, and is superimposed on, either a familial or a marital conflict. In *El jardín de al lado* either the figure who actually writes or the one who tries to write is a figure who has won his or her authorial position in a contest. At the same time, his or her opponent is also his or her partner. In this embattled partnership, to narrate is to suppress the voice of one's opponent so as to become the text's singular subject. To write is to usurp the place of another author whose position of textual dominance one would appropriate through one's own activity. In addition, to cease writing or narrating is to surrender one's position to the accomplice-adversary whose powers are also rooted in one's own defeat.

One can posit Julio and Gloria's relationship in terms of such a contest of discursive rights, and as a competition for authorial powers, since each is thus engaged with the other in several spheres at once. Moreover, the economy of this quasi-militaristic model, according to which the shifts in their relationship might be viewed, is suggested by both Gloria's and Julio's narratives. Such are the terms in which they themselves characterize their relation to one another; such are the metaphors they use to describe and analyze their own attempts to become authors. (One might consider, for example, pages 30, 36, 44–46, 118, 241–42, where, among others, terms such as "derrotar" ["to defeat"], "vencer" ["to conquer"], "esclavizar" ["to enslave"], "víctima" ["victim"], and "verdugo" ["victimizer" or "executioner"] are used to describe the various combative relations in which these authors seem compelled to engage with their agents, rival writers, and spouses.)

Indeed, the novel focuses on how one may become a writer or succeed as an author. It studies how an author's performance is rewarded and how his or her status as an authority is attained. Julio's entire narrative develops such an inquiry. It sketches (authoritatively, at first) his struggle to become engaged in successful authorial activity. His chapters chronicle the intricate shifts in his relation to his wife (the novel is also an "anatomy of a middle-age marriage").[11] However, they also describe the summer writing project he claims he wants to complete, but which he defers repeatedly. Not until the fifth chapter of the novel, and the last month of their stay in Madrid, does Julio tell how he fulfills his professed intentions, which, once realized, also become the emblem of his failure. What is significant here is not so much what Julio writes as how he seems to do so, how he ultimately assumes his precarious position of authority and his role as an author. Significantly, he reveals somewhat self-consciously that his ability to write is grounded in an illusion of authority. His authorial position and performance issue from a fiction of victory and control over a special, and, one later discovers, apparently more authoritative, adversary.

The combatant from whose defeat and virtual capture Julio's ability to write is derived is not one of the literary rivals about whom he obsessively ruminates throughout his narration (that is, the boom authors, the literary fathers and brothers he criticizes, but whom he also seeks to emulate[12]). It is instead Gloria, his spouse, the apparently powerless woman whose work as a translator and whose position as a narrative object would initially situate her in a place of secondary importance. The significant point here is that when Julio describes how he finally begins to write his novel that description coincides with the description of his wife's nervous breakdown and recovery. Indeed, only when Gloria is "defeated" or "imprisoned," only when she has become a dependent figure in relation to whom he may feel more powerful, is Julio's writing no longer blocked. Only then does he no longer defer writing.

Julio is conscious of the positions in which he and Gloria are situated and of what seems to be the power generated by her powerlessness. He overtly describes his own text as a "novela que, con el cautiverio de Gloria dentro de su ahogante depresión, se hace accesible, y avanza mientras vigilo a mi mujer y la cuido" ["novel that, with Gloria's captivity within her own suffocating depression, is made accessible, and progresses while I watch over and care for my wife"] (205). It is as if the possibility of assuming the role of an author were contingent upon the prior (or at least coetaneous) assumption of a homologous role in other relational models they construct together. It is as if Julio's transformation into virtual parent and nurse for his wife, now converted into virtual child and patient, somehow authorized his writing and empowered him to become an author.

Gloria's "defeat," her transformation into a dependent child-patient, does not, however, destroy her powers. Indeed, her defeat can also be read as a preliminary sign of her ultimate authority within the text. Gloria's downfall can also be read as a willful surrender through which she temporarily grants Julio a position of privilege. It is not insignificant that Gloria's depression is partly characterized by a refusal of discourse, or that this refusal is directed at her husband. He is the interlocutor with whom she chooses to discontinue discursive relations and against whom, Julio points out, she indirectly throws her invectives, accusing him of being "el culpable de su vida destrozada, de su incapacidad para enfrentar cualquier lucha, incluso cualquier acción o proyecto que yo la he devorado" ["the one who is responsible for her ruined life, her inability to fight any battle, including any act or project of hers that I have devoured"] (201).

Gloria's silence is precisely what appears to signal Julio's "victory." Her refusal of language allows him to view her as powerless to speak, as unable to assume the role of subject. However, that same silence is also a sign of resistance; it is also an assertion of power. Gloria's refusal to speak to Julio is, in and of itself, a powerful gesture. It also reveals the power she exercises over her husband, whom she punishes with her silence. It is a sign of the control she wields over the mode of their noncommunication; it is a mark of her ability to determine her husband's ability to assume the role of author.

In relinquishing the right to speak to and engage in dialogue with her husband (that is, in asserting her right not to speak) Gloria aids Julio in becoming a subject whose only dialogue is with himself. Julio is permitted (if not forced) by Gloria to assume the authorial role he imagines himself to create while she all the while controls him.[13]

Thus, precisely because she chooses to serve as a silent object, Gloria spurs Julio to become a potent and authoritative subject. Her silence creates the space in which the work of the author-figure, the apparent father of the text, can develop. Gloria can be seen as responsible for Julio's writing and text, for the textual authority he wields, and for the authorship he assumes. But she is also the subject who eventually unmasks his disguise and undermines any authority he might have been thought to have exercised. Indeed, the apparently original and singular authorship of Julio's work is subverted by Gloria both within and outside the story he tells.

That Julio may be read as a figure of textual authority in chapters one to five is suggested by the importance accorded his role as a narrator. By virtue of his function as primary discursive subject and mediator of the narrative, he visibly occupies a privileged position within those chapters. As narrator, Julio appears to be situated at the pinnacle of the novel's discursive hierarchy. While he narrates, he also tells of his project to write a novel (rather, to rewrite a text already written by him but in need of revision), and describes his attempt to complete that composition. Julio's references to his novel suggest that it may well be identical to the one presented to the reader. However, the last chapter of Julio's narrative first offers what seems to be proof of the identification between his text and Donoso's novel, but then verifies the differences between them. When Julio says "voy llegando al fin de mi novela" ["I'm getting to the end of my novel"] (211) at a point when the reader is also approaching the end of Donoso's text, the referent for the word "novela" appears ambiguous. It might designate either the text of the novel being read or the one referred to in it.

The reader is briefly allowed (perhaps even urged) to consider this reading of things. In the end, however, the text reveals that such an identification is impossible, even though at first it appears quite plausible. In the paragraphs immediately following the apparently self-referential statement, the identification of the two texts is nullified when Julio indicates that he has finished his novel (212), while his narrative and Donoso's text continue. From that point on Julio's novel becomes mainly an object of his discourse; his narration has undermined the possibility of equating it with the production of its own narrative. Julio's novel thus remains a somewhat mysterious text one never reads but only reads about.

Until this moment of clarification, then, the text seems to put into question the stability of the boundaries between, as well as the overall hierarchy supporting, what at first might not appear to be distinct narrative levels or different realms of authorial activity. Indeed, the reader's reading of and relation to *El jardín de al lado* and its narrator are affected by the definition of these boundaries and that hierarchy. The difference revealed between Julio's novel and the one read by Donoso's reader reasserts precisely this distinction between narrative levels. (To a degree this is the distance between the positions of subject and object.) But this difference—or distance—will be called into question again by Gloria's narration. In the final chapter the problem of clearly delineating a narrative hierarchy is reintroduced when the divisions of textual authority, presumably reestablished in the last chapter of Julio's narrative, are again put into question by Gloria.

The moment that the nonidentity of Julio's and Donoso's texts is revealed is important for other reasons as well. Precisely because Julio finally undertakes, and then finishes, his textual project—and thereby proves himself already to be, or capable of becoming, an author—he also reveals his "fall" from that primary position. He displays his loss of what seemed to be an authorial control both within the fiction his narration produces and the text that presents his narrative. The gestures through which Julio seems to establish his authorial identity are those through which he discloses the illusory nature of his role as author. With those same gestures he opens himself to defeat by other figures of authority, other author-figures, upon whom he depends for his position. His ultimate loss of privilege is signaled in his descent through the text's narrative hierarchy. His position within the fiction is eroded once he ceases to write, once he must turn to other figures— rival subjects, interlocutors, readers—who evaluate his work and divest it of its potential power.

The moment Julio appears capable of establishing his authorial status is, of course, the moment he finishes his manuscript, which, by definition, would certify his powers and performance as an author. But the moment he completes it is also the moment that he (much like any author, to be sure) ceases to exercise authority over the text he has virtually fathered. In Julio's case, moreover, not only is it a question of losing control over his own text. It is also a matter of having its value negated, its future in print (and thus its very existence) denied. Julio's novel is rejected for a second time by the literary agent at whose recommendation he has rewritten it. For Julio, this rejection signifies a defeat within the arena in which he has desired to compete and win a place of privilege. It constitutes a denial of his right to join the ranks of the renowned Spanish American authors whose success he would deride but, if he were permitted to do so, also gladly share (compare 13, 106, 118). Julio's situation would suggest that he writes so as to become more than a writer (a "modern scriptor"). Indeed, the (traditional) figure of the author—the master figure and father to whom a work would point back upon its completion and publication; the figure whose authority is manifested in the object that also invests him with authority—is the figure privileged by Julio, as well as by other authors, it seems, here in El jardín de al lado.[14]

The undeniable defeat of Julio's enterprise becomes a dramatically instructive, even if also exaggerated, reminder of the author's predicament. The successful completion of his project also signals the necessary limitations of his powers. For Julio's narrative also demonstrates that his power as an author is controlled, if not completely undercut, by his readers. His authorial privilege is eroded by the authority he finally grants to his textual interlocutors. When Julio reveals that he is not quite the author one might have believed him to be, he highlights the loss of control inherent in being the kind of author he actually is. He acknowledges that to finish his novel is no longer to be master over it, no longer to have the power to determine its destiny (212). This power is (and must be) exercised by its readers—by those to whom it is addressed or for whom it is written, by those who bear the responsibility of responding to it.

The end of Donoso's novel takes up the question of the relations between readers and authors and their possible identification with one another. In El jardín de al lado there are two key readers for Julio's novel. They are the two women to whose authority he virtually bows in the end: his wife Gloria and the literary agent Núria Monclús. That each is a significant figure is revealed throughout his narrative (for example, 28–29, 44–46, 178, 205, 225, 241). That he overtly acknowledges them as privileged readers is clearly indicated at its end. After claiming that "Núria Monclús—o su equipo fantasma, los lectores que la informan y sopesarán y valorarán . . . , y dictaminarán sobre ella [his novel]—tiene mi destino en la punta de sus ensangrentados dedos" ["Nuria Monclus—or her phantom team, the readers who keep her informed and who will weigh and evaluate . . . , and pass judgment on it—holds my destiny on the tips of her bloody fingers"], he admits that Gloria's opinion of his novel "es la que más—la única, en realidad—que me importa" ["is the one, the only one that, in reality, matters to me"] (212).

Reclaiming the Author   124

Julio's relation to these readers is figured as a continuous, but also alternating and indirect, dialogue. He writes, in a sense, to respond to their requests and instructions regarding his manuscript, and his work therefore seems to derive as much from their desires as from his own designs.[15] They read partly (perhaps mostly) because he asks them to respond to his writing, to judge the text over which they already have (or have been given) some control, and whose future they will decide.

Although Núria's reading clearly determines Julio's fate as an author, she remains in the margins of the main contest for authority presented by his narration. It is really Gloria's reading that underscores once again the novel's complex staging of the competition for authorial position or authority and the contest between different figures of the author. Just as Gloria's silence seems to transform Julio into an author, Julio's silence forces Gloria to become a reader. That is, when Julio finishes writing and falls silent, as it were, his demand for Gloria's response to his text initiates a type of dialogue. Julio and Gloria eventually reestablish the discursive relationship rejected by Gloria during her breakdown as they negotiate an interaction between his writing and her reading.

In accepting his demand, Gloria both acknowledges Julio's position as an author and reclaims for herself a position of (original) authority. Indeed, her recovery is coincident with her return to discursive exchange with her husband and her assumption of the role of reader for the text he has authored. She is his silent textual interlocutor whose self-insertion into a situation of discourse is generated by his novel—the text that has also been authored, as it were, through her refusal to speak. But the route of that return is a curious one and the model of dialogue through which it is charted is one that puts into question the distances and differences between these interlocutors.

Gloria's reading of Julio's novel is directly mediated by its author. Gloria, the "intelligent" reader or critic upon whom Julio depends for a judgment and whose authority he himself supports (215), will not (or cannot) read it by herself. Julio reads his novel aloud to Gloria. The text presents a scene of reading in which authorial presence is figured as a performing voice, a voice that would speak directly to its listener-reader. This performance would seem to defeat the distance and difference between the author-as-person and the author-as-text. It would appear to put the one figure on an equal footing with the other. However, in this scene the one figure is also called forth from behind the other to assume a place of priority. Indeed, Julio is all that can be heard in this scene, as Gloria silently listens to his novel. But, this resurrection of the figure of the living author in Julio's performance also puts the figure of the lifeless reader in a problematical position. For Gloria also becomes situated as a silent authority who is effaced by, but is also absorbed into the performance of, the author whose voice she, as listener-reader, empowers.

This reading-recitation produces a conflation of authorial and readerly images. The scene both transposes and superimposes Gloria-the-reader and Julio-the-author. For once Julio has read the text to Gloria, she responds not as the reader whose position seems to have been shared by the author, albeit from another "side" of the text, but as another author-figure who also bears responsibility for that text. In fact, she presents herself as a subject who has always been identified with its author. Her proximity to and knowledge of the text thus prevents her from fulfilling the other role in which she has been placed by her husband, who would be situated elsewhere but also alongside her. This reading, then, leaves no room for Gloria's response as a (traditional) reader. She who lays bare the conventional position of reader-listener (that is, the position of the silent partner who receives the text and who, as its addressee, is posited in virtual dialogue with it) renders explicit her inability and/or refusal to read the text for herself, as a critic.

Gloria reminds Julio of something that Donoso's reader might also have noted. In the critical oscillation of subjects that supports this reading project these two figures constantly shift and share positions. Their dialogue continuously raises the question of whether the differences between their roles or positions can be adequately measured, and whether those differences themselves make any difference at all.[16] Here, interestingly enough, from the position of reader-addressee, Gloria seems to negate crucial differences in authority and gender that later, as an author, she will appear to assert.

In speaking to Julio about his novel and declaring that she is unable to serve as its judge, Gloria claims that she is not sufficiently distanced from the text, not different enough from its author, to be able to read it critically. She says: "Para mí lo haces vivir todo porque reconozco los signos cifrados, y puedo romper el código: los llenas con una vida que es mi vida. ¿Pero y los que no comparten con nosotros esos signos? Yo no puedo juzgar, estoy demasiado cerca de todo esto" ["You make it all come alive for me because I recognize the coded signs, and I can crack the code: you fill them with a life that is my own. But what about the people who don't share those signs with us? I can't judge it, I'm too close to all of this"] (216); "[t]u novela tiene todos los elementos, pero no puedo juzgarla porque es tan mía como tuya" ["your novel has everything, but I can't judge it because it is as much mine as yours"] (217).

Gloria's explanation situates her with, or in the place of, the novel's author-owner while it also outlines the poetics of critical reading to which she would subscribe. Her authorial equation is posited in terms of the question of knowledge: to possess a certain amount or type of knowledge is to be (like) the author; to lack a certain type or amount of such knowledge is to be a potential critic. Gloria knows too much to play the role of the critic. According to her reading of the situation, she and Julio are equal in authority, equally authors, who stand together atop the hierarchy of knowledge for this (or "their") text. Only if he is able to identify another reader who has no such knowledge (and whose credentials for evaluating the novel would be established by such ignorance or innocence) will Julio's novel receive the reading he believes it deserves. In *El jardín de al lado* that reader turns out to be someone who is neither ignorant nor innocent, especially about literary matters, as her professional role would emphasize: Núria Monclús, the famous and powerful literary agent. Indeed, Núria enters this textual arena as a formidable and authoritative figure precisely because she is so knowledgeable about and is such a powerful figure in the world of literature.

It is appropriate, then, that Julio surrender his manuscript to Núria, who becomes the final reader of his novel. She would appear to be the subject who fits Gloria's description of its proper reader and whose performance is inevitable. That she has a different kind of knowledge than Gloria is clear. However, it is not clear that her authority over the various texts at hand (that is, Gloria's as well as Julio's) is of a different sort than that wielded by Gloria or Julio. But the power of her reading will be aptly demonstrated for Julio in the end.

Núria's reading is the reading that closes off Julio's narrative. After she rejects his novel he and Gloria take their brief trip to Tangiers where Julio, trying to hide the failure thus far kept secret from his wife, leaves her (and Donoso's reader) at the end of chapter five. The move to the final chapter reveals that these complex shifts have been but a forecast of the inversion of authority disclosed, albeit in a surprising manner, by Gloria. In both sections of the novel (its "body" and final chapter, which can be read as an "endnote" or "epilogue"), however, the shifts prove equally problematical because no stable resolution is reached.

Gloria's narrative in chapter six shifts the focus to a narrative level previously hidden from view. It is there, above and yet alongside the frame of the first narrative, that an authorial narration supplants and silences the narration of a subject (that is, a "first person") who turns out to be but a character (that is, a "third person"). In that chapter Gloria unveils not only the fiction of her husband's authority and her own role in defeating him, but also the pleasures elicited by the knowledge of that failure. Her narration is something of a spousal and authorial confession. She not only reveals the secrets of her authorial designs, which, as noted earlier, have been carried out under the cover of Julio's apparent authority. She also uncovers the strategies of the spousal maneuvers she has developed beneath a mask of powerlessness and subordination—the mask of a mere character in another's story.

Moreover, Gloria asserts that her ascent is tied to her knowledge of Julio's decline. It was "esta derrota final [the final rejection of Julio's novel] lo que más me ayudó a salir de mi depresión: necesitaba verlo menos fuerte" ["this final defeat that helped me to get out of my depression: I needed to see him as less strong"] (255–56). She also admits feeling "un componente de vengativa alegría ante su fracaso" ["an element of vengeful joy at his failure"] (255), even though she declares her compassion for him. Gloria thus acknowledges her desire to bring down this male figure of authority who has held the position she now claims as her own.[17]

Julio's final defeat also signals Gloria's last victory. His failure means her success, as the reversals in her narrative suggest. Gloria openly appropriates the author's position only after Julio appears no longer to be able to defend it as his own. Julio surrenders that position to her; he gives up a position Gloria appears to have authorized him to fill but to which he ultimately has no authoritative claim. And, Julio assumes at the same time the identity of a literature professor and translator, the potentially secondary and subordinate positions to which he is assigned and returned in her text.[18] Gloria's accession to the place of the primary subject of authority leads back, however, to some of the problems signaled by Julio's narrative. Although Gloria emerges as the primary author-figure, the relation between her narration and that of Julio (that is, the relation of chapter six to chapters one to five) is still unclear, and her dialogue with her own approving reader still problematical.

That is, the question of Gloria's place as an author, her position as an authoritative figure, remains.

The figure of Núria Monclús reenters the fiction at the novel's end, where she is cast in a significant role. The final chapter situates Núria in a place from which she reads and responds authoritatively to the last text with which we are concerned. She is given, moreover, what seems to be the last word. Núria is the literary agent whose powers ultimately appear to surpass those of the novel's other authors. That is, as an agent (one whose job is to act in the place, or under the auspices, of others; one who has the authority to act for those in whose name she exercises a power that is also not originally her own) she also acts over and above them, seeming to dispel the authority of the authors whom she would presume to represent. Moreover, Núria seems to represent rather well in one arena even the author whom she would refuse to represent in another.

For Núria is not only the reader who rejects Julio's novel in Gloria's text and accepts Gloria's text in Donoso's novel. She is also the agent whose position and performance at the novel's end virtually reduplicate those of both the authors who precede her, and after whom she appears to have the last authoritative word. But it is in part also her final position that leads one to consider the boundaries of her authority, as well as the limits of Gloria's powers, just as it is Gloria's performance that allows one to see the limits of Julio's position. Moreover, given her ambiguous status as a character who performs mainly as an interlocutor in the last chapter, Núria is as difficult to fix as the author whose text she has read and with whom she speaks. Not unlike Gloria, then, Núria responds to, but also seems to be responsible for, the novels around which Donoso's text revolves. She is the reader or interlocutor who makes endings possible for those texts, as she assumes her place of authority at their end. Yet she is but a figure already written into those texts as their outside judge.

The last chapter of El jardín de al lado actually begins with Gloria's description of Núria Monclús. Gloria prepares for the final reversal as she says: "Ninguna de las terribles leyendas que circulan sobre ella son verdad: es fina, encantadora, generosa, sensible. Pero también sabia, y autoritaria pese a su vocación por la intimidad y lo ha leído todo" ["None of the terrible stories that circulate about her are true: she is refined, charming, generous, sensitive. But she is also shrewd and authoritative, in spite of her capacity for intimacy; and she has read everything"] (247). This version of Núria contradicts Julio's, of course.

As noted earlier, in his narrative she is a cruel judge and executioner for whose verdict he waits after finishing his novel. She is a manipulative, vindictive, even sadistic, authority to whom he is nonetheless bound, much as he is to his wife Gloria.

Regardless of the version privileged by either Gloria or Julio, one fact remains. This "superagent" (Julio uses the term "superagente" on 35, 44) is viewed by each of them as a "superreader." She is the seemingly omniscient and omnipresent reading subject, the authoritative reader, with whom these writers must, in reality or fantasy, deal.[19] Núria is the reader for whom each of these authors writes. She is the final judge of their texts, the omnipotent evaluator whose reading potentially determines whether one or the other will succeed or fail. One can recall that Núria instructs Julio to rewrite his novel and then rejects it after it has been rewritten, and that her rejection means his failure. Her negative judgment defeats his performance as an author and dissolves his position of authority within the fiction, as Gloria's contiguous narrative affirms. However, as the opening of chapter six indicates, Gloria sees Núria in quite a different light: Núria is a benevolent reader, a supportive authority with whose activity Gloria's identity as an author is intricately interwoven. Núria not only appreciates and praises Gloria's manuscript; she also appears to desire to share responsibility for its authorship. In fact, Núria appears to authorize an ending for Gloria's text, and that ending, oddly enough, would seem to be constituted by Núria's final appearance in Donoso's novel.

When, at the end of chapter six and their conversation, Gloria finishes her narration of the story of the summer in Madrid and the return to Sitges, Núria says "Bueno, ¿no es éste el capítulo que falta, el que no has escrito . . . ?" ["Well, isn't this the chapter that's missing, the one you haven't written . . . ?"] (264) in the very last line of *El jardín de al lado*. There, at least two texts seem to end with Núria, and it is she who appears to suggest their endings. However, when Núria appears to authorize closure for a story that has already ended and to provide an ending for a text that is virtually closed by her authorization for closure, the limits of her position and the problematical nature of the novel's end are exposed. For when Núria says "Bueno, ¿no es éste el capítulo que falta, el que no has escrito . . . ?" in the text's final lines, the narrative moves away from closure, away from a path out of the novel. Instead, attention is focused back on the text, on the narrative *mise en abyme* that reopens the novel at the end of the chapter.

The last chapter has an equivocal status. Some of the reader's understanding (or even misunderstanding) of the novel's hierarchy of authority is founded in the unresolvable ambiguity surrounding the nature of that chapter's text and its possible readings. For this chapter can be read either as a set of notebook entries that will become the material for the end of Gloria's novel, or as (a form of) the text of the final chapter itself. There are a number of questions concerning Gloria's notebooks and their relation to her own novel. However, because the reader has no access to those notes (in this regard they are not unlike Julio's novel), those questions cannot be answered. In fact, the resolution of those questions is denied to both Gloria's and Donoso's readers by each of the novel's authors. When Gloria and Núria discuss the notebooks, Núria's request to read them is refused by their author: "todos tenemos derechos a nuestros secretos y los míos allí están" ["we all have a right to our secrets and mine will remain secret"] (262).

References to the notebooks' contents are made in connection with Gloria's second novel, the one she may (or may not) also be writing with the aid of the notes (263). But Gloria's description of the composition of her own text as (at least partly) an act of copying pages or passages from her original notes (249) suggests a significant connection between the notebooks and her novel. The novel, it is suggested, may well be a partial, if not complete, reinscription of her preliminary writings. Indeed, her novel may be but an "authorized" or more (or less) authoritative version of her notebook entries, which, in her function as her own *scriptor*, she merely reinscribes. Thus the priority of the one or the other text is difficult, if not impossible, to decide.

If one were to read the chapter as private notebook entries, Gloria, the author, would be seen as the narrator of a story that she has presumably lived but has not yet written in the form of the end of her novel. (She has not yet written it in that form because she herself does not yet see it as ending.) The only position from which knowledge of that ending could be acquired, chapter six suggests, is, paradoxically, that of Gloria's own addressee—the position filled by Núria within the fictional conversation and by Donoso's reader outside it. Núria's authorization for that ending thus seems to posit her as an omniscient interlocutor. From her position of apparent exteriority, she would appear to be in a position to see what the author with whom she dialogues is unable to see or know (and is only able to repeat) within her transcription of their conversation. Gloria would thereby survive as the author who tells all she knows but who doesn't know for herself all that she tells. And Núria would be viewed as the subject who seems to know what Gloria tells before Gloria herself knows it, but who is not in a position to tell it without her interlocutor.

If one were to read this text as Gloria's last chapter from the novel begun by Julio and concluded by her, Gloria would appear to retain her privileged position in an equally problematical fashion. As narrator of her own text, she remains atop the discursive hierarchy governing this chapter and the novel as a whole. She is the authorial subject who speaks and writes throughout it, even if first she appears under the cover (as the character) of another subject. The chapter's ending reveals this reality in a peculiar way. When Gloria grants Núria (the reader) the authority to tell her (the text's apparent author) what to do, while also seeming to do (by writing) what Núria tells her, it is difficult to decide who, if anyone at all, can be assigned the role of author, or which of the two is a more authoritative figure.

As noted earlier, in the very last lines of Donoso's text Núria authorizes what will be (or already seems to be) a closing for Gloria's novel. It is certainly not insignificant that she has the authoritative last word and that those words give not only instructions to the author about how to write but also advice to the reader about how to read. Moreover, the mention of her name as the novel's text literally comes to a close places Núria in a significant position. (After Núria's suggestion concerning the end for Gloria's novel, the words "preguntó Núria Monclús" ["asked Núria Monclús"] [264] appear as the last words in El jardín de al lado.) Even though these final words confer upon Núria a certain authority, they also situate her as a figure subordinated to others. Those words also signal, of course, the virtual presence of the other subjects of authority (Gloria, the narrator-author; Donoso, the implied author; and even Donoso, the empirical author) who allow Núria to appear in that position.[20] But Núria is still the subject upon whom Gloria, as author, depends for the surprising, paradoxical, and powerful end to her own text. The author-figure within the fiction, if not also around its borders, empowers a character upon whom his or her own authority also depends.

Given the contradictory readings suggested by the final chapter and the novel as a whole, one may remain uncertain about how to read the ending of El jardín de al lado. One may be unsure of how to determine the status of its various figures of the author. For one sees that the question "who is speaking?"—which here gets turned into "who is the author?"—becomes a question to which the text provides a concrete but nonetheless problematical answer. Indeed, the problem of authorial identity pervades the novel as a whole, as well as its final pages. Though the text would seem to destabilize the place of the author, first one, then another figure arises to make a claim for, if not actually to reclaim, traditional authorial privilege and position.

If Donoso's novel suggests that any figure of the author ought to be read as an inherently unstable and duplicitous subject, it also anchors that figure as a finally established and straightforward entity. If the text suggests that the author be seen as an artfully self-effacing subject, it also positions that subject as a figure whose identity cannot avoid detection. The ending of *El jardín de al lado*—where this reading began—reinserts the author's figure into a frame that is designed to disguise its appearance precisely by disclosing its face.

7

Facing the Author

Telling Stories in Mario Vargas Llosa's El hablador

When contemporary authors appear to entangle the public with the private, or the personal with the professional, they reconfigure the author in ways that are at once traditional and unexpected. They pose questions similar to the ones suggested by a text such as "Borges y yo" regarding the boundaries between different critical concepts and figures. Should we read the author as a disembodied, textualized figure or as a figure of biographical significance? Should we read the author as a de-faced figure or as a corporealized entity readily accessible to any reader?[1] Should we read the figure of the author as a transparent cover for the face of a particular individual or as a mask that hides nothing in particular because there is nothing behind it to hide? Though such questions may elicit predictable answers from readers assured of the unconditional "death of the author" or from readers persuaded of the empirical author's critical survival, some Spanish American writers would again pose them in suggestive ways.

The writing of Mario Vargas Llosa—one of the most visible of authors who have also become public figures—has at various times raised such issues. Known because of his political as well as critical and literary activities, he has shaped some of his work around both private and public affairs. Moreover, in some of his novels the figure of the author is constructed as an unmistakably textualized figure at the same time that it is presented as a recognizably autobiographical entity. Even though Vargas Llosa's work would appear to develop a personal, as well as professional, portrait of the author, it would also implicitly ask, what does an author look like? What kinds of faces might an author's work disclose? The confusion of faces and figures fostered by Vargas Llosa's writing serves to identify or re-face, but also to disfigure or de-face, one or another figure of the author.

Vargas Llosa's recent *El hablador* [*The Storyteller*] (1987) develops such a confusion or confounding of authorial figures and faces.[2] In a way, this novel gets at the questions suggested above by implicitly posing a variety of other queries around them. In *El hablador* the modern literary author becomes identified with the traditional teller of tales. The one figure appears to mask and to uncover the other, to disfigure and to define the other's face. The modern figure is presented as an inventive, original author whose personal tale and narrative practices may not finally appear so different from those of the traditional storyteller. The teller of collective stories appears as a depersonalized figure whose individual, and apparently modern, story still needs to be told in order for him to establish his authority as a traditional teller of communal tales.

Following in the path of other of Vargas Llosa's novels that play upon the possibility of reading the author's fiction in relation to the facts of his life story, *El hablador* posits authorial activity as a familiar, and apparently consumingly personal, undertaking.[3] The dramatized author's voice is heard as that of a particular individual whom readers may be tempted to identify as Vargas Llosa himself.[4] However, that voice is also exposed as but the echo, and the authorial face as but the specular figure, of the traditional (and unidentifiable) teller or speaker of stories named in its title. Moreover, the titular figure's performance suggests that the traditional storyteller is the voice not only of a cultural collectivity but also of an individual entity who becomes audible, if not altogether visible, in Vargas Llosa's novel.

El hablador is the story of *el hablador*: it tells both the story about a figure called "el hablador" and the story told by the "hablador" himself.[5] It also tells the story of the telling of those stories, which together comprise the narrative material of Vargas Llosa's novel. The novel, divided into eight untitled chapters, has a symmetrical narrative structure, which situates the stories and their tellers in specular relation to one another as the telling of their tales alternates back and forth. Chapters two, four, and six contain the story told by the unidentified, but seemingly identifiable, narrator (aka "Mario Vargas Llosa"?) about his friend Saúl Zuratas (aka "Mascarita" ["Mask Face"]). Chapters three, five, and seven contain the narrative attributed to the tribal hablador, the figure into which, the novel would have its readers believe, Saúl has transformed himself.

The narrator's restrospective narrative, told in the central chapters, evolves in a generally chronological order. It first focuses on the period 1953–56: he and Saúl become friends; he first learns about the Machiguengas, a tribe of Amazon natives, from Saúl; he pursues the study of literature and history, while his friend becomes involved in ethnology. It then deals with his 1958 trip to the Amazon region where the Machiguengas live: he becomes more directly acquainted with the tribe; he first hears about their tribal hablador from two linguists (the Schneils) working in the area. Near the end it concentrates on his return trip to the same region in 1981: he again meets with the linguists, from whom he discovers more about the figure of the hablador; he learns that Saúl, whom he had thought to have emigrated to Israel in the early 1960s, seems to have disappeared.

Throughout, the narrator makes references to the temporal and spatial frame of narration and writing (1985, Florence), in which he remains situated in the final chapter. There he speculates on the outcome of his mnemonic effort and narratorial, if not also authorial, activity. Such references not only situate the narrator's narration temporally and spatially but also characterize his activity as scriptural rather than oral. And, as the novel closes by citing what appear to be the places and dates framing El hablador's composition ("Firenze, julio de 1985" ["Firenze, July 1985"] and "Londres, 13 de mayo de 1987" ["London, May 13, 1987"] [235/246]), the first of which correspond to the narrator's situation, the suggested identification of the narrator as author of the novel is hard to ignore.[6]

The hablador's narrative comprises a series of traditional tribal stories (that is, cosmogonic and etiological myths), tales of contemporary events from the lives of the tribe's nomadic members (the hablador visits them on his official wanderings), and, finally, an autobiographical tale that purports to tell how this hablador came to assume his tribal role. At the end of the personalized story the text appears to reveal that the hablador is in fact the narrator-author's friend Saúl (224/234). Moreover, based on the corresponding nominal evidence provided at the end of both chapters six and seven, the reader is to presume that Saúl's transformation into a traditional storyteller is also the result of a personal conversion. (Both chapters end with the pronouncement of the name "Mascarita," the first ending prefiguring, the second repeating, the other. "Mascarita" is pronounced by the narrator-author at the end of chapter six, when he refers to his friend in a 1981 conversation with an associate, who knows of him principally by that nickname. At the end of chapter seven, the hablador pronounces "Mascarita" not as his own name but as that of his parrot, through whose presence and parroting performance the storyteller master—that is, the hablador whose discursive performance is presented in the chapter—would thus seem to be identified.)[7] In that conversion one identity is exchanged for or masked by another.

Both stories are framed by the telling of how the stories that are read become the material for what appears to be the novel entitled El hablador. Chapter one, a kind of prologue, focuses on a scene of recognition that precipitates the narrator-author's remembrance of and writing about the figure of the hablador while in Florence during the summer of 1985.[8] Chapter eight, a kind of epilogue, closes the text with the narrator-author's ruminations about the perplexing story of his friend. He has come to identify that friend with the compelling figure of the hablador (230/240), the memory of whom has been triggered by a photograph that precipitates the telling of his story (chapter one). The novel alternates between the two narratives and narrators, and as it does so it also erodes the apparent distances between them and their stories.[9]

By the end of the novel the term "hablador" becomes a term that identifies not only the subject one may suppose fulfills a traditional function in chapters three, five, and seven, and is compulsively considered by the narrator-author in his narrative, but also the subject who tells how the other, apparently more traditional, teller has become an hablador. Indeed, the narrator-author also situates himself as a storyteller whose desire to repeat what he has been told, to tell again what he has heard, is manifested by his own narrative. (It comprises mainly the retelling of conversations and the personal queries and analyses of what the narrator remembers and retells.) He is also connected to the traditional teller as he is placed in narrative situations in which, as either listener or speaker, he assumes precisely those narrative roles identified with the figure of the hablador.

The identification between the narrator-author, or other characters, and the tribal hablador is made through the activity of listening as well as through that of telling. For, as the tribal figure asserts, his role is that of audience as well as storyteller. His is an aural as well as enunciative responsibility, and each activity is as significant as the other. He must listen to and thereby learn from others so that he may remember and repeat what he has heard [127/131]. Some of the narrator-author's descriptions of narrative situations in which he is the listener as well as teller appear to acknowledge consciously the chain of repetitions and the shifting roles that ultimately identify different listening and telling figures in the novel. Moreover, in using the verb "hablar" to describe his actual or potential performance as a narrator, he also equates his narrative activity with that of the figure around whose performance his narrative revolves.[10] Although the identification between the two subjects becomes more apparent as the novel advances toward its ultimate nominal revelation, a number of questions arise concerning the identity of, and differences between, these tellers.

The novel ends by collapsing the distances between the traditional storyteller (the speaker of stories) and the modern author (the writer of novels), though some kind of residual distance remains between them. The novel thus makes the question "what is an author?" as significant as the question "what is an hablador?" Indeed, the one question virtually becomes an interrogation of the other, since the question "what?" leads directly into, and even seems to include within its own interrogative gesture, the question "who?" in Vargas Llosa's novel. The narrative path constructed by the narrator-author, whose activities are organized by his impulse to investigate, interpret, and also invent, leads from one interrogative to the other. The novel becomes a way of answering, however provisionally, the query "what is an hablador?" But the answer it provides is also the answer to another question, a question not about the whole class of subjects designated by the term hablador but about one in particular—the novel's eponymous narrator.

The novel's title initially appears to refer to the individual storyteller whose tales are incorporated into its text, where the other narrator (that is, the narrator-author) also tells his story. By finally presenting the storyteller as an individual, rather than as a collective, subject, the novel would seem to provide not only the answer to one question ("*what* is *an* hablador?") but also the solution to another ("*who* is *the* hablador?"). As it slips from one query and answer to the other, the text also makes it possible to slip from one storytelling frame to the other. *El hablador* thus directs the reader's vision from the figure of the storyteller to the figure of the author, and back again.

The first chapter, which, as noted above, serves as a narrative frame for the stories that follow, also prefigures, and retrospectively seems to repeat, the novel's overall narrative development. As this very brief chapter (four pages) moves through the narrator's unexpected encounter with a European exhibit of photographs of Amazon natives (that is, the Machiguengas), during which his viewing of the photographic series leads him to the figure of the hablador, it plots a narrative return to Spanish America.

However, this initial chapter, which opens by proclaiming the narrator's desire to forget his homeland (7/3), also turns the novel toward his personal, Peruvian story. Though his narrative begins in Europe, it returns to Spanish America, whose geographical, cultural, and political realities are turned into both foreign and familiar images for the novel. His narrative pursuit (that is, the pursuit of the story of the hablador) is an attempt to grasp the figure of the hablador. But that figure, upon which the narrator (and the novel as a whole) focuses with such determined interest, would resist both verbal and photographic efforts to capture it as a fully identifiable figure.

The photographic narrative is reproduced by the description of the narrator's viewing of it and by the introductory verbal narrative itself. Each duplicates the narrative conclusion of the other sequence, at the end of which the hablador makes an appearance as either an image or a word. However, when the first chapter ends with the narrator's assertion of certainty about the identity of the figure presented among the last photos of the visual narrative ("Sí. Sin la menor duda. Un hablador" ["Yes. No doubt whatsoever. A storyteller"] [10/7]), the hablador makes an equivocal appearance. It is precisely this appearance that will be duplicated at the end of the text, where the novel as a whole, repeating its first chapter's narrative trajectory, appears to identify in one form or another the hablador.[11]

The photographic and verbal narratives converge on the appearance of a figure and the revelation of a name or title that foreclose the story of the hablador, because they seem to identify, precisely by seeming to name, the mysterious figure. But they open that story for investigation, because they fail to establish directly—through a legitimate proper name—the hablador's individual identity. The first chapter reveals this figure and leads to other revelations about it; the rest of the novel further uncovers this figure but keeps it somewhat out of focus. Much as the storyteller would seem to be presented directly to his listeners or readers, El hablador reveals him (either as a visually or aurally perceptible object) as a figure of indirection. However, it is precisely because of its indirect appearance that this figure is able to attract so much attention in Vargas Llosa's novel.

The novel situates the hablador as an equivocal figure whose presentation would belie the mediating devices that make its appearance possible both in the preliminary setting of the first chapter and in other settings that follow. In the initial frame chapter the figure of the hablador appears as a photographed figure that is recognized by the narrator at an exhibit he encounters by chance in a gallery on Florence's Via Santa Margherita. He situates this encounter as occurring after having visited some famous sites (for example, Dante's house) in that city. The reference to well-known sights in Florence may be read as devices utilized to present as real and immediate the experience that precipitates the telling (and perhaps writing) of the novel's story. However, like subsequent references, it may also be read as a gesture of indirection that uncovers as much as obscures the scene's status as a fabricated literary enclosure.

(The sighting occurs precisely in the spot where Dante was supposed to have first seen Beatrice. Dante's name appears in El hablador as the name of one of the Italian authors [the other is Machiavelli] whom the narrator-author intends to reread while in Florence, but whom he mostly defers reading as he becomes involved in remembering and, apparently, writing the novel's story [see 7/4, 88/90, 226–27/236–37]. However, when he reveals that he has been reading the Divine Comedy in the original Italian while in Florence, it is to point out the reverberations between Dante's text and the Machiguengas' cosmogonic tales [103/105]. The privilege granted to Dante, if not also to a number of other authors—especially, Kafka, whose Metamorphosis is, for Saúl, a virtually sacred text [see 19/17, 22/20, 196–200/203–7], suggests an image of the author as reader, especially as reader of other authors whose texts reverberate in El hablador. One might also wonder whether there might not be other ways of considering how the [fictional, fictive, or empirical] author inscribes [his reading of] the medieval author and his work into El hablador. It may well be that the reflection of the writing of the one in that of the others also reverberates with the figures of direct or indirect repetition, or vision, that appear to be of some consequence in Vargas Llosa's novel.[12])

When the narrator sees the photographs in the gallery he sees them as both things and as signs. He emphasizes that the presentation of the photos is an arranged, and thus artificial, construct that someone has authored (perhaps the photographer himself, an Italian named Gabriele Malfatti [8/4]). At the same time, his description of what he sees in them would erase the figure of the artist-author from around their borders. It would present the scenes as unmediated by the photographer whose aims, nonetheless, the photos appear to achieve. He sees the photographs as signifiers that give at once direct and indirect access to their models.

The narrator-author's description of the photographed scenes (or rather of his viewing of them) seems to aim to present a reality unmediated by artistic activity or foreign intention, a reality free of "demagogia" ["demagoguery"] and "esteticismo" ["aestheticism"].[13] This is, he asserts, precisely what the photographer himself has aimed at and accomplished (9/5). The photographs thus appear to speak for themselves, as unmediated images. However, much as the narrator-author accepts what appears to him as a virtually direct communication, he still acknowledges the activity of the person responsible for their production. Indeed, he wants to meet personally and talk with the photographer. Such contact between photographer and viewer, however, would contradict the artist's interests. For his intention has been to disappear from around the borders of the pictures he has aimed to have stand on their own, to efface himself as a personal figure.

The "death of the author-as-photographer" is, in fact, literalized by the novel. The end of the chapter, where it is revealed that the photographer is already dead, figures the artist-author as an irretrievable entity, an irrecuperable source. When the narrator learns of the photographer's death from the gallery attendant, the figure she describes is thus a familiar figure: "Era un fotógrafo de modas, había trabajado para *Vogue*, para Uomo, revistas así, fotografiando modelos, muebles, joyas, vestidos. Se había pasado la vida soñando con hacer algo distinto, más personal, como este viaje a la Amazonía. Y cuando al fin pudo hacerlo y le iban a publicar un libro con su trabajo ¡se moría!" ["He was a fashion photographer: he'd worked for *Vogue* and Uomo, that sort of magazine, photographing models, furniture, jewelry, clothes. He'd spent his life dreaming of doing something different, more personal, such as taking this trip to the Amazon. And when at last he was able to do so, and they were just about to publish a book with his work, he died!"] (10/6).

This figure is familiar not only because it concretizes the critical death suffered by the idea of the author as an empirical entity and source of meaning to whom a reader of a visual or verbal text might turn for explanations. It also appears to figure the author of the novel's stories, the author whose tale repeats, as much as it prefigures, the stories of other authors and tellers. The photographer is, much like the narrator-author and the hablador as well, but a "narrative-man."[14] That is, he is not only a figure of the author as absence but also a figure of the author as character or story. In this novel, he is the story of a journey from Europe to Spanish America, and back again; he is the story of reiterated desires and dilemmas that are repeated by other figures in the novel. The photographer's trip to the Amazon, his encounter with the Machiguengas, his presentation of the figure of the hablador also predict the narrator's own story and foretell the story of his friend Saúl.

Moreover, the foreign photographer is seen indirectly as he virtually discovers himself through his encounter with a people foreign and yet familiar to him. In his viewing of the photos taken by the Italian, the narrator not only repeats the photographer's gesture of self-recognition in his past encounter, materialized by the photographs. He also reproduces his own previous Amazon experiences, which can later be seen as both precursors to and repetitions of the experience of the photographer-author whose work is first seen at the beginning of the novel.

The photographs, viewed in Florence by the Spanish American narrator, return him to his country of origin, which he recognizes immediately in the foreign scenes they present to their European viewers. What he sees is thus familiar; and, seen in a foreign setting, those scenes lead him to see, as if for the first time, images that he has literally seen before. (That the narrator has visited not just the general area but precisely those places shown in Malfatti's photographs is emphasized as he mentions having recognized specific individuals, and one in particular: a child whose physical disfigurement identifies him as the same child seen on an earlier trip to the same region [9/5, 162/168]. The first mention of this figure seems to prefigure, and the second to repeat, the disfigured Saúl/Mascarita's appearance among the Machiguengas. The disfigurement of the child recalls the birthmark that distinguishes Saúl/Mascarita's face—more on this later.) His distance from the familiar is undone by the chance encounter with images that might otherwise appear to be foreign. For he sees the familiar, in a way, defamiliarized by the distant frame, which, nonetheless, indirectly returns him to his home territory ("me devolvieron, de golpe, el sabor de la selva peruana" ["[they] suddenly brought back to me the flavor of the Peruvian jungle"] [7/3]).

This sighting of the photographs, then, directs his vision elsewhere, to that which is far in space and time but close in cultural identification. It leads him, indirectly it seems, to a kind of self-encounter, which is also an encounter with the figure of the hablador. The photographs thus become figures of return and repetition, as well as figures of indirection. For as they lead the narrator to tell his own story, which is simultaneously the story of another (that is, his friend Saúl, the supposed hablador), they already repeat the return that his storytelling will later produce as if never before seen or told.

We recall that the death of the photographer detaches the visual texts from their apparent originator and forces the narrator to read them, as it were, on their own terms. It forecloses the possibility of viewing them through the eyes of the author to whom the narrator originally wishes to turn for information about how, when, and where the photograph of the hablador had come to be taken. The death of the artist dismisses the artist-author as an authoritative artistic figure or psychophysical entity, whose own story (if it could be told and heard) might explain more, if not all, about the hablador.

Nonetheless, the demise of the photographer-author within one narrative register seems to trigger the appearance of another author-figure around it. For it is precisely after the pronouncement of the photographer's death that the narrator reaches his conclusion about the identity of the photographed storyteller (it literally concludes the text of chapter one) and that the text initiates (in chapter two) his retrospective and seemingly authorial account of his friend Saúl's apparent conversion. As he remembers and reconstructs, through a sustained narrative analepsis, the story of his friend and, consequently, that of the novel's titular figure, the narrator also assumes an equivocally authorial role within the rest of the novel.[15]

(The proposal of authorial status for the narrator also posits another reading of the novel. When the narrator declares that "He decidido que el hablador de la fotografía de Malfatti sea él [his friend Saúl]. Pues, objetivamente, no tengo manera de saberlo" ["I have decided that it is he who is the storyteller in Malfatti's photograph. A personal decision, since objectively I have no way of knowing"] [230/240], and reviews why one might accept or reject such a conclusion, he raises the possibility of reading the hablador's chapters as his own inventions. Such a reading would radically alter the status of the hablador's narrative.

That is, if the narrator of chapters one, two, four, six, and eight were seen also as the author not only of these chapters but also of the tales apparently told by the hablador [three, five, and seven], the hablador's story, which otherwise appears to be presented directly as a set of authentic, traditional, tribal narratives, would be seen—or heard—not as truthful but merely as verisimilar.[16] The implied or putative author figured by the text as a whole would then become the figure who reduplicates himself in the narrator-author. The latter's activity might then be read, according to his confessions, as only provisionally authoritative, since it also derives from a more privileged, knowledgeable, and authoritative author. Such a reading would place the to and fro movement between one kind of author and another primarily between different narrative registers.)

The death of one kind of author inevitably seems to lead, in El hablador at least, to the birth of another. This apparently authoritative figure is also promoted as a figure who would write himself into the text as a familiar and yet foreign subject, a subject divided, it seems, between different stories. The space opened for the activity of the narrator in the role of an author is an equivocal space. The move from the one to the other position would seem to establish an unbridgeable difference of positions that no text, or teller, could hide. But it is precisely this question of difference, which, of course, is also a question of identity, that Vargas Llosa's novel raises for consideration. The figure of the hablador is at the center of this question, which it begins to pose as the first chapter comes to a close. Indeed, it is the identity of this seemingly authentic storyteller that the novel will appear to disclose indirectly, if not also conclusively, near the end. However, as this disclosure occurs it would also repeat the deceptive revelation that ends the novel's initial chapter.

When the narrator-author concludes the introduction with the words cited above, he names a figure that has been seen, in fact, only indirectly—from the stories told and the photographs taken by others.[17] We remember that the hablador is seen out of focus—his body and face a silhouette, a profile—at the center of a group of listeners whose attention is focused on him: "Todas las caras se orientaban, como los radios de una circunferencia, hacia el punto central, una silueta masculina que, de pie en el corazón de la ronda de machiguengas imantados por ella, hablaba, moviendo los brazos" ["All the faces were turned, like radii of a circumference, toward the central point: the silhouette of a man at the heart of that circle of Machiguengas drawn to him as to a magnet, standing there speaking and gesticulating"] (10/6). But his presence is nonetheless inferred by the narrator, who recognizes in the photograph the figure with which, it is later revealed, he has for a long time been obsessed. (This is precisely the figure, he reveals also near the end of this chapter, he had hoped to see from the moment he entered the gallery [9/6].)

However, the identification of the storytelling figure apparently seen in the final group of photographs described at the chapter's conclusion becomes visible only as a word: hablador. The naming of this enigmatic and compelling figure, whose generic name also functions as the novel's title, resolves very little. Moreover, the naming of this figure, which is but the naming of a function, the performance of which the novel and narrator will throughout attempt to re-present, also poses other questions about it. Indeed, one is led to wonder about what this name actually names, and about what kind of figure or function it is supposed to designate.

If one follows, first, the narrator's story, one sees that, although the word hablador first appears in the novel's opening chapter as the last word virtually spoken, but literally written, in it, it does not make another appearance in his narrative until chapter four. There he tells how the hablador was first mentioned to him during a 1958 trip to the region where the Machiguengas live. The narrator recounts how the Schneils, two linguists connected with the Summer Institute of Linguistics, told him about the Machiguengas, and about how, at the end of an evening conversation about the tribe, they came to mention the hablador (88–89/90–91).[18]

The word hablador, as it turns out, is an approximation in Spanish of a Machiguenga word that resists transliteration or transcription, if not also translation. It is a word that only indirectly gets at the word it would replace; it is a word to whose meaning no one seems to have direct access. In the novel's text, the indigenous word can only be described as a set of sounds.[19] It cannot be put into writing in its original form since, characteristic of oral cultures, the language of which it is a part knows no such form.[20] (A phonetic transcription, of course, would merely reproduce, in a form of writing aimed at characterizing sound rather than representing or producing meaning, the sounds of the word and not its sense.)

The original word pertains to the sphere of the spoken, to the oral and preliterate society of the Machiguengas, whose culture, the novel's many discussions emphasize, may well be in danger of disappearing. The inability of the narrator-author to write the word pronounced as a group of strange sounds by his interlocutors, so as to render it familiar to himself (or to any reader), seems to recognize not only the fundamental gap between the two systems of language, but also the constitutive difference between the oral and the written, which Vargas Llosa's novel nonetheless would seem to (attempt to) bridge.

That the original word, though pronounceable, is essentially unwritable the narrator's description of his conversation and the text's rendering of it would demonstrate. That the word, or its sense, cannot somehow be communicated, even if only indirectly in scriptural form, the performance of the hablador would belie. As the term is used in the narrator's story, it functions as an approximate translation of the original word's sense, rather than as a rendering of its sound. Though the word hablador becomes familiar in the text, it also retains something of a foreign nature. For it persists as the name of a figure whose features, if not also function, seem inscrutable, no matter how much anyone learns about it.[21] However, as it appears in the narration of the hablador it takes on the appearance of a directly apprehensible term, emanating as it does from within the storyteller's own discourse.

The proximate nature of this substitute term, about which the narrator and his interlocutors ruminate, may well serve as a mark of the elusive but durable nature of the oral tradition to which the storyteller pertains and of the culture that his storytelling performances keep alive. Indeed, according to the Schneils' conjectures, the hablador (either as an individual or as an institution) serves as the community's memory, as its vehicle of communication about its own members, myths, and history. (The narrator is personally affected—indeed, he is emotionally moved—by this image of the hablador as the source of the Machiguenga's cultural survival [see 91–92/93].) In Vargas Llosa's novel, moreover, the term hablador would itself seem to hold things together between one narrative frame or textual division and the other.

The Schneils come up with a word, then, that stands as a translation of a term that in some sense cannot be translated, at least not directly from one system (the oral) to another (the written). But this term that would seem to defy adequate representation nonetheless seems to acquire—through its repetition within one and another frame—a fullness, a meaning, that initially seems difficult, if not impossible, to grasp. What cannot be transcribed or translated properly nevertheless seems to present itself in the direct performance of the novel's hablador.

In order to consider that performance, however, the reader is also led to consider how the novel frames any reading of it, how the text actually presents the speaker or storyteller, and how the storyteller's stories may be related (or not) to the stories that frame the telling of his tales. As the novel moves between two different, but closely related, narratives, it shifts between an apparently authentic performance of an hablador (that is, a seemingly direct, naturalized set of discursive instances for which the storyteller functions as the subject) and a narrative that tells, from the outside or indirectly, what such a figure would tell. The hablador is thus a figure seen alternately, if not simultaneously, from within and from without. The figure is presented as a speaking subject or narrator who produces an unmediated discourse. At the same time it is also offered as the object of another's recollection or narration.[22]

The hablador's narrative would present itself as the narrative produced by a subject whose voice is that of an entire tribal community, the collective voice through which the Machiguenga culture is passed on among its members, and thus preserved. If he speaks as an individual it is as an individual whose only function is to speak as an hablador, as one who tells the tales told to him about the tribe's collective history or about how individual stories have come to be told. While El hablador's hablador tells his stories, he appears also to tell the story of collective memory itself, even if from within the story of the specific memories collected by him. This would be the fiction proposed by the text, this would be the natural effect, as it were, of the storyteller's discourse.

Indeed, it is by telling things in his own voice, which is also the traditional, collective voice of the tribal storyteller, that the novel's hablador becomes the most direct source of what appears to be reliable information about this figure. However, this figure also emerges indirectly, from around the edges of the other narrator's story with which its appearance alternates. In telling his own stories, the hablador frequently draws attention to his position as subject and to the process by which he learns of and repeats the stories told to him by others. After closing off the novel's first chapter, the term hablador does not reappear in the narrator-author's narrative until he tells of his conversation with the Schneils in chapter four (as noted above). However, it makes what seems to be a natural appearance in chapter three, where the first narration attributed to the hablador himself is presented.

The hablador's first chapter, which begins in medias res as it seems to continue the telling of a creation myth (38/37), turns not only to the realm of traditional tales but also to the situation of the hablador as their teller. Between finishing one episode and beginning another, the hablador briefly shifts his focus from the utterance to the narrative situation, from the mythic world of his narrative to the discursive setting of his narration. And as he does so, he speaks himself, as it were, into the narrative frame from which his position as speaker is otherwise distanced: "Aquí estamos. Yo en el medio, ustedes rodeándome. Yo hablando, ustedes escuchando. Vivimos, andamos. Eso es la felicidad, parece" ["Here we are. I in the middle, you all around me. I talking, you listening. We live, we walk. That is happiness, it seems"] (41/40).[23]

That the storyteller calls attention to the scene in which he tells his stories is significant for a number of reasons. Indeed, he characteristically positions his own figure as straddling, if not obliterating, the boundaries between the situation of telling and the material that is told. Theoretically, the hablador's performance would efface the individual subject as a personalized voice, for it is in the nature of the traditional teller to repeat not only the stories he hears from others but also the formulas of telling that any hablador employs. These formulas and formulaic repetitions are precisely what mark the performance of the traditional speaker.[24]

Such an erasure of the individualized subject, in place of which would be heard, as it were, the collective voice of the community, is equivocally rendered in this text. The "yo" ["I"] of the storytelling subject (like that of any discursive subject, of course) appears throughout as a function of discourse. Indeed, the anonymity of the speaker would highlight that the subject has no individual identity, but is to be identified as the function performed by any such teller.[25] However, the final chapter of the hablador's performance would privilege another frame of reference. It would appear to personalize the subject whose individual, rather than collective, voice would finally be heard in the novel's text as well as through the hablador's tale. That is, in Vargas Llosa's novel the tribal storyteller ends his performance by appearing to reveal himself as an individual biographical entity, and by seeming to disclose his own identifiable and utterly distinguishable (here that also means disfigured) face. Though he may well seem to present the voice of a collectivity, in the end he also speaks principally from a personal position. Indeed, it is his own story that he finally aims to tell, even when he would mask that story with the stories of others.

In the apparently unmediated narrations of the hablador, it also appears that what gets told is the act of telling itself. As the speaker moves from telling stories about others to telling a story about himself (specifically, about how he has become an hablador) the text shifts from the display of collective tales to the production of a personal narrative. In reading the hablador's chapters as a narrative sequence that finally allows the speaker himself to appear, one sees this equivocal subject situate himself on one and another side of things. He is as much a figure of individuation as he is a figure of repetition.

As a performer of the telling of traditional stories, the hablador is but a subject who repeats, as he retells, what others tell him. He asserts that he has learned a good deal, if not most, of what he knows and then tells from others who know more (especially the *seripigari* figures, the good witch doctors; see 189–90/196). Such assertions would situate him as a secondarily authoritative figure. However, it is precisely by fulfilling the function of the repeating teller (that is, the parrot—more on this figure later) that his authority as an hablador (whose function is to tell again what has been told by, or what has happened to, another subject) is repeatedly affirmed. He thus establishes his own credibility and authority precisely by telling about how he has come to know and repeat his tales.[26]

Within the novel's fiction, then, this figure appears to preserve the storyteller's traditional tribal function as an authoritative office at the center of oral culture. However, the means by which those traditions appear to survive link that culture and the storyteller's figure to literary tradition. The survival of the Machiguenga traditions (as presented by Vargas Llosa's novel) seems to depend upon modern as well as traditional practices.[27] That survival here appears not only within a frame of experience that might be thought of as real or truthful but also (if not essentially) within the borders of the fictional or the literary—that is, in the text of *El hablador*.[28] There, the storyteller performs as a marginal figure whose role is assumed or reclaimed—assimilated and appropriated—by a character who is himself presented and perceived as a figure of marginality.

Indeed, Saúl Zuratas, also known as Mascarita, is, as the narrator repeatedly emphasizes, an exemplary outsider, a foreigner as well as a foreign figure. From the first, Saúl is introduced, as he had, the reader is told, once introduced himself, as a marked or disfigured figure ("tenía un lunar morado oscuro, vino vinagre, que le cubría todo el lado derecho de la cara" ["[he] had a birthmark the color of wine dregs, that covered the entire right side of his face"] [11/8]). Nicknamed Mascarita ("—Me dicen Mascarita, compadre. A que no adivinas por qué" ["They call me Mascarita—Mask Face. Bet you can't guess why, pal"] (11/8), Saúl bears not only a mark of physical disfigurement that sets him apart but also the signs of cultural difference that marginalize him: he is also half Jewish. A figure of divided identity and affiliation, Saúl seems to identify himself with others similarly situated on the edges of Peruvian culture and society. Indeed, it is precisely this feature of his identity that, according to different but not mutually exclusive interpretations (one psychological, the other religio-cultural), allows him to identify with the marginalized indigenous cultures with which he becomes involved.[29]

The story of Saúl is, of course, also a thematic device in Vargas Llosa's novel. The summarized or reconstructed conversations between the narrator and his friend (for example, 18–31/20–29, 92–100/94–102), or between the narrator and other interlocutors with whom he discusses Saúl's interest in the study of the indigenous culture (for example, 31–34/29–33, 75–77/76–78), provide a space in which the text introduces a discussion of, if not also debate about, pressing cultural and political issues. Whether Vargas Llosa's novel answers or takes a definitive position about the many questions implicitly or explicitly asked may be a matter of interpretation. But it can hardly be disputed that pressing questions are raised and that, in a sense, the novel, in telling the story it does in the way it does, tells both a personal and a public tale.

The telling of the traditional tales first appears as the performance of a subject who would efface himself through the projection of a collective voice. But, in addition, it soon reveals the story, if not also the countenance, of an individual subject. If the telling of the story of Saúl appears also as a cultural fable through which Vargas Llosa would appear to expose an issue debated in contemporary Peru, it also is presented as a personal story about telling and about writing. It is also a

Reclaiming the Author

story about becoming or being a teller of oral or written tales, and about what it means to be an author. When the novel ends, the stories of those disparate tellers converge, as do the traditions from which they would appear to have arisen.

That the recuperation of an oral tradition is made possible by the activities of a subject who comes to that tradition from an altogether marginal, if not utterly foreign, position suggests a number of questions. That the representation of such a recovery of an oral figure is made possible by the activities of a subject who writes so as to author (and further authorize) such a figure and the tradition from which its own activities are distanced presents other problems as well. Indeed, that the hablador who speaks in Vargas Llosa's novel is a product of written culture and that the novel's apparent project of recuperation is put into question by that same figure would suggest that the story of the hablador inevitably leads one to question both its collective and individual appearance, its relation to both the oral and the written.[30]

As noted above, the hablador's traditional story evolves into an autobiographical tale, which virtually reveals a face all too easily recognized as that of the narrator-author's friend Saúl. His own story is somewhat disfigured by, as it is filtered through, the storytelling mode of the hablador. It is also masked by the stories he appropriates, but also reauthors, in order to tell his own original story. Indeed, as he reclaims Kafka's *Metamorphosis*, which he retells as the story of his life as a marginal and marked figure (196–200/203–8), or as he retells the story of the survival of the Jews, whom he disguises as an anonymous tribal community from which he has emerged (207–11/215–20), his autobiographical tale conflates the literary and oral traditions, and identifies an audience of modern readers with a circle of tribal listeners.[31]

This appropriation and repetition of stories from written culture situate the teller outside the oral community that his activity as an hablador would aim to preserve. Nevertheless, as he combines those stories with or incorporates them into tales of tribal beliefs and cultural practices, he fashions tales that become assimilable to the collective stories traditionally told by the indigenous hablador. This foreign storyteller, then, would appear to do precisely what is familiar to an hablador: remember and repeat, record and retell, represent and reinvent. But, these are also the activities that describe the narrator-author's performance in the even-numbered chapters surrounding those of the hablador, and, additionally, that of the author somewhere above the text as a whole. To discover the identity of the hablador, then, is to rediscover his specular identification with the narrator-author who tells the novel's other story and with the figure of the author that surrounds them. To unmask one face—though it be the face of a disfigured figure—is potentially to disclose the faces and functions of others.

Indeed, it is not only a personal identity but also a discursive or textual function that is identified when the hablador tells how he has come to assume his tribal role or when his role is further clarified through associations with other tellers. When his story ends with a virtual confession of an individual identity, it also proposes a figure that fits the collective identity of an hablador. For as he identifies himself as an individual (an individual to whom the reader of Vargas Llosa's novel may be led to believe a proper name can be given) whose story restores his identity (that is, his difference), he also establishes his identity as a storyteller, which is all the identification his performance as a tribal figure would seem to require.

The virtual naming of the hablador at the end of the novel becomes an equivocal identification. The final words uttered by the hablador—"Mas-ca-ri-ta, Mas-ca-ri-ta, Mas-ca-ri-ta" (words that echo—or, more appropriately, parrot Saúl's parrot's habitual chatter [12/10], as well as the naming at the end of chapter six, as noted above)—establish what appears to be a definitive nominal connection between the anonymous speaker and Saúl Zuratas, the narrator-author's friend. The identification of this figure as Saúl—suggested cryptically in the novel's first chapter and advanced in the Schneil's description of an hablador, which virtually matches that of Mascarita (175–76/181–82)—appears to be completed and certified through this final act of naming. Though the narrator-author ruminates about the viability of his interpretation (that is, his reading of the photograph, which initiates the recollected and recorded narrative, and the reasoning that leads from that initial reading to this final identification [230ff./240ff.]), the nominal repetition in the text would lead to another reading of things.

The "transformación del converso en hablador" ["transformation of the convert into the hablador"] may well appear to the narrator-author to add "lo imposible a lo que era sólo inverosímil" ["what appeared impossible to what was merely improbable"] (233/244). But such an implausible conjecture is precisely what becomes a credible conclusion in the text. The final identification appears as a logical and persuasive resolution to its narrative, even though the narrator-author

Reclaiming the Author

underscores his own uncertainties about the reasoning that has led him to believe that his friend has become an hablador. Everything, in fact, he tells in, and the reader reads around, his story seems to lead to that revelation. And, of course, everything Vargas Llosa has done to set up the telling of things in the novel seems to have been designed to make believable (while also allowing for the narrator's questions about) the identification of the hablador.

One is still left to consider what the pronouncement of the name Mascarita says, directly or indirectly, at the end and how the appearance of that name directs (or not) one's reading. The name appears as the name of the hablador's parrot, whose totemic value his personal narrative would appear to explain.[32] The hablador parrots the bird's pronunciation of what seems to be a repetition of his own name, so as to induce the bird to repeat (that is, parrot), and thus pronounce, it. But, in parroting the pronouncement of the parrot's name as the parrot himself would pronounce it, the hablador virtually echoes what would also appear to be not only a repetition of, but also a cover for, his own. Therefore, the appearance, or pronouncement, of the name seems to identify and deny identification to the hablador by repeating a name that is at once his own and that of another.

The name revealed by the hablador is originally but a nickname, given to Saúl, as nicknames are, as a substitute tag that metonymically identifies him with, as it also reduces him to, the differentiating and disfiguring mark he bears on his face. The nickname, which intermittently supplants the proper name "Saúl" throughout the narrator-author's narrative about his friend, is given as the proper name of the parrot, whose figure can be taken as a figure of identification and of substitution.

The name Mascarita masks and unmasks a complex set of identifications that metonymically link the storytelling figures in Vargas Llosa's novel. In referring to Saúl, the nickname would appear merely to refer to the person so named through a description of a part of him. It would serve as a secondary tag that supplants an ancestral, authorized proper name, which identifies him as a member of a particular family. This substitute name masks an identification that he will renounce as he proclaims his allegiance to one tribe (the Machiguengas) over another (the Jews). That renunciation may well mark but another identification. For the perceived similarities between the positions of the two marginal groups and their members appear to play a considerable role in Saúl's shift in identity.[33]

In referring to the parrot as Mascarita, the hablador reveals the name he has given the bird, whose chattering and repetitive reproduction of the sounds emitted by others is also described by his human companion's title. For, as noted above, "hablador" can mean not only a speaker (and, in the tribal context, teller of stories) but also a talkative person, a gossip. It would appear that both senses of the word prevail when the term is used as a modifier of "lorito" ["little parrot"] in the text (for example, 12, 25 [the English text elides the diminutive]). For the talking parrot is a bird that chatters and repeats sounds, a speaker that says nothing except what has been said to him. It is a talker that repeats things merely for the sake of repeating them, and that, in the end, may say very little or make hardly any sense at all. The parrot's talk would make of what it says but a sequence of signifiers without meaning. Its talk would direct attention to the process of talking itself, rather than to any kind of sense it might be thought to make. Thus, the link between the parrot and the hablador, established in so many other ways as well, is revealed as a link of reciprocal identification—an identification whose significance the final disclosure of the name Mascarita would further concretize and complicate.

(In addition, the parrot is both an odd and an apt figure of identification here. For this parrot allows one to wander not only among the storytellers within the text but also toward other telling figures around it. For example, Vargas Llosa's parrot seems to openly connect itself to, while also masking, the parrot(s) of Flaubert [that is, those in "Un coeur simple," Salammbô]. And though Flaubert's name is never mentioned in El hablador, there is ample reason to consider the virtual presence of this other, and especially authoritative, voice or figure, given Vargas Llosa's early dedication to and identification with the author [see especially La orgía perpetua: Flaubert y "Madame Bovary" 15–146]. Since Vargas Llosa's parrot engages in little more than nominal repetitions, it may appear to figure such an exchange of authorial names and authority, as well as a play between foreign and familiar figures.

Moreover, the parrot of the one and the other author is also a familiar and foreign figure. For, if one reads Vargas Llosa's—or Saúl/Mascarita/the hablador's—parrot as Flaubert's parrot, and thus as an "emblem of the writer's voice" [Barnes 19, 183], or as a "mirror" of a fictional character [that is, Félicité in "Un coeur simple"] who is herself a figure of repetition [Felman, La folie et la chose littéraire 164], that figure also returns to the Spanish American context. For in "Un coeur simple" [47], the parrot is introduced as an exotic and foreign—precisely, an American—figure that soon becomes familiar, if not entirely at home, in its French setting. To read the parrot as Vargas Llosa's masked homage to one of his own masters [that is, Flaubert], some of whose figures of writing the Spanish American author might appear to repeat, is to see the feathered figure's American origins also point one's reading in different directions—directions that lead back, or forward, also to *El hablador*.)

As the name Mascarita is spoken by the hablador to name not himself but another figure, the parrot, which is a figure of repetition, also comes to figure the hablador. Moreover, the parrot is seen—or heard—as a figure of the hablador both generally (that is, all storytellers are represented, and somehow repeated, by the parrot, which is, in turn, refigured by them) and specifically (that is, the individual storyteller—the subject who would also appear to have once been called Saúl and who speaks in *El hablador*—is embodied by this, or any, parrot).[34] The name Mascarita is a pivotal term for the identification of these figures, who, in turn, give additional meaning to that name.

"Mascarita" is both a proper name (of the parrot) and a nickname (of Saúl Zuratas). But the referents for this name are not only the parrot and the person presumed to be designated by either the name Saúl or the title hablador but also the nickname itself. For "Mascarita" (literally "little mask," though translated as "Mask Face" in the English) is a name that also designates a role or function, an attribute or quality. In characterizing specific characters or entities as it does, this name would also seem to be parroting, by repeating, literary or critical clichés about telling stories or writing novels more generally.

"Mascarita" also refers back to itself. It is a reflexive tag that calls attention to the function it performs, and, in its descriptive capacity, also repeats (by renaming in identical fashion) the roles with which its referents are also identified. (As a nickname it is also a cover and substitute, and thus mask, for the proper name—Saúl or Saúl Zuratas—it would displace. As a proper name it would situate itself as proper to but not as the sole property of its apparent referent—the parrot—whose name unmasks the identity of its owner, whose name it would seem to repeat.) To be a storyteller is to cover or mask one's own identity, to become identical to any other teller of tales who would similarly perform this traditional function. "Mascarita" is, therefore, both tenor and vehicle: it literalizes its own metaphoric value, and metaphorizes its own literal function.

El hablador might thus appear to present the storyteller as someone who loses his identity behind a mask that is nothing more than an empty shell into, or behind, which the storyteller interjects himself. The nickname would thus appear as a nominal cover for a name that never appears (indeed, no name, except the name given to every figure in the traditional tales—that is, "Tasurinchi" [the name of the Machiguenga god-creator], is ever given as that of the hablador),[35] and for the role of the storyteller itself. But the name Mascarita is also a mask of nonidentity, a cover from under which the identities of various tellers would emerge in Vargas Llosa's novel. Indeed, when the hablador reaches the end of his performance in the text, it is precisely the question of identity that his narrative raises. It is precisely his own individual and individuating story that he would reinsert into the framework of the traditional collective tale through which he identifies himself as virtually identical to other tellers.

The hablador, who is indirectly named and identified at the novel's end, also directs attention to the other storytellers—indeed, other habladores—around him. As one can see, the novel sets up an identification among all these telling figures: between the figure of the hablador generally and the hablador as Saúl/Mascarita; between the figure of the tribal storyteller and that of the novel's narrator-author; and between the narrator-author within the novel and the author-figure or author-person around it. This identification leads one to consider how it might resituate the figure of the author. For, if it characterizes the author's performance mainly, if not entirely, as that of a teller of repeated tales, it might seem to propose a redefinition of authorial activity and authority. Such an identification or characterization may also seem to resituate the figures of Vargas Llosa as well.

In a sense, the novel's presentation of the figure of the hablador and the performance of the narrator-author is a meditation about authorial activity as a product of both narrative principles and individual personality. It is also an interrogation into the authorial activity and identity of its own author. Indeed, Vargas Llosa's performance as both a literary and a political figure, and his presence as both a public and a private personality in Spanish America today, may well make it difficult to read a text such as El hablador, which plays on its author's plurality of roles and positions, without figuring (or being tempted—if not compelled—to figure) the "real" Vargas Llosa into it.

To address contemporary issues, as Vargas Llosa does when he has the narrator-author and his friend describe, discuss, and debate the questions surrounding the Machiguenga's exemplary situation and status, is to implicate (in all senses of the term) an authorial figure for whom such issues are anything but marginal concerns. Moreover, the nonexistence or invisibility of the narrator-author's name, as much as the plurality of names given to his friend and to the hablador, allows the name of the novel's author to insinuate itself around, if not within, those figures.[36]

No doubt, one may read El hablador as an authorial response to the question of how Peru (and other Latin American countries as well) has dealt, or might yet deal, with the matter of its indigenous populations, and the possibilities offered by different political systems for some kind of responsible resolution to those problems. Given Vargas Llosa's recent political activities, it may seem impossible to read the text without privileging such points. It may seem necessary to supplant the textual subject with the empirical figure.

What might be significant about such a turn in reading, however, is not so much that it may aim to privilege the extraliterary over the textual figure, but, perhaps, that it might merely (and unwittingly) reproduce the conflation of figures and images that texts such as Vargas Llosa's bring about. If the figure of the author as a biographical, and sometimes a public, figure has begun to reenter critical discussion, the invitation for that apparent reentry has been extended by works of narrative fiction themselves. But such an invitation is extended in the name of an author whose figure inevitably remains balanced between one and another concept and frame.

The masked name in El hablador would designate the author as both a textual and an empirical figure. It would identify not only a figure that is an unoriginal parrot-scribe (such a figure could be viewed as a copyist or scriptor, as a follower of other masters, as suggested above) who would repeat the stories of others. It would designate also an authoritative and original writer (such a figure could be viewed as a modern auctor) who would invent the characters and stories that may nonetheless appear to repeat the appearance of others. El hablador suggests that each of these figures is at once very modern and very traditional. Indeed, the novel suggests that the modern author is but a modern storyteller, a storyteller who, on the one hand, repeats the traditions and figures of other authors but who, on the other hand, also originates different, and ever original, stories and frames for such repetitions.

As Vargas Llosa's novel proposes the figure of the author as a traditional storyteller, his text would reclaim for the author a position of traditional authority. His novel suggests that authors assume this position the moment they begin to tell their stories. In playing such a central role within modern culture (as does, or did, the tribal hablador, the "keeper of culture" for the oral tradition), the modern author would seem to disappear as an individual, as a personal story that could be read over and above (or as a grid for) the stories that come to form literary tradition.

However, in El hablador the authority of tradition also seems to rest on the authoritative performance of an individual who establishes his identity and authority as a storyteller precisely by returning to his own personal tale. Though that identity is in some sense irrelevant to the telling of stories in the novel (indeed, the absence of a name for the narrator-author would suggest that individual identification matters little, if at all, for the narrative's tales), the apparent discovery of the (masked) name at the novel's end makes a difference. The hablador's self-revelatory tale, along with the narrator-author's reflexive commentary, suggest that the story of why or how the storyteller has come to perform his role, as well as some explanation of his identity, is critical. It may well be that the storyteller is granted authority by his community and culture precisely because of such stories.

Vargas Llosa's novel figures a competition between authorial anonymity and identity. It is a competition that his own position as a Spanish American author reinvigorates rather than resolves. Indeed, El hablador is a text around, if not in, which the figure of the author as a powerful individual (both personally and politically) also emerges. Over the years Vargas Llosa's writing has inevitably been telling stories about becoming or being an author.[37] If one such story may seem to work through a personal tale of passion (for example, La tía Julia y el escribidor), another appears to turn its attention to a more public and political frame (for example, Historia de Mayta). The story told by El hablador is a story about a turn away from and also a return to the figure of the author. It is a story about both modern and traditional storytelling figures, whose identification with one another necessarily situates those figures at the center of their respective communities and cultures.

The apparent literary self-rendering proposed by a text such as El hablador, along with the meditation on issues current within modern literary and political debates, takes the reading of the author in contemporary Spanish American narrative in directions that might otherwise seem difficult to reconcile. If the author has in some way been recalled from the grave in Vargas Llosa's recent work, it has by no means been restored to an uncomplicated life. El hablador, like other Spanish American texts, reclaims that figure, but also returns it to a problematical existence. In doing so, this novel, like others, continues to reframe how one might look at or listen to the author in contemporary fiction.

Afterword

Even though the present study comes to a close in this afterword, the question of the author remains open to discussion, and to projects that might frame the question somewhat differently. I would, therefore, like to conclude this account of how Spanish American narratives raise the question of the author by reviewing some points made in the preceding pages and by speculating about related, though somewhat different, ways of reading this figure.

If one were to read the foregoing chapters as the parts of a story that I have told about the figure of the author in Spanish American fiction, one could view my study as attempting to describe what some of the contemporary figures of the author look like and how those figures tell their own stories. These readings of texts by Cortázar, Poniatowska, Fuentes, Puig, Donoso, and Vargas Llosa have also aimed to show how their work generates a dialogue among figures that can be taken as both eccentric and established models of authorial activity and identity. Moreover, Spanish American narrative reveals how such figures commingle and compete not only within any particular text's pages but also around its borders.

My study's conclusion would suggest that the author reappears in these texts (as much as it disappears from them) as a figure of considerable authority. Yet what emerges in this appearance is not a traditional concept universally triumphant in a contemporary setting, but rather a figure that is drawn in dialectical relation to the notion of the author as a disappearing, if not defunct, entity. In performing a critical reexamination of "the author," Spanish American fiction opens up a space for the appearance of that concept's contrary—but nonetheless compatible—figures. These figures emerge within different frames, as well as in different forms and fashions, around texts such as those I have discussed in the preceding chapters.

I have suggested reading *Rayuela* on its own as well as in conjunction with other texts by Cortázar or other authors, so as to consider the figures of the author produced by the circulation of authorial names and images around that text. Cortázar's novel and the names of the author it draws into its orbit plot the figure of the author (whose name inevitably leads from one to another figure) as a privileged, though destabilizing, force that continues to command considerable authority. Though the name of one or another author readily signals the tenuous condition of its referent, the author's name—as read around *Rayuela*—also persists in preserving the figure's customary position. Thus, even in a text that has generally been regarded as having undermined the author's traditional place and powers, and which would present its most suggestive author-figure (that is, Morelli) as both a textual and a narrative character, the author becomes a confounding composition of uncontainable figures.

In reading Poniatowska's testimonial novel, I have argued that there is substantial authority still attached to the nominal authors of diverse forms of contemporary narrative. Oddly enough, *Hasta no verte Jesús mío* suggests that this is especially so in texts that would seem to transcend the traditional role of the author—as they transform it—by dividing the author's conventional responsibilities between different textual and personal figures. Poniatowska's writing reveals how the testimonial novel problematizes the position of its author as it attempts to present an apparently self-evident truth. This text and the author's writings around it raise questions about authorship and originality, and thus pose problems specific to the testimonial genre as a whole. However, this novel also reveals that if, on the one hand, Poniatowska's text appears to unseat the author as a figure of original activity and authority, on the other, it seems to enthrone the author as an authoritative figure of truth and testimony.

Terra nostra's author-figures seem to be placed in equally, if not more, precarious and suggestive positions. The absolutely authoritative and firm ground sought within the novel's pages, especially by its organizing monarchal figure, eludes not only its readers but apparently also its author, whose literary plan and precepts this text would both advance and erode. Fuentes's novel shapes a contest between different figures of authorial possession, masterful figures whose empowerment the novel makes readily visible but whose defeat its story and narrative structure also design. The contest between author- and reader-figures, which is plotted within its pages and which figures the parallel encounter around its textual frame, proposes the author as an adversarial and possessive figure. In the end that figure's considerable powers are not to be ignored, even if they fail to produce the absolute mastery the novel's personal, textual, or fictional author-figures would aim to embody.

One may read Puig's *Pubis angelical* as situating the problem of authorial property and mastery, or the image of the author as owner or master of a text, through the question of authorial word or style. The author appears and disappears as both an idiosyncratic and conventional figure, as both a personal and popular image. This image is produced by the novel itself and also by the author's apparently authoritative words around it. As they are read around this text, such words address significant questions about it. The figure designed by these texts also appears as a figure of stolen languages and styles, of appropriated conventional models that seem to be permanently taken, rather than temporarily borrowed, from popular culture. Read through a novel such as *Pubis angelical* and other words around it, then, Puig becomes identified as the originator of the words of others, as the proprietor of authorless styles which nonetheless seem to find their perfect author in his writing.

The question of the author appears to expose itself rather dramatically in Donoso's *El jardín de al lado*. Indeed, as it implicitly poses and provisionally answers the questions "who is speaking?" and "who is writing?" this novel suggests that any text's author may become visible as an individual figure situated both within and beyond its borders. The contest for authorial position and authority between the novel's competing author-figures within the fiction at once disguises and discloses the competition of figures around it. The revelation of the author's identity at the end of the text, where the above questions are retroactively posed, suggests that authors cannot but reveal themselves, even when they would devise ways to disguise who they are. Donoso's novel also suggests that the disclosure of the author's identity within the text, the revelation of his or her face or name, is but a textual disguise that would fashion other authoritative images of the author—images at once personal and textual—around it.

The questions asked by Vargas Llosa's *El hablador* about the author are also questions of identity. The responses they elicit fashion figures that would identify the author both as an anonymous, traditional teller of collective tales and as an individualized, biographical, and personal writer. As the novel implicitly moves from the question "what is an hablador?" to "what is an author?" it identifies the figure of the one with that of the other, while also setting those figures against one another. In *El hablador* the figure of the modern author is recuperated as a figure of significant value through its identification with the eponymous storyteller. At the same time, the tribal teller of tales becomes a striking, literary figure, whose image is fortified by its association with a contemporary author. The text opens a dialogue between apparently different concepts and potentially equivalent figures of the author. Moreover, it also suggests that the face of the author himself—that is, Vargas Llosa—surfaces within the virtual exchange of stories and figures, and that the author thereby stages a dramatic, personal appearance.

As I conclude this brief recapitulation of points made earlier, I am aware that the story apparently told by the readings contained in the previous pages—and repeated, however reductively, in the paragraphs above—may have produced its own figures of the author. I am aware that, as I have read these texts (whose order, as I noted in the preface, has been determined by their dates of publication), my virtual narrative has moved from the question of the author's name to the question of the author's face. The gradual (and somewhat indirect) shift from name to face may seem to have generated the appearance of a personal, perhaps even empirical, figure of the author—and, of course, also my own authorial figure above or around it.

That such figures may have emerged, or been reclaimed, not only from out of the pages of the texts I have been discussing but also from within the discussion I myself have fashioned serves to recall several points. It is a reminder that this figure continues to appear within Spanish American fiction, and that there are other directions in which the discussion of the author might be taken. Indeed, the question of the author inevitably calls to its horizon the figure of the empirical, real-world writer along with other figures produced through the writing of any author. That figure has been situated outside the frame of this study, though it might well fall within the frame of other discussions.

Indeed, there are various avenues one could follow with the real-world figure. One might, for example, address the question of how, precisely, the real-world author's status has shifted (or not) within Spanish American culture and whether any such shift can be correlated with or counterposed to the production of authorial images by works of literature themselves, and especially by narrative fiction. If such an inquiry were to focus mainly on recent developments, it would also likely consider whether the empirical author's role or status in Spanish America differs (or not) from that of authors in Western culture more generally, and precisely what are the circumstances to which any such differences might be attributed. Within that context, one could also analyze the forms of representation through which real-world authors have been situated in the public arena, particularly in recent decades. One could consider, for instance, how the role of the author-superstar has been constructed by modern culture and how, perhaps, it has been lived by some Spanish American authors.

If, for example, one were to consider a case such as Vargas Llosa, with whose writing I have ended my readings, one could explore both the matter of the author-superstar, which in his case becomes a political as well as literary figure, and the problem of reading the figure of the author in a contemporary setting. Rather than solidifying the borders between one and another kind of figure, however, I suspect that such an inquiry would further confound them. I expect that one would inevitably have to face the phantasmatic, textual dimensions of the empirical author's appearance, even when that figure seemed to appear as an unmediated, accessible presence on the stage of world politics or culture.

On the other hand, if one were to look at the authorial presences projected by real-world writers around their texts and the apparently personal images produced by their writing, one would also be reminded of the variety of images of the real-world author that are now being produced by Spanish American narratives. Moreover, it would appear that the diversity of authors' images around Spanish American fiction has produced a dialogue of figures that in some way matches, and may be mapped onto, the dialogue of critical figures within it.

Were one to recall the variety of trends and traditions that have become more visible in Spanish American writing in recent years, and the challenge to received critical concepts and literary conventions they would represent, one could begin to see the spaces within which the virtual dialogue among disparate figures has emerged. Were one to consider the diverse forms of narrative incorporated into modern Spanish American literature, or the heterogeneous sociocultural contexts and personal situations from which Spanish American authors have emerged or from which they have been writing, one could begin to see the frames within which those authors' real-world appearances have been fashioned. It may well be that one might then be able to understand better some of the fictions and textual figures with which Spanish American authors have become identified.

If, as some would argue, the predominant image of the modern Spanish American author has been an essentially homogeneous one (that is, that of an educated heterosexual white male figure schooled in European and Anglo-American currents and bound to urban high culture), it is also the case that a diversity of visages and voices have arisen to challenge the monolithic image. Over the past several decades Spanish American fiction appears to have transformed itself not only through the deployment of unconventional narrative strategies, discursive forms, and thematic concerns during the first wave of the new narrative, but also through the projection of disparate authorial voices and faces within its pages. Those voices and faces would seem either to derive from or to map themselves onto a variety of real-world Spanish American figures who have become more visible and audible in the last several decades.

Thus if one were to try to describe what a Spanish American author looks like these days, one would have to look at a variety of faces; if one were to try to describe what a Spanish American author sounds like, one would have to listen to a variety of voices. The faces one would see and the voices one would hear would be those of both mainstream and marginalized figures that have become recognizable through a variety of enterprises. Along with the voices of the most well-known and celebrated authors, one would hear voices of less resonant figures; along with the faces of the most famous and recognizable authors, one would see the faces of less familiar figures.

That is, one would also hear the voices of women, projected by authors whose personal appearances might seem to coincide with the private and public concerns explored within their fictions: for example, Claribel Alegría (*Luisa en el país de la realidad*, 1987), Rosario Ferré (*Papeles de Pandora*, 1976), Elvira Orphée (*La última conquista de el Angel*, 1977), Armonía Somers (*La mujer desnuda*, 1967), Marta Traba (*Las ceremonias del verano*, 1966), Luisa Valenzuela (*Cambio de armas*, 1982), and Ana Lydia Vega (*Encáncaranublado*, 1982). One would also see the faces of ethnically and racially diverse subjects, uncovered by authors who would seem to speak from their own personal or professional experiences and perceptions: for example, Benita Galeana (*El peso mocho*, 1979), Isaac Goldemberg (*La vida a plazos de Don Jacobo Lerner*, 1978), Luis Rafael Sánchez (*La guaracha del macho Camacho*, 1976), Jacobo Timerman (*Preso sin nombre, celda sin número*, 1981), and Manuel Zapata Olivella (*Changó, el Gran Putas*, 1983). One would also confront figures for whom the question of sexual preference or orientation plays an important, if not central, role in their stories and indelibly marks the principal subjects of their narratives: for example, José Lezama Lima (*Oppiano Licario*, 1977), Sylvia Molloy (*En breve cárcel*, 1981), Cristina Peri Rossi (*Solitario de amor*, 1988), Rosamaría Roffiel (*Amora*, 1989), and Severo Sarduy (*Colibrí*, 1983). And one would also hear the testimony of witnesses and victims from different countries, classes, and cultures, whose faces and voices tell both individual and collective tales: for example, Arturo Arias (*Después de las bombas*, 1979), Miguel Barnet/Esteban Montejo (*Biografía de un cimarrón*, 1968), Elisabeth Burgos-Debray/Rigoberta Menchú (*Me llamo Rigoberta Menchú y así me nació la conciencia*, 1984), Roque Dalton (*Miguel Mármol*, 1972), Alicia Partnoy (*The Little School*, 1986), Doris Tijerino/Margaret Randall ("*Somos millones . . .*": *la vida de Doris María, combatiente nicaragüense*, 1977), Hernán Valdés (*Tejas Verdes*, 1974), and Rodolfo Walsh (*Operación masacre*, 1957).

It could be argued that the plurality of authorial voices and faces suggested by such writers and their work has undermined the assumption that the Spanish American author can be represented by any single image or figure. The texts I have discussed might also reveal that the homogeneous image produced by some of the most distinguished authors not only belies the diversity of real-world figures that have been active throughout the boom and post-boom years and the variety of topics with which Spanish American authors have become engaged. It also disguises the differences among the famous figures

Afterword   **166**

themselves. Some of the most acclaimed authors' work would have us recall the inroads that have been made not only by less well-known figures but also by some of the most prominent writers. Indeed, it would seem that the authorial projections of celebrated figures subvert as much as support the idea of a uniform or completely representative figure one could recognize as "the Spanish American author."

Perhaps one might be able to tell yet another kind of story—a story about the changing figures of the Spanish American author— through the texts with which the previous chapters have dealt. Such a story could give some idea of how diverse images of the author have been introduced, while conventional images have also been cultivated, by these Spanish American authors. Such a story could move from the texts of Cortázar and Fuentes, to that of Vargas Llosa and then Donoso, to that of Poniatowska and, finally, to Puig, as follows.

If Cortázar's *Rayuela* (1963) and Fuentes's *Terra nostra* (1975) problematize the figure of the author (by simultaneously destabilizing the author's name or position as an authority and solidifying the author-figure's powers), they also appear to support the image of the author as a traditional, and traditionally authorized (that is, male, first-world, high-culture), figure. Whether such an image is produced through the figure of Morelli or that of El Señor—representative figures of such an author—each would seem in one way or another to become identified with (even if appearing as an unstable or unsuccessful image of) the authors of Cortázar's and Fuentes's texts. Whether one is tempted or not to identify the author-figures in these fictions with the real-world writers responsible for their production, one might still see in these texts reflections of the real-world positions and assumptions characteristic of their authors. Theirs are the sorts of faces and voices, it might be argued, that seem to have shaped the prevalent image of "the Spanish American author."

Vargas Llosa's novel might appear to reinforce this dominant image and to elaborate it as that of a "real" Spanish American author— indeed, as that of Vargas Llosa himself. For this novel situates an arguably autobiographical author-figure, who is also a famous literary personage, at the center of its fiction. However, one recalls that *El hablador* (1987) also attaches the voice of an indigenous, unlettered figure to that of the famous boom author. In so doing, the novel may well insert into the author's space other, less canonical, figures. In orchestrating this convergence, if not also contamination, of images, *El hablador* seems to create a space for both traditionally familiar and singularly strange figures of the author. The indigenous and unfamiliar figure (the hablador) is appropriated for literary purposes by a well-known and familiar writer, who performs his act of ventriloquism within and around the novel. The superimposition of figures draws attention to the diverse traditions from which Spanish American narratives and narrators are drawn, and with which the well-known, lettered figure would also identify himself. These are currents about which, Vargas Llosa's novel suggests, not only mainstream authors but also marginalized figures may have a good deal to say. These are the currents from which the author's appearance as a new and old figure is formed.

Donoso's *El jardín de al lado* (1981) renders problematical the idea that texts by famous boom figures unequivocally reinforce a homogeneous image of the Spanish American author. Indeed, as it explores the relation between authorship and gender, superimposing and confounding images of male and female authority, Donoso's novel offers a critique of and correction to the dominant image of the author in Spanish America. The figure of the author is here an embattled figure, which counterposes different faces and voices of the author with each other. One might argue that, by putting forward the face and voice of another, less recognizable—because female—author, Donoso potentially undermines the authority of the boom-author image, and playfully problematizes his own position.

The texts of Poniatowska and Puig serve as additional reminders of the diverse orientations and origins of real-world writers from Spanish America, and the different personal images also projected by their work. *Hasta no verte Jesús mío* (1969) not only problematizes the concept of the author for testimonial texts. It also puts forth at least two female figures whose faces and voices differ markedly from the established faces and voices that may have once shaped the image of Spanish American authors. The appropriation of authority by such figures, as well as their challenge to the established social or literary order, exemplifies the inroads made by testimonial novels, for example, within modern Spanish American narrative. Though it is arguable whether her writing in *Hasta no verte Jesús mío* (among other of her testimonial texts) subverts the authority of a traditional author-figure, Poniatowska's presence around her text, as well as the figure of Jesusa within it, has helped to introduce several competing images of the author into the Spanish American scene.

The dis-appearing figure presented by Puig has upset the standard image of the Spanish American author partly because of the cultural models and social concerns with which his writing is engaged. Indeed, Puig's performance through *Pubis angelical* (1979) has fashioned a face that is filtered through the faces of Hollywood fictions and science fiction fantasies, and a voice that is heard through the voices of psychoanalysis and feminism, popular culture and contemporary politics. This text, as well as others by Puig, projects a voice that is raised to talk about different forms of social, political, and sexual repression, as well as to spin tales taken from the otherwise devalued realm of popular art. *Pubis angelical* exemplifies Puig's activity in the name of the popular, on behalf of low models or figures otherwise put down by the high. His performance also suggests an author who might be read through, if not identified with, some of his fictions' female figures and fantasies. It projects an author who situates himself as a sexually ambiguous figure. Puig dis-appears as a figure whose identity is difficult, if not impossible, to imagine, and whose position with respect to the established order seems to keep shifting. That dis-appearance is emblematic not only of his idiosyncratic image. It is also representative of the unstable and varied images of "the Spanish American author" more generally.

This other story told by the Spanish American authors I have selected underscores that, while a monolithic image of an established figure may seem to prevail, both the textual and real-world images of the Spanish American author have for some time been quite diverse. Like the texts within which we have seen the author dis-appear, this story shifts things from the realm of the textual to the realm of real-world activity and back again. The story of the authorial encounters within each text would frame the author as a problematical figure in one and the other domain. Indeed, each of these Spanish American authors, as well as the authorial theories or concepts encountered through their texts, appears as something of a figure at the crossroads—a figure anchored at a problematical but nonetheless productive site. It is a site at which different stories one might tell about "the author" intersect; it is a frame within which different personal and public images intermingle.

To situate the figure of the author in one or another context, it appears, is to confront a fundamentally complex and confounding figure. This figure is inevitably altered by the different contexts by which it is framed. However, the shift of focus from one context to another, like the shift from one story to another, reframes provisionally rather than redefines absolutely the question of the author. In figuring the author as they do, these Spanish American texts attach that question to both the textual and the real-world figures that emerge from them. The question persists in a variety of guises as it continues to be asked and answered by Spanish American fiction.

At this end of my study, then, one might say that, in posing questions about the author, Spanish American narratives not only stage an encounter of critical concepts more generally and authorial theories in particular. They also perform a way of reading between different figures and frames, between disparate concepts and contexts. To read the author in Spanish American fiction is also to read how one might read that figure elsewhere. Indeed, the stories about the contemporary figures of the author told here and in the preceding chapters are stories I offer as a way of telling about how "the author" might be read. But they are also—perhaps essentially—about how Spanish American fiction might allow us to read.

Notes

1 Situating the Author

1. Except when indicated that translations are mine, throughout this study references to both the Spanish and the published English texts will be provided, with the respective pagination differentiated by a forward slash. Where no published English version exists, all translations are mine.

2. That the question of the author becomes a question of significance within Borges's writing overall is emphasized most inventively by Kadir 39–69, with whose observations some of this discussion coincides.

3. See McHale 200, 202 for related comments, which, by accepting but then putting into question the text's apparent conclusion, virtually mirror the problematical ending of "Borges y yo." Mignolo and Aguilar Mora, among others, read the text as the demonstration of an exemplarily Borgesian effect (189). However, the Borges text that has perhaps received the most attention for its proposals regarding the figure of the author and problems of authorship is "Pierre Menard autor del Quijote" ["Pierre Menard, Author of the Quixote"] (see 444–50/96–103). The related observations about that text and the question of the author that I found most

suggestive for this discussion are those in Borinsky, de Man's "A Modern Master," González Echevarría's "Borges and Derrida," and Molloy 52–59.

4. Although my reading, and subsequent characterization, of this text's emblematic value were developed independently, McHale also uses the term "parable" to discuss related ideas, but takes his reading in a somewhat different direction (200). References to the concept of the author as a critical category or trope or theoretical principle, and also to the "poetics of the author," throughout this chapter have been aided by Siegle's discussion of similar, if not sometimes identical, notions (169–223).

5. That such propositions and performances might be situated squarely under the rubric of postmodernism is still a debatable point; see Manzor-Coats for the most detailed consideration of Borges and postmodernism, and González Echevarría (*La ruta de Severo Sarduy* 243–54) for one proposal about how to describe recent Spanish American fiction in terms of that category.

6. In using the word "precursor" to situate Borges's text in relation to those of Barthes and Foucault, I am of course alluding to Borges's own propositions in "Kafka y sus precursores" ["Kafka and His Precursors"] (see 710–12/242–46). That Borges has been read by a good many French literary critics and theorists, and that, moreover, his writing seems to have served as a suggestive, if not also directly influential, springboard for some of their thinking about literature, is by now a well-acknowledged fact; see Rodríguez Monegal's "Borges and La Nouvelle Critique," and González Echevarría's "Borges and Derrida" for different, though related, comments on this point. Following this vocabulary, one might situate Gass's identically titled response to the 1968 essay by Barthes (who becomes Gass's precursor) as an attempt to respond to and challenge Barthes's piece by repeating its title (265). In addition, see Gass 265–88 for points that dovetail with observations in this chapter.

7. In the original 1968 essay Barthes uses not the Latin *scriptor* but the French *scripteur* (an uncommon term, it emphasizes the act of writing as inscription or copying). The use of scriptor underscores the French word's etymological link with the Latin term, from which it derives, and thus casts the writer's activity not as authorial (i.e., original or originary) but as merely scriptural. We might also note that the italicization of the term in the 1986 translation (*Rustle of Language* 49–55) marks a linguistic difference that Barthes's original does not propose so violently. For although *scripteur* is not a neologism its uncommonness already sets it apart from the words surrounding it, perhaps not unlike the uncommon sense of the scriptor that Barthes here proposes. I have, therefore, preferred to follow the 1977 translation (*Image-Music-Text* 142–48), which more subtly adheres to the linguistic and semantic shift in Barthes's essay. Cf. the opposition between the author [*écrivain*] and the writer [*écrivant*] proposed in his *Critical Essays* 143–50.

8. The modern scriptor is a figure tied to (better yet, inherent in) the text, which, unlike the work, does not bear a fixed meaning that is authored, or authorized, by the author. It therefore cannot be characterized as closed by the activity of a creator. The scriptor is situated in a relation of simultaneity, rather than anteriority, with the text, whose meaning, as we recall, is not to be "deciphered" but only "disentangled" by the reader ("The Death of the Author" 147).

9. These shifts in terminology are, of course, shifts in the privilege granted to one or another critical notion or term. As such, in Barthes's proposal the figure of

the modern scriptor emerges to supplant, if not also to suppress, that of the Author, whose "dethronement" his essays propose and plot out. It also finally empowers the figure of the reader. But, as Kamuf remarks about this final privileging of the reader over the Author (and over the Critic), this is an "exchange [of] the 'tyranny' of the idea of the Author for that of the reader" (10).

10. As we recall, Foucault also summarizes the major questions and issues that ought to inform an examination of the author: " 'How, under what conditions and in what forms can something like a subject appear in the order of discourse? What place can it occupy in each type of discourse, what functions can it assume, and by obeying what rules?' In short, it is a matter of depriving the subject (or its substitutes) of its role as originator, and of analyzing the subject as a variable and complex function of discourse" ("What Is an Author?" 158).

11. On the literary creation of the authorial figure, rather than the biographical personage, by literary biographies, see Tomashevsky, whose views on the author as a subject of literary biography are compatible with other Russian Formalists' (in particular Tynianov) conception of the author in terms of the proper name (Steiner 132). In addition, see Mukařovský's consideration of the personality of the artist versus that of the author and their relation to the notion of literary development; and Bakhtin's notion of authorial utterance as a specific "conception of the world" rather than a manifestation of "inimitable individuality" (Todorov, *Mikhail Bakhtin* 61–62). Compare also to Eliot's "[i]mpersonal theory of poetry" (148–51).

12. On the distinction between the author's name and the author's signature, see Derrida's "Signature Event Context," and "Limited Inc abc . . . ," Kamuf, and de Man's "Autobiography as De-facement" (922–23).

13. Recent polemics about the author revolve precisely around the powers, as it were, attributable to such a person or figure and, in particular, around the question of intentionality. At issue is the possibility, or necessity, of legitimizing such a notion for the reading of literary texts. See, for example, Bruns's "Intention, Authority, and Meaning," Derrida, Juhl, Hirsch, Kamuf, Knapp and Michaels, and Hobbs for a sample of the recent interest in this and related issues. Cf. Bakhtin's *The Dialogic Imagination*, 259–422; and Suleiman. Oddly, precisely when traditional features of "the author" (as an authorizing critical notion) initially become controversial within the field of literary studies, the category is recuperated (through the terms "auteurism" or "*auteur* theory") as a legitimizing concept for film criticism. (I owe this observation to David Wills, from comments following a paper delivered at the University of Southern California in February 1989). See Caughie's collection for a review of the development of theories of authorship in film studies, from auteurism onward. For a very brief introduction to how the concept of the author has been questioned in art history studies, see Krauss.

14. Here I am drawing on de Man's well-known distinction between the rhetorical and the literal (*Allegories of Reading* 3–19).

15. The construction of this history aims to indicate in very general, and necessarily schematic, terms how the critical concept has shifted (or not) within a variety of critical currents. That I am aware, this "story" does not seem to have been told as a discrete tale by any anthology or history of critical or literary theory currently available. However, as the volume compiled by Jefferson and Robey attempts not only to discuss modern literary theory in terms of the general principles underlying

Notes   **173**

different trends but also to point out, where possible, the positions taken by those trends regarding specific issues—one being "the text and the author" (14–15), I wish to acknowledge that their volume has aided me in composing this brief narrative about "the author."

16. See Ehrlich.

17. However, it ought to be remembered that, within the context of the discussion of literary history, the Formalists also allowed for a consideration of the author as a person whose education, social status, etc., also intervene in the development of literary forms; see, for example, Mukařovský 161–79.

18. I refer of course to Wellek and Warren's opposition between "intrinsic" and "extrinsic" approaches to literary studies in *Theory of Literature*. See Wimsatt 3–18 for the well-known Wimsatt and Beardsley essay.

19. Robey recalls I. A. Richards's early formulations about the author's "consciousness" and contrasts his formulations to those of more recent literary theorists (Jefferson and Robey 76–78).

20. See, e.g., Barthes, "The Death of the Author" 146–48; and Culler 30, 116–18.

21. See, e.g., Derrida's *Of Grammatology*, "Signature Event Context," and "Limited Inc abc. . . ."

22. See Kamuf.

23. Compare Tompkins, Suleiman and Crosman, and Iser.

24. We might note, however, that reception theory—i.e., the theory of literary history as of the history of literature's reception by its readers—allows a place for the author as an historically situated entity whose work, like the reader's reading, is shaped by the "horizons of expectations" that determine both the production and the reception of literature; see Jauss.

25. See his "Criticism and the Experience of Interiority."

26. See, e.g., his *Validity in Interpretation* and *The Aims of Interpretation*. Hirsch's position represents one side of the critical debate about the question of intentionality, which, perforce, also revolves around the figure of the author (see also note 13). Concerning the reading of narrative fiction in particular, see also Rabinowitz on "authorial reading" (29–46).

27. See, e.g., Lukács's *Writer and Critic and Other Essays*; Goldmann's *Towards a Sociology of the Novel* or *Cultural Creation in Modern Society*; Macherey's *A Theory of Literary Production*; and Bakhtin's *Problems of Dostoevsky's Poetics* or *Speech Genres and Other Late Essays*. The mention of the above names and titles, of course, aims only to suggest—and in no way to encompass—several of the tendencies and texts that might be considered representative of some currents in Marxist criticism; the same holds for mention of references to feminist criticism and theory below.

28. See, e.g., their *The Madwoman in the Attic* or *No Man's Land*.

29. See her manifesto of sorts in "The Laugh of the Medusa."

30. See, e.g., McGann's "The Significance of the Biographical Context" for proposals for such an orientation and the attendant recuperation of the author's biography as a framework for critical discussion.

31. For a summary of views of the subject, see Smith.

32. The word author has its origins in the term *auctor*, which is derived from the Latin *augere* (to grow, to augment). But its meaning appears also to be related to other terms in both Latin (*agere* to act, to do, to perform; *auieo* to tie) and Greek

Notes   **174**

(*autentin* authority) (Minnis 10; see also Whinnom 212, and Dante 252–53). *Auctor* seems originally to have meant someone who produces or makes something (especially a book) or someone who is a performer (especially of the act of writing). The term was therefore used in a more specialized way than was *actor* (from *agere*), which meant a maker of things more generally. But *auctor* was also affected by its association with *auctoritas* (authority). Indeed, for the Middle Ages *auctor* came to mean "someone who was at once a writer and an authority, someone not merely to be read but also to be respected and believed" (Minnis 10), "someone who, by virtue of some kind of recognition or endorsement, has had his views validated, so that they are thereafter accepted as part of the great chain of 'authority,' leading back ultimately to the Scriptures" (Whinnom [paraphrasing Chenu] 212).

33. The question of authority early on becomes a key component of the idea of authorship inherent in the term *auctor*, from which our modern notions derive. Moreover, the role of the *auctor* was often distinguished from that of other literary figures (e.g., the *scriptor*, *editor*, *compilator*, and *commentator*) precisely because it carried greater authority. On the gradation of responsibility and authority of these different figures and functions, see Minnis 94–95, 102; on the origins of authority in Roman politics and culture, see Arendt 91–141; on the medieval association between *auctor* and *auctoritas*, and the confusion between *auctor* and *actor*, see Chenu 83, 86; on the medieval *auctores* as authorities for the medieval curriculum, see Curtius 48–54, 56; and Minnis 13. See also Said 81–100, on the possible relations between the terms author and authority, the limitations on the authority inherent in authorship, and the application of such a perspective to a reading of narrative fiction. For a general introduction to the question of authority, see, e.g., De George; for an examination of the question of authority (and in particular the author's authority) in specific texts from Augustine to Faulkner, see Flores; and for an attempt to problematize the question as a general issue for literary studies, see Everman.

34. On the identification of the *auctor* with the origin and as a founder, and on the differentiation of the *auctor* (author, the one who founds or inspires a work) from the *artifex* (maker, the one who carries out the idea), see Arendt 122; and Minnis 86.

35. The following brief review of some aspects of this development aims only to map out some general, and thus necessarily schematic, features of this part of the author's story. See also Pease (whose essay came to my attention after having completed this project and whose overview dovetails in some ways with this discussion) for another version of both the critical and cultural stories of "the author"; see Braudy for the possibility of telling the tale as part of the history of fame.

36. On medieval biblical commentators' shift in focus away from the divine and toward the human *auctor* from the twelfth and through the thirteenth centuries, see Minnis 5.

37. Here is meant personal biography or personality as separate from and outside the context of theology, wherein questions about the *auctor's* life revolved around theological issues and were related to models of moral activity (see Minnis 103–12).

38. The comments on poetic license draw principally on Miller; see also the essays in West and Woodman concerning imitation.

39. This opposition between established tradition and the individual writer,

between traditionally authorized and individually sanctioned literary practices, seems to have been evident already in the way that some medieval writers began to exercise a form of poetic license, primarily by focusing on specific uses of language (Miller 27). On the issue of originality "among the ancients" and its relation to the question of authority and other concepts, see also Bruns's *Inventions* (44–59, 186–87).

40. On this debate, whose general outcome was the development of "an essentially secular view of literature," see Quint 219.

41. The mark of this shift may be revealed partly in the shift from thinking about writers mainly in terms of the notion of (divine) inspiration to conceiving of their authorial activity as evidence of the exercise of imagination, a notion which gains currency after the Renaissance; see Guillory for an extensive discussion of this topic.

42. On the "unadulterated pride of authorship" evident in the twelfth century, and on the customs surrounding the suppression or revelation of the author's name in the medieval period, see Curtius 516–17. On the history of authorship as the history of the economic and social conditions that have supported or deterred authors' activities, and which have fostered systems of patronage or allowed for the professionalization of the writer, see Laurenson.

43. "Scientific discourses began to be received for themselves, in the anonymity of an established or always redemonstrable truth; their membership in a systematic ensemble, and not the reference to the individual who produced them, stood as their guarantee. The author-function faded away, and the inventor's name served only to christen a theorem, proposition, particular effect, property, body, group of elements, or pathological syndrome. By the same token, literary discourses came to be accepted only when endowed with the author-function" (Foucault, "What Is an Author?" 149).

44. On medieval interest in the lives of *auctores*, and for a discussion of an exemplary case (that of Ovid), see Ghisalberti. On the proliferation of pseudo-authorial materials see Paul Lehmann, *Pseudo-Ankike Literatur des Mittelalters* (1927; rpt. 1964).

45. Barthes begins his essay "Authors and Writers" with such a characterization of "authors" (writers of literary texts), as opposed to "writers" (i.e., "intellectuals"), who begin to emerge around the time of the French Revolution and to "appropriate the authors' language for political ends" (*Critical Essays* 144). This essay addresses the role of the author from a different angle than does "The Death of the Author," whose publication it precedes by some eight years.

46. For another perspective on authorship in the eighteenth century, see Stallybrass and White's comments on the English figure of the master-poet (the author as separated from and superior to "low" culture) and on the relation between authorship and cultural hierarchy (80–124).

47. See Tomashevsky on this and other related points concerning the emergence of literary biography and its role in creating an image of the author during the eighteenth and nineteenth centuries; see also Wellek and Warren 75–80.

48. Given the proliferation of conflicting discussions that have entered into the debate around the term "postmodernism" and the concept of the postmodern (compare, for example, Fokkema and Bertens, H. Foster, Hutcheon, Huyssens, and Lyotard), I have considerable reservations about using the adjectival form here, although I recognize that it may serve as a more or less recognizable signpost for

Notes   176 some readers. However, in spite of these terminological and conceptual difficulties (and my own reluctance therefore to categorize these texts in such terms), I have found that my consideration of "the author" (mainly through readings of recent Spanish American fiction) has led me to formulate independently some notions and terminology (i.e., the author as a "problematical" figure or concept) identical to those proposed by Hutcheon (see especially 224ff.). Although I encountered the Hutcheon study only after having devised a vocabulary that seemed to me appropriate to, because it was generated by, the Spanish American texts themselves, and after having written the major portion of this book, I do wish to note the coincidence of terms.

49. As suggested above, the critical polemics surrounding the author seem to have arisen mainly around the question of how one is to read the relationship between the author-person (and additionally the author's name) and the work he or she is understood to have produced. Disputes about the author are thus not so much disagreements about whether there is a person, a psychophysical entity, that might properly be identified as an author, but rather they focus on questions concerning theoretical concepts and critical practices, the concepts and practices through which "the author" itself has been reviewed and revised over the years. See also note 13.

50. Booth's introduction of the concept of the implied author defines it as "the image [the author] creates of himself" (395); "the 'implied author' chooses, consciously or unconsciously, what we read; we infer him as an ideal, literary, created version of the real man; he is the sum of his own choices" (74–75); the "implied author's character dominates [the reader's] reactions" (215). Further proposals relating to or incorporating the notion include, among others, those of Chatman 147–51; Genette, *Narrative Discourse* 213, 258–59; and Todorov, "Point of View in Fiction" 329–30. Though a phrase such as "gestural vocabulary" (Rabinowitz 122) would subsume this notion as well as others mentioned below, it would not resolve the problematical connections noted here.

51. See Siegle 180ff. for a recent attempt to clarify such a notion; see Thiher 121–55 for a response to related, though different, questions about the "voices" of postmodernist fiction.

52. The complexity of such critical phrases or terms as are mentioned here and below is also addressed by Bakhtin (*Speech Genres and Other Late Essays* 109–12, 116–17; see also Todorov's discussion of that critique in *Mikhail Bakhtin* 51–52). In addition to the terms mentioned here, one might also consider the relations among the phrases "fictional author," "fictive author," "text author," and "text-act author," as proposed by Spires 11, 73, 137n.

53. If one chose to work with such vocabulary, the inherently critical or theoretical nature of Spanish American fiction (which many critics have acknowledged and which I aim to elaborate around the concept of the author) might be taken as evidence of how that tradition might be mapped onto theories of the postmodern (e.g., Hutcheon 14, 148, 226–29). However, I hesitate to perform such a mapping because that maneuver would too easily subordinate literary texts to theoretical explanation, and too readily dilute the differences and particularities that characterize what we call "the literary"—especially Spanish American fiction.

Notes

2 In the Name of the Author

1. See also Mac Adam, *Modern Latin American Narratives* 54–56. Cortázar, one of the most well-known writers of Spanish American new narrative, is the author of a sizable body of fiction, both novels and short stories. *Rayuela* is the second of his novels, which also include *Los premios* [*The Winners*] (1960), *62: modelo para armar* [*62: A Model Kit*] (1968), and *Libro de Manuel* [*A Manual for Manuel*] (1973). His volumes of short narrative include: *Bestiario* (1951), *Final del juego* (1956; 1964), *Las armas secretas* (1959) [*End of the Game and Other Stories*/*Blow-Up and Other Stories* includes texts from these first three volumes], *Todos los fuegos el fuego* [*All Fires the Fire, and Other Stories*] (1966), *Historias de cronopios y de famas* [*Cronopios and Famas*] (1969), *Octaedro* (1974), *Alguien que anda por ahí y otros relatos* (1977) [*A Change of Light and Other Stories* includes texts from these last two volumes], *Un tal Lucas* [*A Certain Lucas*] (1979), *Queremos tanto a Glenda y otros relatos* [*We Love Glenda So Much and Other Tales*] (1980), *Deshoras* (1982), and *El examen* (1986).

In other instances of Cortázar's writing the author also appears as a question of names and figures, as it does in *Rayuela*. One might also consider, for example, *62: modelo para armar* or *Libro de Manuel*, whose prologues would seem to speak in the name of a single author but whose narrative structure or discursive composition would divide and disperse that figure's appearance.

2. From the earliest readings of *Rayuela*, critics have talked about the ludic features of its complex narrative structure. For representative examples, see Barrenechea, "La estructura de *Rayuela*, de Julio Cortázar," and Giordano, "Algunas aproximaciones a *Rayuela*, de Julio Cortázar, a través de la dinámica del juego"; for other titles dealing with this topic, as well as information on the vast critical bibliography devoted to Cortázar's work, see Carter.

3. However, this appended sentence (which, in those imprints where it is included, follows the opening line cited directly above) has been omitted from the English translation, which appears to follow the 1963 original.

4. For discussion of *Rayuela's* theory of reading, see, e.g., Barrenechea ("Estudio preliminar" 107–11), Brody (31–35), Mac Adam ("*Rayuela*: la cuestión del lector"), and Ostria González.

5. See, e.g., Barrenechea ("Estudio preliminar" 85 and "La estructura de *Rayuela*"), Brody (26–36), and Ortega ("Morelli on the Threshold").

6. On the inherently relational quality of any exercise of authority, see, e.g., De George; on some of the differences between being in authority and being an authority, see, e.g., Peters and also Winch.

7. This reading of the tablero draws on comments I have made in Kerr, "Leaps Across the Board." See also Castro-Klarén and also Sarlo for complementary readings of the instruction table and the author-reader relationship in the novel.

8. Readers unfamiliar with the "discovery" of Borges outside Latin America (a foreign discovery which, some have lamented, preceded his later, and thus delayed, recognition at home) should consult Rodríguez Monegal's "Borges and La Nouvelle Critique," and Alazraki's *Critical Essays on Jorge Luis Borges*.

9. See Kerr, "Leaps Across the Board" and Merrim's "Desire, and the Art of Dehumanization" 52, for readings that put into question such a coincidence of theory and practice in Cortázar's novel.

Notes　　　　　　　　　　　　　　　　　　　　　　　　　　　　　**178**

10. Among the other authors whose names appear to identify texts apparently cited, if not appropriated, by Morelli (and/or Cortázar) are: Claude Lévi-Strauss (chapter 59), Meister Eckhardt (chapter 70), José Lezama Lima (chapter 81), [Hugo von] Hofmannsthal (chapter 102), Anaïs Nin (chapter 110), Clarence Darrow (chapter 117), Malcolm Lowry (chapter 118), [Lawrence] Ferlinghetti (chapter 121), [Antonin] Artaud (chapter 128), Georges Bataille (chapter 136), [Witold] Gombrowicz (chapter 145), and Octavio Paz (chapter 149).

11. The naming of the chapters according to their assigned numbers in the text is deceptive, of course, since the reading sequence supplied by the table of instructions resituates, as it renumbers, them according to its own numerical and narrative scheme. Thus, chapter 154 is the thirty-first chapter after chapter 22, which is the forty-fourth chapter in the reading "à la rayuela"; or, viewed another way, chapter 22 is really chapter 44 and chapter 154 is really chapter 75. On the deliberate, and consequently meaningful, ordering of chapters in the tablero, see Holsten.

12. Mac Adam reads the text as presenting Morelli "dying in the hospital" (*Modern Latin American Narratives* 57); Barrenechea notes Cortázar's plan to represent Morelli's hospital death scene and Oliveira's vigil over, as well as subsequent identification with, the dead author ("Estudio preliminar" 86); see also the reproduction of Cortázar's original notes for the scene (Cortázar and Barrenechea 210). If one were to read the novel's chapters in chronological order, that death would appear to be imminent only in its final pages, since the text ends with chapter 155. However, if one were to read them "à la rayuela," this fatal scene would appear in the middle of the narrative as well as in the middle of the text as a whole. For, once Oliveira arrives in Buenos Aires, the "capítulos prescindibles" interspersed with chapters 37–56 no longer advance directly Morelli's literary theories, as noted above. See Alonso ("Julio Cortázar") for a different, though related, way of reading the "death of the author" and the text of Cortázar.

13. Mac Adam reads this as Cortázar's attempt to invent not only a magisterial figure absent from the Latin American tradition, but also a conventional or "traditional" model against which he—or his own text—could react and in relation to which he (or Morelli) could propose "innovative" and "transgressive" literary ideas (*Modern Latin American Narratives* 53–55). That the master to whom Cortázar alludes through the figure of Morelli may well be, or is in fact, Macedonio Fernández (1874–1952), whose *Museo de la novela de la eterna* (posthumous publication 1967) could be identified as the model for or fulfillment of *Rayuela's* proposals, is suggested by Engelbert (xi, 153–54n.), Lindstrom (59), and Merrim ("Desire, and the Art of Dehumanization" 48, 52, 62n).

14. Among others, see Brody, and Barrenechea ("La estructura de *Rayuela*").

15. Oliveira has been read as the first-person narrator-author by Barrenechea ("La estructura de *Rayuela*" 212) and Mac Adam (*Modern Latin American Narratives* 52). References to the Oliveira-Morelli identification, sometimes connected to the Cortázar-Oliveira composite figure, can be found in, for example, Barrenechea's "Estudio preliminar" (56, 62, 65, 85–86) and "Los dobles en el proceso de escritura de *Rayuela*" (812), and in Sarlo (945).

16. Brody, among others, literally hyphenates the names (32), after referring to Morelli as the author's "alter ego" (27), and Mac Adam refers to him as an authorial "surrogate" (*Modern Latin American Narratives* 54). Barrenechea's description of Morelli

as "la máscara que se construye Cortázar para exponer su 'poética' " ["the mask that Cortázar constructs for himself in order to present his 'poetics' "] ("Estudio preliminar" 85), and Alazraki's declaration that "Morelli, después de todo, representa la conciencia novelística del autor" ["Morelli, after all, represents the author's novelistic consciousness"] (Prólogo lxii), are good examples of the identification assumed by many readers.

17. On the author as "begetter," "originator," or "creator," and related notions, see Said 81–100.

18. See note 9, and Sarlo.

19. This character-author is referred to only with a surname in *Rayuela.* He has no given name either in the novel or in Cortázar's notes. Moreover, in Cortázar and Barrenechea, *Cuaderno de bitácora de "Rayuela,"* one finds no authorial comments about the name itself nor any indication of what its original significance might have been. Thus, besides considering whether "Morelli" may be but a cover for "Macedonio" (see note 13), one might also speculate about Morelli's onomastic antecedents (if not fictional models or thematic sources) in texts by other Argentine masters whose work Cortázar knew well, or in their sources—in Borges's Morell ("El espantoso redentor Lazarus Morell," *Historia universal de la infamia* ["The Dread Redeemer Lazarus Morell," *A Universal History of Infamy*] [1935]), or Bioy Casares's Morel (*La invención de Morel [The Invention of Morel]* [1940]), or Wells's Dr. Moreau (*The Island of Dr. Moreau* [1896], on which Bioy Casares is presumed to have drawn for his novel). One may also wonder whether Cortázar, who translated all of Poe's prose works (*Obras en prosa de Edgar Allan Poe* [1956]), may have somehow derived the name from the American author's "Morella" (1834–35), which, aptly enough, can be read as a fable about the propriety of the proper name.

20. Some of these suggestions draw in a limited fashion on Derrida's "Signature Event Context" and "Limited Inc abc. . . ."

21. The information provided about Morelli and his method draws on Damisch, Ginzburg, Previtali, Spector, Wind (32–51, 138–51), Wollheim (177–219), and Zerner.

22. Morelli's interest in scientific matters would appear to originate in his training as a physician. See, e.g., Wind (especially 36–38, 138–39 n. 61) for information about his life and works, and for contrasts between the method of Morelli ("a clear-headed amateur who did his work so exceedingly well that it passed almost imperceptibly into the work of his professional successors" [34–35]) and that of earlier connoisseurs. The relation between Morelli's method and that of scientific disciplines of his era is taken up by Ginzburg and by Spector.

23. Schor's comments on the relation between significance and insignificance, especially with respect to "the detail" (36–39), could frame a discussion of Morelli's method. (Aptly enough, Morelli is actually mentioned, if only in passing, at the beginning of Schor's discussion of "the detail" in Freud [68, 158–59 n.1].) See Wind on Morelli's "cult of the fragment" in relation to the recovery of a "lost original" and within the context of Romantic thought (42–43). In his insistence on such material details, habits, or tics of individual style, Morelli might also be situated among the initiators of the "formal method" of analysis, according to Damisch's "La partie et le tout."

24. Wind (37) and Wollheim (185) provide the information about the transla-

tor's name and the translated variations on "Morelli," also noted parenthetically in my text. For sources on Morelli's work as a whole, see Wind 138–39 n. 61. When I ventured to obtain a list of Morelli's publications, I found that a number of titles in different languages, and their attributions of authorship or translation, suggested an array of problems concerning the author's name. For others who might share my fascination with this "case," I cite some examples: Ivan Lermolieff, *Die Werke italienischer Meister in den Galerien von München, Dresden und Berlin. Ein kritischer Versuch* (Leipzig: Seemann, 1880); Giovanni Morelli, *Italian Masters in German Galleries. A Critical Essay on the Italian Pictures in the Galleries of Munich, Dresden, and Berlin*, by Giovanni Morelli, translated from German by Louise M. Richter (London: G. Bell and Sons, 1883) [microform]; Giovanni Morelli, *Le opere dei maestri italiani: nelle gallerie di Monaco, Dresda e Berlino: saggio critico de Jvan Lermolieff*, translated from Russian into German by Johannes Schwarze, and from German into Italian by Baroness Di K . . . A . . . (Bologna: Nicola Zanichelli, 1886); Giovanni Morelli, *Italian Painters: Critical Studies of Their Works by Giovanni Morelli (Ivan Lermolieff)*, translated from German by Constance Jocelyn Ffoulkes, with intro. by Right Hon. Sir A. H. Layard (London: J. Murray, 1892–93); Giovanni Morelli, *Della pittura italiana: Studii storico-critici—Le gallerie Borghese e Doria Pamphili in Roma* (Milan: Treves, 1897)/Giovanni Morelli, *Della pittura italiana: le Gallerie Borghese e Doria Pamphili in Roma, studii critici / di Giovanni Morelli (Ivan Lermolieff)* (Milan: Fratelli Treves, 1897).

25. Wind declares not only that Morelli was considered to have caused a "revolution" with his method, which aspired to ground connoisseurship in science (38–39), but also that he "disliked artistic conventions. Whatever smacked of academic rule or aesthetic commonplace he dismissed as deceptive, hackneyed and unrewarding" (43). However, Morelli's "scientific" theory of connoisseurship is not unconnected to the theory of Giovanni Battista Cavalcaselle, another art historian with whose "empirical" method of attribution Morelli's theory could be compared and against which, it has also been suggested, Morelli was concerned to establish his own authority. Cavalcaselle traveled with Morelli while the latter developed his theory and, though three years his junior, he may have been viewed as Morelli's intellectual elder (Previtali 27–28). Thus, Morelli's relation to the traditions from which his own models are drawn and the scholars whose works lay the foundations, if not also the competing theories, for his theory of attribution seems to raise openly the issues of originality and authority. See Spector on Morelli and scientific tradition (especially Morelli's critique of Crowe and Cavalcaselle); see also Zerner.

26. Questions about the concept of originality, the notion of an original work, and, by extension, the very foundations of connoisseurship, to which Morelli's name is attached and with which traditional art history has been concerned, have been raised within some circles of art history studies in recent years; see Krauss for a brief introduction to these developments.

27. The comments on Freud's relation to Morelli's work draw especially on Spector and on Wollheim 177–219.

28. Ginzburg brings together as principal authors and practitioners of this paradigm Morelli, Freud, and Sherlock Holmes, aiming to "show how, in the late nineteenth century, an epistemological model . . . quietly emerged in the sphere of the social sciences" (81).

29. For related speculation, which moves into a detailed discussion of Freud's reading of the Moses statue, see Damisch's "Le gardien de l'interprétation."

Notes   **181**

30. The *Cuaderno's* text comprises a reproduction of Cortázar's handwritten and variegated notes, whose originals were personally entrusted to Barrenechea by him (9) and whose copies form the body of the logbook itself (139–260). It also contains a set of additional "pre-textos" ["pre-texts"], which include the novel's originary episode called "La araña" ["The Spider"] (this episode was elided by the author from the original novel but later published separately in *Revista iberoamericana* [1973]) and other typed manuscript materials and handwritten notes (261–88). The materials authored by Cortázar are appended to the original logbook pages, along with a lengthy "Estudio preliminar" ["Preliminary Study"] composed by Barrenechea (7–138). Though the volume's contents would attest to its essentially heterogeneous nature, one reviewer sees the *Cuaderno* as a "book of criticism" published by Barrenechea (Goodrich 571). I see the matter of authorial and generic identity as somewhat more problematical.

31. The organization of the 1983 book places Barrenechea's own text before that of Cortázar. Her "Estudio preliminar," which presents both a preliminary reading of Cortázar's logbook in virtual dialogue with *Rayuela* and a theoretical introduction to her own reading and his logbook texts, comes ahead of the notes first authored by Cortázar. Barrenechea's writing becomes its own "pre-texto" for the "pre-textos" that have occasioned her preliminary study, along with the publication of the logbook itself. At the other end, the *Cuaderno* closes with what Barrenechea calls "otros pre-textos" ["other pre-texts"], the last of which is the originary episode or chapter of *Rayuela* ("La araña"), which is recuperated and once again revealed by Barrenechea, in the fashion of Cortázar, who preceded her. (As noted above, Cortázar first revealed and simultaneously restored this chapter some ten years after the novel's original publication.) She situates it (appropriately enough, one might argue) at the very end of the 1983 text (281–88). Indeed, that the text ends with "pre-texts" that are themselves finally punctuated by an originary chapter is quite fitting for a volume dealing with *Rayuela*, to whose disruptive textual order its title openly alludes.

32. However, that the name Cortázar has greater value because of its presumed priority may well be declared, as convention would have it, by the book's title (the logbook named there is of course the text originally composed and owned by Cortázar) and the ordering of names on its title page. But within the text edited and authored by Barrenechea, this order and privilege are also reversed: Barrenechea's texts occupy approximately the first (7–138) and Cortázar's the second (139–288) half of its pages; and the index, which separates the names of the authors by placing each one over the list of texts attributed to him or her, literally exposes the division of authorship by textually distancing each name from the other (289).

3   Gestures of Authorship

1. A few words about terminology. I am using the phrase "documentary fiction" as the general term to encompass all those texts that purport to function as documents concerning the social, political, or historical realities they take as their referents, and which do so in ways that have been read as literary. I am using the more specific "novela testimonial" or its English equivalent partly because Poniatowska identifies her text in those terms (see below) and partly because it is the

phrase most widely used in Spanish to classify a variety of texts that fall into the "testimonial" or "documentary" category. Various discussions of the loosely defined genre would implicitly or explicitly address the matter of generic terminology, but the end result has yet to clarify or normalize the vocabulary. Different terms mean different things to different readers; different texts elicit different labels from different critics: in English, compare the uses of "documentary fiction" (Foley), "documentary narrative" (D. Foster), "documentary novel" (Barnet translated by Bundy and Santí, Foley, González Echevarría [*The Voice of the Masters* 110–23]), "testimonial literature" (D. Foster), "testimonial narrative" (Beverley), "testimonial novel" (Beverley); in Spanish, "novela-testimonio" (Barnet), "narrativa de testimonio" (González Echevarría [*The Voice of the Masters* 110–23]), "novela testimonial" (Beverley), "testimonio" (Beverley). The case of Poniatowska's text is exemplary but not representative of all the texts that would fashion personal testimony into a form of writing that gets taken as more or less literary. Indeed, the matter of classification rests as much (if not more) with critical response as with authorial intention. Sklodowska's review of the critical theory of Spanish American "testimonio," which came to my attention after completing this chapter, demonstrates that point as it offers a comprehensive perspective on the terminological and conceptual problems at issue.

2. Beverley would counterpose "testimonio" to existing literary forms such as new narrative, while D. Foster would establish the (mainly formal) points of contact between them.

3. Poniatowska has published a variety of texts, including works of fiction, journalism, and criticism. Among the best known of her titles are: *Lilus Kikus* (1954), *La noche de Tlatelolco: testimonio de historia oral* [*Massacre in Mexico*] (1971), *Querido Diego, te abraza Quiela* [*Dear Diego*] (1978), *Fuerte es el silencio* (1980), *Domingo 7* (1982), *¡Ay vida, no me mereces!: Carlos Fuentes, Rosario Castellanos, Juan Rulfo, la literatura de la onda* (1985), *De noche vienes* (1985), *La "flor de lis"* (1988), and *Nada, nadie: las voces del temblor* (1988).

Other of Poniatowska's testimonial publications present direct documentary compilation or citations of multiple voices (*La noche de Tlatelolco, Fuerte es el silencio, Nada, nadie*), rather than narratives derived from testimonial materials. One might also consider how such texts also problematize the figure of the author. Perhaps the author's voice can be heard around, though more often it vanishes behind, the voices of other testimonial witnesses; and the author's hand can be seen giving shape to the words of others, though those words also appear to come forward on their own. The critical reflection on the question of truth and authorial authority of the sort found in and around *Hasta no verte Jesús mío*, however, seems to be tied to Poniatowska's more "literary" testimonial writing.

4. I aim to emphasize how a particular novela testimonial can be read not simply in terms of its referent but as a text that, consciously or not, reflects upon its own status as testimonial literature. In that Poniatowska's text virtually demands such a double reading it would establish its proximity to, as well as distance from, texts customarily considered to be reflexive or more properly literary. For two rather different views on the literary status of testimonial fiction or its relation to the tradition of literature more generally, see Beverley and also González Echevarría (*The Voice of the Masters* 110–23). See also Foley's consideration of the documentary novel for a complementary discussion.

Notes

5. With these comments, and others below, I am thinking also of Said's discussion of the duplicity, the "molestations of authority," inherent in all narrative fiction, and especially in the role of the author (81–100).

6. The general question of the truth-value of works thought of as either testimonial or documentary may be taken up in different ways, and indeed has been considered by a number of critics in different forums. See, e.g., Barnet, Cavallari, D. Foster, González Echevarría's *The Voice of the Masters* (110–23), and Prada Oropeza, on Spanish American writing, and Foley, on European and Afro-American models.

7. If one were to accept González Echevarría's description of the two trends in the Cuban documentary novel (the "epic" trend and the "account of the marginal witness") as representative of the dominant forms of the novela testimonial more generally, Poniatowska's text could be grouped with the second of those trends— "the *petite histoire*, a sort of cultural history dealing with everyday life and folk traditions" (*The Voice of the Masters* 116), presented by the protagonist's own narration. Cf. Kiddle's categorization of the testimonial novel in Mexico and *Hasta no verte Jesús mío* within it (85), and Feal's discussion of some testimonial novels as ethnobiography ("Spanish American Ethnobiography and the Slave Narrative Tradition").

Poniatowska's character is read from different angles as a representative figure by Davis (225–26), Fernández Olmos (70, 72), Lemaître (135), and by Poniatowska herself ("Jesusa Palancares" 11, and "Testimonios" 159). On the other hand, Franco reads her story as unique rather than representative, and thus as unassimilable or incomparable to other such testimonies (*Plotting Women* 178). See also Poniatowska's conversations with Méndez-Faith (57) and with Roses (59–60).

8. On the novel's resemblance to the picaresque, see Jaen, Tatum; on its differences from that model, see Beverley 15–17.

9. However, Poniatowska emphasizes the difference between her text and a social science or journalism project, for which similar techniques may be utilized. She says:

> Para escribir el libro de la Jesusa utilicé un procedimiento periodístico: la entrevista. Dos años antes, trabajé durante mes y medio con el antropólogo norteamericano Oscar Lewis, autor de *Los hijos de Sánchez* y otros libros, Lewis me pidió que lo ayudara a 'editar' *Pedro Martínez, la vida de un campesino de Tepoztlán.* . . . Este [sic] experiencia sin duda ha de haberme marcado al escribir *Hasta no verte Jesús mío.* Sin embargo, como no soy antropóloga, la mía puede considerarse una novela testimonial y no un documento antropológico y sociológico.
>
> [In order to write Jesusa's book I used a technique of journalism: the interview. Two years earlier, I worked for one and one-half months with the North American anthropologist Oscar Lewis, author of *The Children of Sánchez* and other books, and Lewis asked me to help him to "edit" *Pedro Martínez, A Mexican Peasant and His Family.* . . . This experience undoubtedly must have marked my writing of *Hasta no verte Jesús mío.* Nevertheless, since I am not an anthropologist, my novel can be considered as a testimonial novel and not as an anthropological or sociological document.] ["Jesusa Palancares" 10]

See also her conversation with Méndez-Faith 56–57; cf. Kushigian.

10. Indeed, the following statement by the author would also suggest that the

Notes

text must in some way be read as a literary production: "Utilicé las anécdotas, las ideas y muchos de los modismos de Jesusa Palancares pero no podría afirmar que el relato es una transcripción directa de su vida porque ella misma lo rechazaría. Maté a los personajes que me sobraban, eliminé cuanta sesión espiritualista pude, elaboré donde me pareció necesario, podé, cosí, remendé, inventé" ["I used Jesusa's anecdotes, ideas and many of her expressions but I couldn't affirm that the story is a direct transcription of her life because she herself would reject it. I killed off superfluous characters, I eliminated however many Spiritualist sessions I could, I expanded wherever it seemed necessary, I pruned, I sewed, I mended, I invented"] ("Jesusa Palancares" 10). Lagos-Pope emphasizes that such literary activities are precisely the strategies that enable the author to present the text as if it were an authentic documentary. For other discussions of the interplay of literary technique and factual material, see Fernández Olmos 70–71, Kiddle 84–85, and Kushigian 667.

11. See Foley 25–41 on the matter of the generic borders of documentary fiction.

12. This discussion assumes distinctions among the real, the true, and the verisimilar (i.e., le réel, le vrai, and le vraisemblable), as proposed by Kristeva 211–16. The first term refers to what is called material or objective reality, which is self-evident and entails no discursive mediation. The second (i.e., the true) and the third (i.e., the verisimilar), on the other hand, refer to types of discourse and their effects. The true is a discourse that resembles the real; the discourse of the true produces an appearance of reality, but is itself not the real. The verisimilar is a discourse that resembles another discourse (that is, the true, or the discourse of the true), which is the discourse that resembles the real. The verisimilar is therefore at a second remove from the real, which it might appear to resemble through its resemblance to the true but from which it is in fact doubly distanced. To read the true as the real is not to see the true as a discourse; to read the verisimilar as either the true or the real is not to see it as an effect of discourse. It is also to be blinded to the discursive mediation inherent in the appearance of the true or the verisimilar, which such witting (or unwitting) blindness would lead one to take for something they are not.

13. I am grateful to Alvaro Ramírez for his helpful suggestions regarding all translations of passages from the novel. Poniatowska cites the first sentence of this statement also in "Jesusa Palancares," commenting before it that "Y se me va a morir, como ella lo desea; por eso, cada miércoles [the day on which Poniatowska would interview her each week] se me cierra el corazón de pensar que no podría estar" ["And she's going to die on me, just like she wants; therefore, each Wednesday my heart just breaks at the thought that she might not be there"] (9). Moreover, many other, though not all, quotations that appear in this piece also appear in the novel's text, sometimes with some variation (e.g., compare her comments on Villa or Carranza in the novel [95–96, 136–37; cited below in notes 23 and 24] with those in "Jesusa Palancares" 6). Such variations, of course, raise questions about how to identify the original words of Jesusa: are they the words cited in the novel, but somehow copied incorrectly by the author later in her explanatory statements? Or are they the words that appear in Poniatowska's comments, returned to their original state after having been altered by the author for inclusion in the novel? Or are both instances of citation but alterations of Jesusa's original words, recorded

Notes   **185**

accurately by machine or remembered and written up either adequately or inadequately by the author?

14. That the narration, which appears as Jesusa's monologue, is situated within (and apparently occasioned by) a dialogue exchange is only revealed intermittently, when Jesusa addresses an interlocutor, whom Poniatowska, in her statements about their interview sessions, would identify as herself (see, e.g., 171, 173, 271, 313).

15. Even though she says she wanted to learn to read, Jesusa remained illiterate throughout her life; she notes as much in her own narrative (e.g., 52–53, 286) and in statements cited by Poniatowska in the author's testimonies about their conversations ("Jesusa Palancares" 9).

16. Although Franco discloses that Jesusa's real name is Josefa Bórquez (*Plotting Women* 177), Elena Poniatowska has more recently provided the correct given name as Josefina. At Josefina's request, Poniatowska agreed not to reveal her name while she was still alive, and therefore has only been at liberty to disclose it after Josefina's death in 1988. (I am grateful to Cynthia Steele for first sharing the information about the name Josefina with me, and to Elena Poniatowska, who confirmed the correct information in a personal conversation.) In a number of ways, then, a lying of sorts becomes a condition of possibility for the novel's existence.

17. Jesusa's theory situates the subject within the question of the true both as a reader and as a producer of her own discourse. Hers is a solipsistic theory of truth, in which each subject would become its own self-validating teller of truth and in which the discourse of the true would also seem to validate itself. The listener or reader of such a discourse could therefore have only a skeptical relation to truth, a relation that would run from faint doubt to full-blown denial; this is what seems to happen in the case of Jesusa herself, as noted here.

18. A characteristic example of Jesusa's view of the inherently untruthful aims of a good many speakers, and an instance of how she contradicts and corrects information given by others (of which more examples are presented below), is the following response to things she has heard said about Chihuahua: "Puras mentiras. La gente decía que en Chihuahua no había cristianos sino puros apaches. . . . Los de allá son como los de aquí, lo que pasa es que a la gente les gusta abusar, contar mentiras, platicar distancias y hacer confusiones, nomás de argüendera. Yo nunca vi un apache" ["A pack of lies. People used to say that there weren't any God-fearing people in Chihuahua, just Apaches. . . . People over there are just like people here, what happens is that people like to abuse, tell lies, talk nonsense and confuse things, just gossip. I never saw an Apache [there]"] (95).

19. For other examples, see also 46, 73, 100, 124–25, 164.

20. This truth, she assures her addressee, has been recorded accurately in her memory, to which her own testimony would also appear to remain transparently faithful. For example, Jesusa states: "yo tengo el defecto de que todo lo que oigo se me queda en el pensamiento, todo, y a mí se me grabó aquello [a scene to which she has just been witness]" ["I'm cursed with this memory, everything I hear stays with me, everything, and that [scene] got engraved in my mind"] (161).

21. On verisimilitude as a masking of itself, see Todorov, *The Poetics of Prose* 83–84.

22. Chevigny has commented on Jesusa's relation to authority (55–56); Davis has taken up Poniatowska's interest in her as an exemplary "defiant woman" (226);

Notes   **186**

Lemaître has considered her in the context of patriarchal society (131–32); and Tatum has pointed out her resistance to traditional social roles (54–57).

23. Jesusa's invective against Villa is triggered by an announcement of plans to honor his name:

> Oí que lo iban a poner en letras de oro en un templo. ¡Pues los que lo van a poner serán tan bandidos como él o tan cerrados! Tampoco los creí cuando salió en el radio que tenía su mujer y sus hijas, puras mentiras pues qué. ¿Cuál familia? Eso no se los creo yo ni porque me arrastren de lengua. . . . Ése nunca tuvo mujer. Él se agarraba a la que más muchacha, se la llevaba, la traía y ya que se aburría de ella la aventaba y agarraba otra. Ahora es cuando le resulta dizque una 'señora esposa,' y dizque hijos y que hijas. ¡Mentira! Ésas son puras vanaglorias que quieren achacarle para hacerlo pasar por lo que nunca fue. ¡Fue un bandido sin alma que les ordenó a sus hombres que cada quien se agarrara a su mujer y se la arrastrara! Yo de los guerrilleros al que más aborrezco es a Villa. Ése no tuvo mamá. Ese Villa era un meco que se reía del mundo y todavía se oyen sus risotadas.
> [I heard that they were going to put his name up in gold letters in some temple. Well the ones who are going to put it there are probably just as crooked and hardheaded as him! I didn't believe them either when they said on the radio that he had a wife and daughters, a pack of lies, and what? What family? I don't believe that even if they dragged me by the tongue. That guy never had a wife. He used to grab the youngest girl he could find, carry her off, take her around with him and when he'd get tired of her he'd throw her away and grab another. Now they talk about his so-called "wife," his so-called sons and daughters. What a lie! These are the "glorious deeds" they want to give him credit for to make him look like something he never was. He was a heartless bandit who told his men to grab any woman they wanted and carry her off! As for myself, of all the fighters the one that I detest the most is Villa. That guy was a real son of a bitch. That Villa was real scum who mocked everyone and you can still hear his horselaugh]. (95–96)

24. Her skepticism about what is told on the radio, as evidenced by what she says they have not chosen to tell, shows up in the following comments:

> [Carranza] se apoderó de la mayor parte del oro que había dejado Porfirio Díaz en el Palacio. Hiza [sic] cajas y cajas de barras de oro y plata y se las llevó. Adelante de la Villa, en Santa Clara, los obregonistas le volaron el tren, le quitaron el dinero y lo persiguieron y él cayó en la ratonera, allá en su rancho por Tlazcalaquiensabe. . . . Nomás que eso tampoco lo dicen por el radio. Anuncian lo que les parece pero no aclaran las cosas como son. No dicen que el Barbas de Chivo [Carranza] siempre andaba de escape, siempre de huida.
> [He got most of the gold that Porfirio Díaz had left in the Palace. He filled up boxes and boxes with bars of gold and silver and took them away. Before the Villa, in Santa Clara, Obregon's men blew up the train, took the money away from him and chased him and he fell into the trap, there in his ranch in Tlazcalawhoknowswhat. . . . Only they don't say that either on the radio. They tell what they want to but they don't clear up how things are. They don't say that the Goatbeard was always on the run, always running away.] [137]

Her distrust of newspapers arises from an instance in which a news report contradicts what she herself has seen at the scene of her friend Sara's death: "cuando

Notes 187

hablan los periódicos, no les creo porque en aquella época dijeron que Sara Camacho había muerto en la Comisaría en las primeras curaciones y son mentiras, porque la sacamos muerta de debajo del tren" ["when they write in the newspapers, I don't believe them because back then they said that Sara Camacho had died at the police station when they were first attending to her and that's a lie, because we pulled her out dead from under the train"] (260).

25. For related comments on marginality and the "testimonio," see Beverley.

26. One might also note that the original source of the novel's discourse—the figure who could be referred to as Josefina—is but another displaced figure. For she is dislodged to a marginal, if not altogether invisible, position by Jesusa (the textual figure) and Poniatowska, both of whom cover her up at the same time that they create a space for her story.

27. Franco, *Plotting Women* 178. Compare Franco's reading, which bypasses explicitly the problematical hierarchy of authority from which the figures of Poniatowska and Jesusa—and even Josefina—may confront one another either within the text of the novel or among the fabric of testimonies of which the novel is but one document.

28. Such documentary statements may surface in materials appended to the body of the testimonial text in the form of a prologue or introduction (see, e.g., Miguel Barnet *Biografía de un cimarrón [Autobiography of a Runaway Slave]* [1967], or Rigoberta Menchú/Elizabeth Burgos, *Me llamo Rigoberta Menchú . . .* [1985], or Alicia Partnoy, *The Little School* [1986]), or in separately published essays, interviews, formal statements (this is the case for *Hasta no verte Jesús mío*) or theoretical proposals (see Barnet's "La novela testimonio").

29. The most detailed of Poniatowska's statements about *Hasta no verte Jesús mío* can be found in "Jesusa Palancares" and "Testimonios," cited throughout this chapter. Related, if not similar or identical, material also appears in her conversations with Durán and Durán and with Méndez-Faith.

30. Her account of how Jesusa came to her attention and sparked her interest is also a telling one: "La conocí en la cárcel. . . . [L]a Jesusa iba continuamente a la cárcel, pero no para visitar, sino porque caía presa, y yo la escuché hablar y la escuché también hablar en un lavadero en un edificio del centro y dije: '¿Pero qué mujer es ésta?' Porque le hablaba a la otra lavandera con un gran vigor y le decía: '¡Qué tonta eres! . . .' y yo dije: '¿Quién es esta mujer? Yo quiero conocerla, verla, oírla.' Entonces le pregunté a la portera dónde vivía y así la fui a ver." ["I met her at the jail. . . . Jesusa was always in but not to visit anyone, but rather because she just always ended up in jail, and I heard her speak [there] and I also heard her speak in the washing area of a building downtown and I said: 'Who is this woman?' Because she was speaking to the other laundress so forcefully and was saying to her: 'You're so stupid! . . .' and I said: 'Who is this woman? I want to meet her, see her, hear her.' Then I asked the doorwoman where she lived and that's how I went to visit her."] ("Testimonios" 157.) On the author's research and composition techniques, see also notes 9, 10.

31. Poniatowska's description of her relationship with Jesusa (she uses that name for Josefina in her authorial testimonies) is also a confession of her self-discovery (e.g., the discovery and solidification of her Mexican identity) through

Notes   **188**

the development of their special friendship and her identification with the woman who, to her mind, is so extraordinary ("Jesusa Palancares" 9–11, "Testimonios" 158, and interview with Méndez-Faith 57). On some of the textual consequences of this complex relation between author and protagonist-informant, see Kushigian 667–69, 675; see also Chevigny 54, and Fernández Olmos 72.

32. If one were to read the author's testimony as belonging to a class of writing that could be defined generically, it might be considered in terms of Todorov's, rather than Kristeva's, discussion of verisimilitude, and specifically in terms of his description of generic verisimilitude (*The Poetics of Prose* 80–88). In such a reading, however, it would be difficult if not impossible to map the one theory entirely onto the other, since Todorov virtually dispenses with the category of the real, explaining such verisimilitude entirely as a relation of discourses.

33. Gestor literally means manager, promoter, administrator, representative, or business agent. Barnet proposes this term as a substitute for "autor" in his seminal discussion of the "novela-testimonio" ("La novela testimonio"), a manifesto of sorts about the aims, techniques, and meaning of the modern genre, of which his own *Biografía de un cimarrón* figures as a founding text. Barnet's terminological proposal, however, entails a slippage in terminology. Though he uses the word when he defines the characteristics of the genre, he does not focus on the term itself, either to define it or contrast it with "autor" (author) or to take up its theoretical or ideological implications. Barnet merely introduces the word by virtue of using it in place of the term it displaces. (The substitution begins in the section entitled "El fenómeno histórico" ["The Historical Phenomenon"] and runs throughout the rest of the essay.)

Oddly, the essay's abridged version in English fails to recognize—indeed, erases—this crucial terminological shift within Barnet's discourse. Wherever "gestor" appears in the original, the term "documentary novelist" is used in the English text; and in one place the term "author" (28) is reintroduced where not even the term gestor appears in Barnet's text (297). The slippage from one to the other term (and perhaps even the translators' reinsertion of the original word into Barnet's text) may well figure the difficult relation between the concepts to which each might give a name. They may well be considered concepts that inevitably move toward as much as away from one another in both the theory and practice of the novela testimonial.

34. Bruce-Novoa's reading of Poniatowska follows such a characterization (509); cf. Beverley 17–18.

35. See Minnis 100–102, as well as the discussion in chapter 1 above.

36. Such a depersonalization (Barnet's term) entails, in a way, a repersonalization—a personalization of the gestor as another person, as his interlocutor-informant, whose personal experience he also appropriates: "Se produce también una despersonalización; uno es el otro ya y sólo así podrá pensar como él, hablar como él, sentir entrañablemente los golpes de vida que le son transmitidos por el informante, sentirlos como suyos" ["There must also be depersonalization. One has already become the other and that is the only way one can think and speak like him, feel deeply all the blows in life that he tells you about, feel them as if they were all your own"] (Barnet 297).

Notes 189

4   On Shifting Ground

1. *Terra nostra* is considered one of the most important works authored by Fuentes, a prolific writer of fiction, drama, and essays. He is perhaps best known for his novels, which also include the following: *La región más transparente* [*Where the Air Is Clear*] (1958), *Las buenas conciencias* [*The Good Conscience*] (1959), *La muerte de Artemio Cruz* [*The Death of Artemio Cruz*] (1962), *Cambio de piel* [*A Change of Skin*] (1967), *Zona sagrada* [*Holy Place*] (1967), *Cumpleaños* (1969), *La cabeza de la hidra* [*The Hydra Head*] (1978), *Una familia lejana* [*Distant Relations*] (1980), *Gringo viejo* [*The Old Gringo*] (1985), *Cristóbal Nonato* [*Christopher Unborn*] (1987), and *La campaña* [*The Campaign*] (1990). His collections of short stories include *Los días enmascarados* (1954), *Cantar de ciegos* (1964), *Chac Mool y otros cuentos* (1973), and *Agua quemada: cuarteto narrativo* (1981) [*Burnt Water* includes stories from the last two volumes], and *Constancia y otras novelas para vírgenes* [*Constancia and Other Stories for Virgins*] (1989).

Fuentes's other works of narrative fiction figure the author in ways related, but not identical, to the example of *Terra nostra*. Indeed, one could consider the virtual presence of a masterful (if not also manipulative) author-figure around texts such as *La muerte de Artemio Cruz*, *Cambio de piel*, and *La cabeza de la hidra*, or the reflexive dramatization of authorial activity in *Una familia lejana* or *Cristóbal Nonato*.

2. Moreover, like the title of the novel around which my chapter heading is formulated, this titular phrase would become an emblem of the illusion that gets propagated by titles more generally. That is, not only titles of novels but also titles of studies written about them would pretend to contain the texts and authors they name, the objects that no individual title (not even their own titular phrases) can contain. And, this is doubly so for a title that would get taken as encompassing *Terra nostra* (a text whose own title already problematizes this matter, as noted immediately below) or encapsulating what might be said about it.

3. See Kadir 107.

4. Fuentes interview with McShane 50. I use the phrase "mystery text" to refer both to texts that characterize a specific mystery genre (i.e., detective fiction) and to the various written texts that compose Fuentes's novel; it may even refer to the novel itself. I am interested in emphasizing not only the enigmas within the novel's story but also the mystery that surrounds, and thereby shapes, the text as a whole.

5. González Echevarría, who also explains some of the foundations of Fuentes's inquiry into Hispanic cultural origins, suggests how *Terra nostra* "renders the link between cultural specificity and literature questionable" (*The Voice of the Masters* 87). Alazraki reads *Terra nostra* as "Fuentes' reply to the history of Hispanic America" ("Coming to Grips with History" 551), as a text that seeks to explain Hispanic America's history in terms of its founding model of authority (e.g., Philip II as paradigm of Spanish American dictators; especially 551–53, 556). For a discussion of the semiotic function of history in *Terra nostra*, see Gertel; for a reading of the novel as guided by a "Marxist conceptualization of history," see Boling; and for observations about Fuentes's fictionalization of history, see Oviedo ("*Terra nostra*: Historia, relato y personaje").

6. The analysis of the question of power draws on ideas from both Foucault's *Discipline and Punish*, and *The History of Sexuality*. The crucial distinction for this discus-

sion, formulated as follows, emphasizes that "power . . . is conceived not as a property, but as a strategy, that its effects of domination are attributed not to 'appropriation,' but to dispositions, manoeuvres, tactics, techniques, functionings; that one should decipher in it a network of relations, constantly in tension, in activity, rather than a privilege that one might possess; that one should take as its model a perpetual battle rather than a contract regulating a transaction or the conquest of a territory" (*Discipline and Punish* 26; see also 27, 202, and *The History of Sexuality* 94).

7. Oviedo ("Fuentes: Sinfonía del nuevo mundo") reads *Terra nostra* primarily as a "mito de todos los mitos" ["myth of all myths"] (22) but also as an historical and literary palimpsest (24).

8. By emphasizing the notion of an original crime or murder, as well as that of a primal parricidal horde, Fuentes appears to follow, among other texts, Freud's *Totem and Taboo* and *Moses and Monotheism* and the theories they set forth about the origins of culture.

9. See Goytisolo, Coover, Oviedo ("Sinfonía del nuevo mundo") and Fuentes interview with Coddou for comments on Fuentes's literary representation of the Escorial.

10. Most of the major entities in *Terra nostra* are fictionalized versions of figures from Spanish and Spanish American history, myth, and literature. Besides Felipe, Tiberius, and Quetzalcóatl, already mentioned, there are Isabel I, Cervantes, Don Quijote, Celestina, Don Juan, Oliveira (from Cortázar's *Rayuela*), and Humberto el mudito (from Donoso's *El obsceno pájaro de la noche*), among others. The English translation provides a list of characters (3–5), whose Spanish names are generally retained in the translation; the list is not included in the original Spanish text.

11. The relationship between univocal and multiple readings or texts is discussed by Fuentes in *Cervantes o la crítica de la lectura*, many of whose passages duplicate passages from the novel; see for example an identical discussion in *Terra nostra* 302–16/295–308. For comments on Fuentes's reading of *Terra nostra* that can be connected with the line of discussion developed below, see García Núñez 103–5. On the problematics of reading Fuentes's novel and essay through one another, see Kadir 122–40, and González Echevarría, *The Voice of the Masters* 87–95; for a different view of the relation between those texts, see Gyurko.

12. E. González describes *Terra nostra* as a "web of despotic trickery" that ends "by enshrining the author as an all-powerful schemer" (149). My reading coincides somewhat with that view; however, through the analysis of both Fuentes and El Señor as authors, I also aim to suggest how that scheming may well betray itself.

13. See, for example, A. González for a discussion of the "totalizing" or "encyclopedic" current that develops in American novels of the sixties (her exemplary texts are *Terra nostra* and Pynchon's *Gravity's Rainbow*).

14. On the "doubling" of characters in *Terra nostra*, see Swietlicki.

15. Durán considers the three as one among many examples of "triplicity [as] the magical key" to the novel's temporal structure (4–5). Fernández Muñoz sees them as the fundamental "triad" of the neo-baroque narrative "spiral" (422–23).

16. Cf. García Núñez 100–101.

17. These comments draw on Genette *Narrative Discourse*, and Bal.

Notes **191**

18. The distance between these characters is also marked linguistically: Polo is an "él" ["he"] in the written text and the narrator an invisible "yo" ["I"]. As Benveniste (195–204, 217–22, 224–30) has shown, the third-person pronoun can be read as the sign of nonperson or the absence of person, that is, as the sign of the person absent from the instance of discourse. Only first- and second-person pronouns, as well as verbs in those persons, mark the presence of person, for they represent the situation of discourse itself. Thus, Polo Febo, as a "he," could also be read as a nonperson, while the narrator, as an invisible "I," could be a sign of person. As such, the narrator would exist in correlation with the narratee-reader, who could be viewed as the invisible "you" to whom the narrator speaks.

19. Following some of Benveniste's theories and the line of analysis suggested above, one could view the narrator (an implicit "I") and Polo (an explicit "you") as existing in correlation with each other.

20. See Benveniste 197, 201, 218, 224–26.

21. See Peden for a comparison of early and final versions of this first chapter.

22. See García Núñez on superimposition as the novel's structuring image and narrative figure.

23. Accepting as factual Celestina's own statement—"todo lo sé; ésta es mi historia; yo la estoy contando, desde el principio: yo la conozco en su totalidad, de cabo a rabo, . . . yo sé lo que el Señor sólo imagina, lo que la Señora teme, lo que Guzmán intuye" ["I know everything, this is my story, I shall tell you everything from the beginning; I know the story in its totality, from beginning to end, . . . I know what El Señor can only imagine, what La Señora fears, what Guzmán guesses"] (257/251)—Goytisolo reads her as the novel's principal narrator and creator of a frame story (21). This is a neat but, in my view, not entirely persuasive reading. Celestina would seem to be a perfect narrator inasmuch as she is, by virtue of her name, the ultimate go-between, the mediator par excellence. But the narrative complexities of *Terra nostra* do not, in the end, confer such privilege or position upon her. Perhaps Fuentes unwittingly disproves structurally what may appear to be asserted thematically in the novel. The author seems to privilege Celestina as "mother" of the "heroes" within the fictional world of *Terra nostra* but ultimately denies her the originary position within a discursive hierarchy. As González Echevarría points out, if Fuentes privileges Celestina "as origin," he is in error in doing so, for he does not "take into account that she is the very negation of origins, given that precisely her major occupation is to restore virginities, to offer the new as patchwork" (Rev. of *Cervantes o la crítica de la lectura* 84). For another perspective on Celestina in the novel, see Siemens.

24. Foucault's formulations about the interdependence of knowledge and power (*Discipline and Punish* 27–28) not only explain but also are explained by these developments in Fuentes's novel.

25. See El Señor's comments also on 505/497, as well as Guzmán's description of the monarch's beliefs on 507/500.

26. See note 6. *Terra nostra* would dramatize the coming into operation of this (Foucauldian) notion of power, which is precisely the dispersion of the absolutist practice. The powerlessness of the absolutist theory is precisely what is figured by El Señor. What is unsettling about the novel is that it keeps dispersing power from a

sovereign author- or reader-figure in ways that do not do away with but, on the contrary, reinforce the power of those figures.

27. El Señor would take his power with him, like the narrator mentioned in Fray Julián's statement (660/655, quoted above). To possess power here means to keep a secret, and vice versa; in Fuentes's novel certain figures of authority appear to have the right to attempt either or both.

28. We recall Barthes's use of the paternal metaphor in his discussion of the Author ("The Death of the Author"); see also Said on the "constellation of linked meanings" that connect the term author with fatherhood (83–84). Said also emphasizes that one cannot speak of authority without implicating the "molestations that accompany it," for molestation "is a consciousness of one's duplicity . . . whether one is a character or a novelist," and "no novelist has ever been unaware that his authority, regardless of how complete, or the authority of a narrator, is a sham" (84). Though apparently aware of such limitations, both El Señor and Fuentes nevertheless seem to plot to overcome them; see also Kadir 124–30, and González Echevarría, *The Voice of the Masters* 93–94, for related observations.

29. Fuentes's readers, along with El Señor, read "Manuscrito de un estoico" ["Manuscript of a Stoic"] (681–704/676–700), a text divided into six parts and whose narrator (one Teodoro) begins by saying: "Escribo en el último año del reinado de Tibero" ["I am writing in the last year of the reign of Tiberius"] (681/676). This text appears to be the one that comes from the past, according to the gypsy (557/551). The second manuscript, entitled "La restauración" ["The Restoration"] (717–39/ 713–34), deals with events set in the 1970s. Depending on whether El Señor or the reader of *Terra Nostra* serves as the point of reference, that text can be read as the one originating in either the future or the present. The knowledge readers may think they have is thus undermined, for one of the texts (which one is unclear) seems to remain hidden. It is even possible that the "hidden" text is *Terra nostra* itself; such an identification would, of course, compound significantly the novel's complexity.

30. Kadir talks about the novel as figuring the "dynamic process of its own becoming" (109) and as extending its "own incompletion, or untotalizability" (140).

31. Josephs speculates on possible sources for the coupling specifically and the final chapter generally.

32. Bersani, discussing Foucault, asserts that "every resistance to power is an exciting counter-exercise of power. There is no protest against power which does not rejoice in its own capacity to control and dominate" (6). Foucault's related comments can be found in *The History of Sexuality* 95–96.

5 The Dis-Appearance of a Popular Author

1. We recall that Barthes suggests that the authority of the Critic is bound to that of the Author ("The Death of the Author" 147); with the Author's death comes also that of his critical partner. One can think of the lower-case figures as their survivors.

2. To some extent, the discussion of Cortázar and Barrenechea in chapter 2 takes note of these possibilities.

3. I am drawing on Bakhtin's comments about authorial discourse and dialogue (see especially *Speech Genres and Other Late Essays* 60–102, 103–31).

Notes   **193**

4. When the term "dis-appearance" (which appears first in this chapter's title) is used, it is meant to convey the synchronic turns between one kind of authorial appearance or disappearance and another, as compared to the stationary situation suggested by the unhyphenated form of the word. It aims to signal the author's simultaneous appearance within and disappearance from one or another arena.

5. Puig's recounting took place in a public appearance at the University of Southern California on January 31, 1989. For Puig, the proposal of such notions and the publication of his writing represent a fortuitous convergence of his idiosyncratic literary output and French critics' theoretical speculation about literary production. His description of this early moment in his literary career, when what mattered to him was merely to be read and become recognized, may also be emblematic of the variety of concerns that shape the activities of a good many authors today. Moreover, in his narration of such an incident he may also manage to appropriate (and perhaps even teach) the lessons once learned from readers and critics who formerly might have presumed to have been taught by him.

6. Puig has described on numerous occasions how he began to write his first novel. In outlining its beginnings he also has seemed to document the literary, cultural, and biographical origins of La traición de Rita Hayworth; see, e.g., the interviews with Fossey (139–42) or Sosnowski (70–72), or his "Growing Up at the Movies" (51).

7. For example, one might consider Puig's challenge to the borders between "high" and "low" art, or to the world of the political and the realm of the sentimental, as I have aimed to do in Kerr, Suspended Fictions. Given that Puig's writing has become identified with some of the generic and thematic models of "low" culture that he has both utilized and analyzed in his work, his writing would seem quite distanced from the currents and discourses of literary theory that many have suggested lie within it. Yet it may well say (as, perhaps, the French critics referred to by Puig were trying to point out) as much as the work of writers regarded as consciously identified with such currents and discourses. (One might consider someone like Severo Sarduy, who, though firmly rooted in Spanish American culture, also writes from within a European theoretical context—examples include his Escrito sobre un cuerpo: ensayos de crítica [1969], Barroco [1974], and La simulación [1982]. On these and other issues related to Sarduy's work see, e.g., González Echevarría's La ruta de Severo Sarduy, and Méndez Rodenas).

8. On this point see also chapter 6 of Kerr, Suspended Fictions.

9. In addition to the references in note 6, see also Puig's interviews with Catelli, Christ, Corbatta, Rodríguez Monegal, and Torres Fierro for his own accounts of how he became an author.

10. If one were to think of such talk as presented only in critical essays and books, Puig would be situated with what seems to be a minority of writers who have not produced such texts. Indeed, most of the other well-known contemporary Spanish American authors have also published works of criticism or theory, some of considerable importance. Consider, for example, the following texts published by some of the authors included in this study: Cortázar's numerous reviews and articles from the 1940s and 1950s, essays in La vuelta al día en ochenta mundos (1967) and Ultimo round (1969); Fuentes's La nueva novela hispanoamericana (1969), Cervantes o la

Notes   **194** crítica de la lectura (1976), and numerous articles; Poniatowska's ¡Ay vida, no me mereces!: Carlos Fuentes, Rosario Castellanos, Juan Rulfo, la literatura de la onda (1985); Vargas Llosa's García Márquez: historia de un deicidio (1971), La orgía perpetua: Flaubert y "Madame Bovary" (1975), and Contra viento y marea, vols. 1, 2, 3 (1983, 1986, 1990).

11. Though he ventured into writing works of drama and screenplays, Puig is known mainly for his novels, which include also the following: La traición de Rita Hayworth [Betrayed by Rita Hayworth] (1968), Boquitas pintadas: Folletín [Heartbreak Tango: A Serial] (1969), The Buenos Aires Affair: Novela policial [The Buenos Aires Affair: A Detective Novel] (1973), El beso de la mujer araña [Kiss of the Spider Woman] (1976), Maldición eterna a quien lea estas páginas [Eternal Curse on the Reader of These Pages] (1980), Sangre de amor correspondido [Blood of Requited Love] (1982), and Cae la noche tropical [Tropical Night Falling] (1988).

As I emphasize elsewhere in this chapter, Pubis angelical is representative of how Puig's writing problematizes the author's figures and raises questions about critical notions subsumed by the term author. One might consider especially his earlier novels (e.g., La traición de Rita Hayworth, Boquitas pintadas, The Buenos Aires Affair) in order to explore related examples of the authorial dis-appearance characteristic of his writing.

12. In general terms, the narrative trajectories are as follows: The fiction center-ing on Ana in 1975 begins in the second half of chapter 1 and runs throughout the entire novel, which comes to an end within this fictional frame. The melodramatic, Hollywood-style tale is developed in part one of the novel; the first chapter opens in that setting and the seventh virtually closes it off. The science fiction tale begins at the end of the first part of the novel, in the second half of chapter 8, and runs through the whole of the second part, ending in the first half of chapter 16, the text's final chapter. (See note 15 for more detail on the textual plotting of these stories and their narrative forms.) Puig's narrative around "la mujer más hermosa/bella del mundo" ["the most beautiful woman in the world"] is a rewriting, in a way, of the telling of the life of Hedy Lamarr, which not only had been fashioned by Holly-wood myth and publicity for the viewing public, but also had already been told by the actress herself in Ecstasy and Me: My Life as a Woman (New York: Bartholomew House, 1966).

13. Puig's comments on the reception of his novels by feminists generally, and on reactions to Pubis angelical in particular, can be found in the interview with Corbatta (619). For readings that take up the novel in relation to Lacan's notions, see especially Merrim's "For a New [Psychological] Novel," and Yúdice.

14. The boundaries of this time period cannot be established, since the text's first dialogue between Ana and one of her two interlocutors (16–22/9–14) contains no concrete calendar reference. However, the novel includes several temporal indicators that allow the reader to identify more or less the time frame for the narrative. For example, "México, octubre 1975" ["Mexico, October 1975"] (23/15) serves as a heading for chapter 2, where Ana's diary entries purportedly begin. There she opens each entry with a reference to the day of the week, and on one occasion includes the date as well ("Hoy sábado 9" ["Today Saturday the ninth"] [29/20]). The reader can thus move backward and forward from that entry to establish the approximate duration of the represented fiction, as noted above.

15. The contemporary story is presented in either dialogue or diary form in all but two of the novel's chapters (11 and 15). Ana's diary pages are presented in

chapters 2, 4, 5, 10, and 13; her dialogues with her feminist friend Beatriz appear in chapters 1, 3, 14, and 16, and her conversations with her political activist/lawyer friend Pozzi are found in chapters 2, 6, 8, 9, and 12. The Hollywood-style melodrama is advanced in chapters 1, 3, 4, 6, and 7; and the science fiction tale unfolds in chapters 8, 10, 11, 13, 15, and 16. The following provides a summary of both the pattern of narrative techniques and the textual chronology of the chapters and chapter sections (separated by blank spaces but unnumbered in the text; here designated as A or B or C) devoted to each tale, which are here identified by their protagonists (Ana, for the 1975 story; Ama/actress, for the 1930s/1940s tale; W218, for the twenty-first-century setting):

Part One—1.A: Ama/actress (third-person narration), 1.B: Ana (dialogue: Ana and Beatriz); 2.A: Ana (diary), 2.B: Ana (dialogue: Ana and Pozzi); 3.A: Ama/actress (third-person narration), 3.B: Ana (dialogue: Ana and Beatriz); 4.A: Ama/actress (third-person narration), 4.B: Ana (diary), 4.C: Ama/actress (third-person narration); 5: Ana (diary); 6.A: Ama/actress (third-person narration), 6.B: Ana (dialogue: Ana and Pozzi); 7: Ama/actress (third-person narration); 8.A: Ana (dialogue: Ana and Pozzi), 8.B: W218 (third-person narration). Part Two—9: Ana (dialogue: Ana and Pozzi); 10.A: W218 (third-person narration), 10.B: Ana (diary); 11: W218 (third-person narration); 12: Ana (dialogue: Ana and Pozzi); 13.A: Ana (diary), 13.B: W218 (third-person narration); 14: Ana (dialogue: Ana and Beatriz); 15: W218 (third-person narration); 16.A: W218 (third-person narration), 16.B: Ana (dialogue: Ana and Beatriz).

16. Lewis comments on the different systems of naming in the three stories (534).

17. Puig's predilection for interruptive narrative techniques and heterogeneous (and thus potentially disruptive) narrative forms is evident in much of his other work (e.g., *Boquitas pintadas*, *The Buenos Aires Affair*, and *El beso de la mujer araña*), and might be considered a characteristic feature of his signature style.

18. The question of identification among other figures either within an individual tale or among different stories may also be read as linking up with, and thus reinforcing the contact among, the three narrative frames. One might consider, for example, characters such as Theo/Thea, LKJS, the industrialist and the movie mogul, Beatriz and Betsy. On the possibility of establishing connections among these and other figures through their names, see Linenberg-Fressard.

19. In another conversation, Puig poses his "experiment" in a similar fashion: "En *Pubis angelical* . . . por un lado avanza la historia a base de lo que la protagonista controla, lo que dice y lo que escribe en su diario. Separadamente va aquello que yo supongo que son sus fantasías reprimidas, sus miedos, sus deseos inconfesados. Yo intenté un experimento: ver qué tensiones se establecían dividiendo estos contenidos" ["In *Pubis Angelical* . . . on one side the story develops on the basis of what the protagonist controls, what she says and what she writes in her diary. Separately, it unfolds what I assume to be her repressed fantasies, her fears, her secret desires. I tried to experiment, to see what tensions were established by separating these contents"] (Puig interview with Catelli 22).

20. See, for example, Corbatta 70–72, 79, or Muñoz 86, 90–91, 93. Compare to Bacarisse (193; the tales are read as three independent stories, with the "Ama" and W218 as projections of Ana's persona) or Solotorevsky (4–5; the relations among

the stories are described in terms of diegesis—Ana's story—and metadiegesis—the story of "Ama" is the first and that of W218 is the second) or Pellón (195–96; the three stories form two narrative lines, and are aligned in paradigmatic relation to one another). Merrim, on the other hand, puts into question the possibility of definitively establishing the provenance of all the stories ("For a New [Psychological] Novel" 152).

21. The question of how to read Ana's analysis also involves a decision about whether or not to take her (or the text's presentation of her) seriously, whether or not to read what she says as a cliché that becomes an object of parody or as a statement that might still have a more direct and less critical sense to it. The manner in which one answers that question of reading will, of course, also determine how, if at all, one reads the novel's (or Puig's) position regarding contemporary issues (for example, feminism; see note 13). Cf. Merrim "For a New (Psychological) Novel."

22. It is fair to say that all of Puig's novels take up the question of sexual politics, addressing implicitly or explicitly (as in *Pubis angelical*) issues of concern to feminists. Though there may be disagreement about whether Puig comes out on the "correct" side of some such issues, his novels interrogate the social, cultural, and sexual models inherent in the traditional orders and institutions that still shape modern society. See the following for examples of how such themes have been discussed by his readers: Green, Lewis, Magnarelli 117–46, Morello-Frosch "La sexualidad opresiva en las obras de Manuel Puig," and Muñoz.

23. Here one may be reminded of the theory and techniques of serial fiction, a popular form on which Puig has drawn in other novels (especially *Boquitas pintadas* and chapters 1, 2 of *El beso de la mujer araña*).

24. Cf. Bacarisse's identification of Ana as a "figure of Puig's own puzzlement" (196). The assumption that Puig has control over his own dramatization of the subject's loss of control appears to run counter to the tenets of some psychoanalytic literary criticism. That the author is inevitably out of control, subject to the unforeseen workings of the unconscious, is a principle with which such criticism has familiarized us. Were one to pursue this kind of insight, one would view the author as "out of control," as incapable of controlling the unconscious effects of his own text, indeed even mastered by them. See Felman's "Turning the Screw of Interpretation" for one of the early, and most enlightening, formulations about literature and psychoanalysis, the author's mastery, and the reading effects that texts are capable of producing.

25. The most helpful reading of the text in terms of this notion, and also regarding the question of pleasure, in this and other of Puig's writings is found in Yúdice, whose terminological borrowing from Foucault is also adopted here.

26. See also notes 13, 22; see, in addition, note 9 for references to texts in which some of the author's explanations of the issues of concern to him appear.

27. I am drawing on Suleiman; her discussion implicitly raises the question of whether an author can suggest, if not explicitly identify, his or her stance on an issue without somehow becoming an authoritarian figure.

28. We remember that the matter of style has traditionally been theorized as one pole of a formal opposition—between "form" and "content," between the "how" and the "what" of a text—and the analysis of the features thought to constitute that pole has been undertaken by stylisticians in a seemingly objective, or apparently

Notes

scientific, manner. That this traditional theoretical opposition, and the subsequent devaluation of style, constitute an "obsolete notion," was suggested early on by Robbe-Grillet 41–47; and that stylistics as traditionally theorized and practiced leads to arbitrary descriptions rather than valid interpretations has been proposed by Fish, "What Is Stylistics and Why Are They Saying Such Terrible Things About It?" For the view of style as the relation between the individual and cultural codes, see Barthes's *Writing Degree Zero* 13–18.

29. Such a figure would be understood mostly in the terms proposed by Booth's phrase "implied author," though other terminology current in studies of fiction (e.g., "putative author," "authorial image") has also been used to refer to such a figure.

30. In these and other references to style as signature, I draw somewhat on Goodman (especially 260–63). Some critics have talked about Puig's writing as a "borrowing" of languages and genres; see, for example, Morello-Frosch's "The New Art of Narrating Films," and Rodríguez Monegal's "A Literary Myth Exploded," on Puig's first novel. I propose, instead, the notion of stealing because it suggests a transfer of ownership implicit in the appropriation of words and styles as well as in the transformation of models characteristic of Puig's writing.

31. Here and below (where mention is made of parody and stylization) I am drawing on detailed discussion in Kerr, *Suspended Fictions*, and especially on its first and last chapters.

32. I am drawing on both Barthes, *Writing Degree Zero* 10–13, and Lang 725–31.

33. I am drawing somewhat on Bakhtin's comments about the relation between generic utterance and individual expression (*Speech Genres and Other Late Essays* 60–102).

34. The reference to the objectification of discourse draws on Bakhtin, *Problems of Dostoevsky's Poetics* 181–204. In the following I am also drawing on points I have made previously in Kerr, *Suspended Fictions*: the possibility of establishing a single textual identity or position (i.e., parody or stylization or a combination thereof) is undermined in *Pubis angelical*, as it is in other of Puig's novels; precisely because its relation to the various models shifts between, or combines within its own reproduction of, the models, aims and effects that would appear to be at odds with one another, *Pubis angelical* also resists such identification.

35. I am thinking somewhat along the lines proposed by Fish in both "What Is Stylistics?" and *Self-Consuming Artifacts* 383–427.

36. See Merrim, "For a New (Psychological) Novel" 154–57, and Solotorevsky.

37. Such a reading, one might argue, is demanded by Puig's novel, which could therefore be read as an exemplary instance of pastiche or "blank parody" (the phrase is Jameson's [114]). I have my doubts about this perspective, as this chapter and also Kerr, *Suspended Fictions* would suggest.

38. See Bakhtin, *Speech Genres and Other Late Essays* 108ff. on the idea of the authorial utterance as unrepeatable, and on the impossibility of the pure repetition of an author's discourse as an identical utterance.

39. I am thinking here also of something like Deleuze and Guattari's notion of the author as a "machine," proposed in their discussion of Kafka (7–8).

40. Cf. Jameson 113–18.

Notes 198

41. It is precisely such heterogeneity that would sabotage an attempt to describe Puig's style in the terms of traditional stylistics; see also note 28.

6 Writing Disguises

1. Donoso has written mainly works of fiction. This novel, his seventh, follows *Coronación* [*Coronation*] (1957), *El lugar sin límites* [*Hell Has No Limits*] (1966), *Este domingo* [*This Sunday*] (1966), *El obsceno pájaro de la noche* [*The Obscene Bird of Night*] (1970), *Casa de campo* [*A House in the Country*] (1978), and *La misteriosa desaparición de la marquesita de Loria* (1980), as well as a volume of short novels, *Tres novelitas burguesas* [*Sacred Families*] (1973), and his two collections of short stories, *Veraneo y otros cuentos* (1955), and *El charlestón* (1960), which have also appeared together as *Cuentos* [*Charleston and Other Stories*] (1971). More recently, he has also published *Cuatro para Delfina* (1982; a collection of short narratives), *Poemas de un novelista* (1981; a volume of poetry), *Sueños de mala muerte* (1985; a drama), *La desesperanza* [*Curfew*] (1986; a novel), and *Taratuta; Naturaleza muerta con cachimba* (1990; two novellas).

El jardín de al lado is not the only text in which Donoso has directed attention to the figure of the author. One might also consider how, for example, others of his works thematize the question of authorial performance and prerogatives (e.g., *Casa de campo*; see also note 20) or produce allegories of authorship within parallel registers of individual or related texts (e.g., *El obsceno pájaro de la noche*, *Tres novelitas burguesas*).

2. The consideration of authority throughout this chapter draws especially on De George, Bruns, and Said (81–100).

3. In Julio's narrative the Madrid garden is paralleled by another in Chile: the garden of the house where he grew up and where his mother is dying as he narrates. The Madrid garden repeatedly triggers images of the Chilean one (Julio even invokes the Proustian *madeleine* as a metaphor for this process [222]). Moreover, through his alternations in the use of the demonstrative pronouns "este" ["this"] and "aquel" ["that"] to designate each of these gardens (e.g., 65), Julio virtually places himself simultaneously in both of them. The two gardens are juxtaposed and conflated into a single illusory and edenic place that has both literal and figurative value. This "lost garden" is the place or space upon which Julio projects as many fantasies of the present and future as memories of the past. The novel's title thus points beyond the garden in Madrid at others, past and present, "here" and "there." And since it has multiple referents, the garden cannot be viewed as designating only one of those places. For other mention of the various gardens, see, for example, 66–68, 86–88, 119, 157–58, 170–71, 198–99. Feal takes up the garden in connection with the novel's "interartistic dialogue" ("Veiled Portraits" especially 407–8); Meléndez reads the garden as a "recurrent trope" (207–9); and Escala considers its closed space as an emblem of exile (295–97).

4. Although the story's chronology is generally clear, the exact dates of its beginning and end are inaccessible. Through a reference to one specific date (June 2, Julio's mother's birthday [78]), one can also determine the dates of their departure from Sitges (Monday, June 4) and their first day in Pancho's apartment (Tuesday, June 5). However, it is impossible to fix exactly the date of Pancho's call and invitation (the significant causal event in the story). Although Julio says "se

Notes

iniciaba junio" ["it was at the beginning of June"] (12) when reporting his conversation with Pancho, it appears that, given the available information concerning various intermediary events (including a conversation between Julio and his friend Carlos on Sunday, June 3), the beginning of Julio's fiction is situated sometime during the last week(s) of May. Likewise, the novel's end cannot be specified in precise calendar terms. The reader is told only that the last narration (Gloria's) occurs "many months" after the couple are in Morocco (248) and that it is being written, presumably, on a winter Sunday (251). (It might also be noted that the fictionality of the June dates can easily be established: in 1980, June 1 was actually a Sunday, June 3 a Tuesday, and June 5 a Thursday. In addition, since the novel is dated "*Calaceite, verano 1980*" ["Calaceite, Summer 1980"] (264), the time of authorial writing is represented as anterior to the ending of the fiction and its presumed composition by Gloria. However, the time of Gloria's writing would not appear to postdate that of the novel's initial publication, which occurred in April 1981.)

5. Their home is more accurately a home-away-from-home. For these characters are Spanish American exiles, displaced persons who live far from their original home, and who also move from one home to another several times in the narrative. In fact, the novel thematizes the question of exile and the situation of Spanish Americans in particular: Julio's narrative takes up many of their problems both in his reported discussions with other characters and in his private ruminations (e.g., 23, 32–33, 50–53, 180). Given Donoso's experience as a Spanish American living in exile in Spain—he left Chile in 1964 and three years later took up residence in Spain; he returned to Chile in 1981, where he continues to live and write (*Poemas de un novelista* is the first text he published there after returning)—this novel might be taken as presenting, in literary form, some of the empirical author's views on the cultural issues and personal dilemmas faced by exiled Spanish Americans. In fact, Pérez Blanco reads the novel as a quasi-biographical text and focuses especially on the issue of exile; Meléndez takes up the question of autobiography, as well as the "ethical/aesthetical conflict" (210), in her reading of the novel as a palimpsest; Escala defines the novel's main theme in terms of the interrelation of aesthetic production and exile (293); see also Bernal and also Burgos. See also Gutiérrez Mouat's discussion of the interrelation of "aesthetics, ethics, and politics" in Donoso's novel and its possible affinities with Mann's "Death in Venice." For Donoso's first-person statements about his life and literary biography, see, for example, "Chronology," the prologue to *Poemas de un novelista* (9–22), and *Historia personal del "boom"*; see Montero for a reading of the novel principally in terms of the last title.

6. This pronoun, as we know, belongs to no one, because it is the "property" of any discursive subject. Here, then, it would virtually equalize, by covering up the distance between, its two principal antecedents. See Benveniste 218–20, 224–26, and Jakobson 130–47.

7. The term "tour de force" is taken from the novel. In what is surely a self-conscious moment in the final chapter, Gloria tells how the literary agent Núria Monclús, in conversation with Gloria regarding her novel, has expressed "su admiración por mi novela, que considera un *tour de force* por haberme logrado meter dentro de la piel de un personaje tan distinto a lo que yo soy" ["her admiration for my novel, which she considers to be a *tour de force* because I've succeeded in putting myself inside the skin of a character so different from myself"] (247–48). The

differences of gender and authority that separate Julio and Gloria parallel those that would also distance Gloria and Donoso.

8. See Benveniste 201.

9. See, e.g., 254–55, where Gloria admits both to knowing certain facts of which Julio has presented her as being innocent and to having plotted (without Julio's or the reader's knowledge) certain moves that position him as the object of manipulation. Here Gloria's authorial confessions reveal that her authority is grounded in the knowledge held by one subject and the ignorance of another. The revelation of the hierarchy of knowledge that structures the text and of the identity of the (authorial) subject who seems to be placed at its pinnacle is, then, also a disclosure of the mechanism through which that hierarchy and that identity are suppressed from view by the text's author (here that may also mean Donoso, as he is figured by the text and as he seems to move more personally around it). Gloria's privilege lies partially in her ability to conceal her own power, her own authority. It might be noted, however, that since the revelations of her secret maneuvers are also cast as confessions (forms of the verb "confesar" are used on 253–55, precisely where she unveils the hidden information noted above), she also unwittingly suggests that her own discourse is subject to the demands, pressures, and powers of another subject (an implied or real interlocutor) whose position would recall the limits (as opposed to absoluteness) of her authorial authority. (This reading of her confessional status draws on Foucault, *The History of Sexuality* 58–63.)

10. See Donoso's description of the well-known literary agent Carmen Balcells, in *Historia personal del "boom"* 115.

11. As it presents this marriage in crisis, Donoso's novel also addresses a number of issues of general cultural and critical interest. The matter of sexual politics receives a good deal of attention; it is both an explicit thematic and an implied political structure in the novel. If one were to read the novel in terms of that problematic, it would be necessary to examine the contradictory implications of the strategic move from the "fiction" of male to the "fact" of female (if not feminist—one recalls Gloria's work as a feminist critic) authority. It would be necessary to consider the position that the "final" author-figure produced by the text (the one to which one might give the name "José Donoso") seems to take regarding this question. That is, it would be necessary to come to terms with the text's presentation of these author-figures as fluctuating, and even unstable, entities, whose politics cannot be viewed as determined only by one or the other position or gender. See Feal "Veiled Portraits" for one approach to this topic.

12. In his many criticisms of the boom and its principal authors (i.e., Julio Cortázar, Carlos Fuentes, Gabriel García Márquez, and Mario Vargas Llosa), Julio seems to be a fictionalized version of the type of writer much mentioned by Donoso in his *Historia personal del "boom"* (see, e.g., 12, 14–15, 62–63, 73, 93, 106, 113)—that is, the failed writer whose sense of exclusion and envy determine his views of those authors (i.e., the literary "mafia" of which he would like to be a member). Counterposed to, but nonetheless connected with, these authors is Donoso's version of a boom superstar, one Marcelo Chiriboga, a writer who, though verbally attacked briefly by Julio (139–40), is presented as a kind of "super-author" (especially 132–33). Donoso's parody (or, might one say self-parody, given Donoso's own position beside the above-mentioned authors?) of both the wor-

Notes   **201**

shipers of the superstars and the boom authors themselves is evident in Julio's description of Chiriboga.

13. That Gloria's silence generates Julio's writing serves as another prediction (which the reader cannot yet read "correctly") of the authorial truth to be revealed later in chapter 6. Moreover, these scenes are themselves foreshadowed in chapter 1 where Gloria, reacting angrily to a comment made by Julio, first refuses to speak with her husband, who then responds with a monologue that fills the space of that silence and, in addition, the text (24–27). There, for the first time, Gloria incites Julio to discursive activity through a silence that becomes, as in chapter 5, a way of punishing and resisting her spouse, and not simply a sign of her own suffering or powerlessness.

14. Here one might read a figuration of the return of a more conventional notion of the author, if not the recuperation of the Author (per Barthes's "The Death of the Author" and "From Work to Text"), placed in opposition to the figure of a less privileged and less authoritative writer. Donoso's text seems to turn between supplanting and supporting each of those figures.

15. Although Julio tries to follow Núria's suggestions about how to rewrite his novel (29, 71, 103, 114, 212), he doesn't succeed. Núria herself points this out to him: "[various publishers] dicen que es pura retórica, imitación de lo que está de moda entre los escritores latinoamericanos de hoy. No tiene vocación para el lirismo. Y toda la adjetivación, demasiado opulenta, suena falsa. La construcción, derivativa de *Conversación en la Catedral*, de Vargas Llosa, y las disquisiciones y el humor, que es muy forzado, parecen arrancados de *Rayuela*" ["they say that it is only rhetoric, an imitation of what is now in fashion among Latin American writers. You don't have any talent for lyricism. And all of the adjectivization is too opulent; it sounds phony. The structure, derivative of *Conversation in the Cathedral*, by Vargas Llosa, and the speeches and the humor, which is very forced, seem to be lifted from *Hopscotch*"] (223–24). The mention of Cortázar's *Rayuela* is ironic, for it is, in fact, because of Gloria (the "real" author who, as a character, says "Quiero que me escribas una *Rayuela*, para mí" ["I want you to write a *Hopscotch* for me"] [34] and whom Julio casts as a kind of "Maga" [the female protagonist of Cortázar's novel] in his narrative) that Julio has perhaps achieved a certain likeness between his own novel and that model. Núria's mention of those two texts constitutes, in addition, a playful and self-critical—perhaps even self-parodic—moment in *El jardín de al lado*. For parts of it can indeed be viewed as "derivative" of those very novels; see especially chapters 2 and 6, where the utilization of a frame conversation, as well as the superimposition of dialogues from distinct temporal levels, resemble substantially the narrative techniques of Vargas Llosa's novel. In addition, this self-referential moment would also reintroduce the problem of the relation between Julio's novel, about which these criticisms are made, and Donoso's—for in different ways the comments relate to both texts.

16. The complex relation between reader and writer in this scene not only allows one to read the novel as figuring the fundamentally dialectical relation between reading and writing (see Meléndez). It also provides a link to earlier (and radically different) positions accorded reader or audience in relation to the author. See Docherty 2–11 on the historically shifting relations of authority between reader and author.

Notes   **202**

17. Gloria reveals that her desire to take revenge on Julio might also be read as part of a more generalized, though also personalized, gender conflict. She asserts that to defeat him (a father-figure in his spousal as well as authorial role) is also to defeat and take revenge on her own father. She suggests that his downfall is also a means of "expiating" her father's crimes against her (as a daughter, she did not receive the paternal support that would have been offered to a son). Thus, she also discloses her pleasure at learning of Núria's defeat of Julio, for "en él nos vengaba a todas" ["in him she avenged all of us"] (256).

18. This shift constitutes another and virtually direct reversal of principal roles for the protagonists. Although Julio shares the role of translator with his wife in his narrative (they collaborate on a translation of *Middlemarch* [13, 248]), it is not the role through which he is identified in chapters 1–5. Feal explains the appropriateness of *Middlemarch* for their project ("Veiled Portraits" 399).

19. It ought to be noted, however, that her omniscience and omnipresence are also illusory (because they are secondary) powers, which are generated by the work of other readers apparently under her control: her own "agents," the readers who form her "equipo fantasma" noted by Julio above. Their very existence would support her image of omnipotence and at the same time reveal its contingent nature.

20. It may well be that such a demonstration of authorial prerogative is a logical maneuver for the end of this, and perhaps any, text, since it is precisely there that the author's authority comes to an end. Donoso's writing attempts to face (perhaps even defeat) this textual reality over and over again; several of his novels call upon a figure of seemingly final authority, a figure of the author, at the end of their own pages. The figuration of the author as an authoritative voice or empirical entity outside the fiction's frame is inscribed in both *Casa de campo*—a text to which, in fact, Julio refers in *El jardín de al lado*, but as if it were a real place (193) and not a literary text—and *La misteriosa desaparición de la marquesita de Loria*. At the end of each of those texts the reader is virtually faced with an author-figure whose appearance signals the fiction's end while also deferring its arrival. In *La misteriosa desaparición de la marquesita de Loria*'s last chapter an authorial subject intrudes momentarily in his own voice to remind the reader that what is being read is only a novel (193–94). And the self-conscious narrator-author of *Casa de campo* ends the novel by inserting himself into the text as a character (396–403) and dedicating large portions of the narrative to a discussion (indeed, a critical analysis) of that same novel's narrative structure and techniques (especially 391–92, 395, 404, 457, 477, 490–93). For another view of Donoso's endings, see Feal, " 'In my end is my beginning' "; for a more detailed analysis of the author-figure and the question of authority in *Casa de campo*, see Kerr, "Conventions of Authorial Design."

7   Facing the Author

1. Though these statements take things in a different direction, I am drawing somewhat on de Man's terminology in "Autobiography as De-facement."

2. Vargas Llosa has written works of drama and literary criticism as well as narrative fiction. His other novels are: *La ciudad y los perros* [*The Time of the Hero*] (1963), *La Casa Verde* [*The Green House*] (1966), *Conversación en la Catedral* [*Conversation in the*

Cathedral] (1969), Pantaleón y las visitadoras [Captain Pantoja and the Special Service] (1973), La tía Julia y el escribidor [Aunt Julia and the Scriptwriter] (1977), La guerra del fin del mundo [The War of the End of the World] (1981), Historia de Mayta [The Secret Life of Alejandro Mayta] (1984), ¿Quién mató a Palomino Molero? [Who Killed Palomino Molero?] (1986), and Elogio de la madrastra [In Praise of the Stepmother] (1988).

El hablador exemplifies, as it repeats in different registers, Vargas Llosa's engagement with the figure of the author in other of his works of fiction, as also noted in the body of this chapter. If one wished to consider other texts, one might look at how the author is figured as a fictive, but seemingly autobiographical figure in some (e.g., La tía Julia y el escribidor, or Historia de Mayta), or as a manipulative textual subject engaged in dialogue with the reader around a mysterious, if not also criminal, scene or story in others (e.g., La ciudad y los perros, Conversación en la Catedral, or ¿Quién mató a Palomino Molero?).

3. One thinks especially of La tía Julia y el escribidor, though a good many readers have aimed to establish the autobiographical relevance of other of his texts (e.g., Historia de Mayta, La ciudad y los perros, and Conversación en la Catedral). On autobiography and La tía Julia, Feal (Novel Lives 94–161), and Alonso ("The Writing Subject's Fantasy of Empowerment") are most suggestive; see Oviedo (Mario Vargas Llosa) for the most extensive treatment of the author's biography and work.

4. Though the novel neither names the narrator-author nor provides all the facts of his biography, certain details revealed in his story suggest identification with Vargas Llosa. The following more or less match details of the empirical author's life story: the narrator-author studied at the Universidad de San Marcos in the 1950s; he studied literature and history, and his preferred authors were Sartre, Faulkner, and Joyce; he took his first trip to the Amazon region around 1958; as a well-known Peruvian writer, he did a television program in Lima in 1981. Such an identification is in fact suggested by Alter (41), and definitively asserted by Franco ("¿La historia de quién? La piratería postmoderna"), who describes the narrator's story as "una narración autobiográfica" ["an autobiographical narration"] told by the author himself (14), and by Rivas, who reads the novel as Vargas Llosa's "autocontemplación... como novelista" ["self-contemplation ... as a novelist"] (191).

5. Following the English version of the novel, I will use the word "hablador" throughout this chapter. Although in the English text one of the characters suggests "speaker" as the optimum translation (90–91), and its title proposes a more resonant alternative (i.e., "storyteller") around which the present discussion also revolves, "hablador" is retained there and here as a term that resists satisfactory translation. Oddly, this word seems to resist such translation and at the same time to lend itself naturally, as it were, to its surrounding foreign linguistic frame, to which its incorporation also does a certain violence. That the term cannot be translated may set in motion a resistance to identification or classification inherent in the subject(s) who would fulfill both its traditional and modern functions. See also notes 19, 21.

6. The narrator not only remembers and narrates in Florence. He also presents himself as taking notes, and perhaps even writing a novel that would appear to be similar, if not identical, to El hablador. Explicit references to writing suggest the possibility of reading the novel either as the text that the narrator-author is composing throughout his narrative or as the materials out of which a future text will be

created (see 35/33, 37/35, 69/71, 88/90, 92/93, 233/244, 234/244). I will intermittently refer to this figure as the narrator-author so as to recall that he is the potential subject of both activities and, therefore, potentially situated within two narrative registers simultaneously.

7. See also note 11. The reading of Saúl's story as a story of conversion (cultural and social, if not also religious) is proposed by the narrator-author's own characterization of his friend's apparent self-transformation (see 21–22/19–20, 29/28, 32/31, 233/243).

8. As underscored by the citations above, in both the Spanish and English texts Florence is referred to in Italian—that is, as *Firenze*. This proper name, perhaps not unlike the noun hablador (see notes 5, 19, 21), persists in its original, seemingly essential or untranslatable, form in both texts, as if it were an untouchable or inviolate term whose transformation is either impossible or improper to produce.

9. The bipartite narrative structure and alternating narrative techniques form part of the characteristic "duplicity" of Vargas Llosa's novels; see Montenegro on the structures of duplicity in Vargas Llosa's earlier work.

10. See, for example, the narrator's repetition of what the Schneils have themselves repeated to him from their own sources, and his comments about what they tell him, throughout chapter 4; his emphasis on his own role as audience for the linguist-storyteller to whom he listens, like a Machiguenga listening to the hablador, on his second trip to the Amazon region (172/177); and his account of how his desire to tell a story about the Machiguenga storytellers impels him also to tell Saúl about his own storytelling intentions (102/104). On the use of "hablar" see also 75/76. More significant, perhaps, is his account of how he listened to Schneil respond to one of his queries and his self-identification with the figure of the hablador, whose performance often went uninterrupted throughout the night: "articulé [the question], con una fatiga grande, como si fuera yo el que hubiera estado hablando toda la noche" ["I managed to ask, with great fatigue, as if I had been the one talking all night"; translation mine] [176/182]).

11. The ending of chapter 1, with its revelation of the word hablador, prefigures the endings of chapters 6 and 7, which, in repeating the name Mascarita and specularly revealing the supposed identity of the text's hablador, also recall the final moment of the novel's first chapter.

12. Indeed, we recall that, although Dante's *Vita nuova* first presents Beatrice as a significant figure, arguably her most notable appearance is in the *Divine Comedy*, where she appears as a mediator of vision, as a figure of indirect vision (see Freccero 39). As it sets this first sighting at a moment when the narrator-author has just seen the place where Dante supposedly first saw Beatrice, the setting suggests an apposite literary frame for the telling of the novel's stories, which are both literary and oral tales retold. For its narrators appear to tell in a seemingly direct fashion what an unexpected experience leads them, indirectly but inexorably, to tell. The reference to Dante's first unsettling encounter with Beatrice, just as the text presents the narrator-author's unexpected encounter with the images in the gallery, not only raises the question of how things are to be seen and told here, and by whom, but it also recalls the process of literary framing that organizes the novel as well.

13. The repetition of "allí estaban" ["there they were"] at the beginning of enumerative clauses replete with gerunds, as well as the use of verbs in the imper-

fect to describe the natives in the photos, both separates the spectator (and thus the reader) from the scenes described and also makes those scenes appear to be directly present to the spectator-narrator (see 8–9/4–5). The illusion implicit in this photographic description, which is itself presented as a faithful transcription of the Machiguengas' activities, is that the Indians are being seen while carrying on with their daily life, which such a description also presents as if it were not observed, intruded upon, or changed by any external figure.

14. I am referring to Todorov's notion, which posits fictional characters as stories or narrative sequences (*The Poetics of Prose* 66–79).

15. As noted above, the reflexive references to the narrator's activity as authorial as well as narratorial emphasize both mnemonic and inventive processes. The inventive process is, in fact, frequently stressed over the former: see, e.g., 37/35, 88/90, 97–98/99–100, 145–46/151, 167/173–74, 233/244.

16. The distinctions between truth and verisimilitude follow Kristeva (211–16).

17. Malfatti's photographs (and therefore the figure of the hablador) seen in 1985, appear first in the novel's text, after the hablador is introduced to the narrator in the story (i.e., in the linguists' verbal descriptions of the Machiguengas and the tribal storyteller). The Schneils' descriptions, repeated by the narrator in his own narrative, provide him with a verbal picture of the hablador, which allows him to recognize the figure captured in the gallery photos (see especially 88–92/90–93, 168–79/173–85). The description of how he virtually sees the hablador, when his activities are described by Schneil, who, having seen, also can describe, the scene to him, is itself both an echo and a prefiguration of what he sees and says when he encounters the photographs in the gallery (see 173/179).

18. Founded by U.S. Protestant missionaries also trained as linguists, the Institute has had a controversial history in Latin America. By some, it has been viewed as but a cover for foreign operations throughout Latin America (i.e., those of the CIA); by others, as essentially a group of missionaries, who have been trained to work as linguists and anthropologists, so as to gain access to the indigenous communities and carry out their evangelical mission; and by others, as researchers whose primary aim is to record and preserve in one way or another the culture of peoples whose transformation, if not destruction, may well be the inevitable result of their countries' economic development and modernization. The background information supplied by the narrator-author's own summaries, as well as by the represented conversations with Saúl, about the Institute and its effect on the indigenous cultures with which its members have lived and worked, raise (though they do not resolve) important questions from outside the novel as well as within the lives of its fictional characters. On the Institute and the Indians, see 69–70/70–72, 85–86/86–88, 93–100/95–102; regarding the effect of one or another political or economic system on the indigenous populations, see also 76–77/77–79, 228–30/239–40. I am grateful to Adalberto Salas for further clarifying some of this information for me. Franco also comments on the polemics surrounding the Institute and its representation in Vargas Llosa's novel ("¿La historia de quién?" 14–16, 20 n. 23).

19. See 88–89/90–91 for the process of translating the indigenous sounds into a comprehensible Spanish or English term. The question of translation is raised again when, during his 1981 trip, the narrator meets the Schneils and recalls their earlier

talk about the hablador, which both linguists seem to have forgotten and which the narrator insists upon recalling for them as he repeats the word. When Schneil finally remembers, he says: "Los habladores. Los *speakers*. Sí, claro, es una traducción posible" ["Habladores. *Speakers*. Yes, of course, that's one possible translation"] (168/173). The insertion of the English word speaker into the Spanish text suggests (from the other side, so to speak) the difficulty of finding an adequate equivalent for "hablador" in any language. See also notes 5, 21.

20. The observations regarding oral culture draw on Ong.

21. The English-language text makes this foreignness more visible as it alternates the Spanish "hablador" mainly with the English "storyteller," and sometimes with "speaker," as noted above. The last is, moreover, but an approximate rendering of one sense of the Spanish word, which commonly means chatterer, chatterbox, or gossip, and which seems only to approximate the indigenous term's meaning. The English text would therefore seem to acknowledge visibly the tricky sense of the original word, since a determination about its exact equivalent seems difficult, if not impossible, to make: no one term of translation seems capable of containing its original meanings or sense. In the Spanish text, where "hablador" is the only term used to designate the tribal figure in that language, this single word also seems unable to account for or contain the senses suggested either by the narrator's conversations with the Schneils, or by his private ruminations, or by the hablador's performance itself. See also notes 5, 19.

22. Information about the Machiguengas is supplied not only by the Schneils, but also by Saúl; the narrator repeats that information in his personal ruminations and analyses (see 78–79/80–81, 81–85/83–84, 87–91/88–93, 103–4/105–6, 151–52/156–57, 155–59/160–64, 165–70/170–75). The descriptions of the tribe's beliefs and history summarize, from the outside, as it were, distant cosmogonic and etiological stories, tribal customs, and recent experiences of individuals or tribal groups. The informative summaries and descriptions both prepare for and repeat, as they indirectly tell, what the hablador himself also seems to tell directly. (The suggested identification or distinction between description and narration draws partially on Genette's *Figures of Literary Discourse* [127–44].) The veracity of the narrator's summaries and of the majority of the tales told by the hablador in chapters 3, 5, and 7 is proclaimed by the authorial acknowledgment at the end of the text (237/247); see also note 24.

23. This statement suggests early in the text (chapter 3) that this speaker is similar, if not identical, to the figure that appears in the photograph seen and described at the end of chapter 1. The scene in chapter 3 also appears as a scene of recognition, for it seems to present for the second time, though from a different angle, the figure that the narrator had already recognized but which the reader sees only for the first time in chapter 1. In telling some of his stories in chapter 3, the hablador already tells much of what the Schneils summarily retell the narrator about what they have learned (and the reader will have already read) about the tribe. These retellings, moreover, also repeat some of the information that the narrator's friend Saúl earlier tells about the same group (chapter 2).

24. The hablador's discourse would appear to follow the syntactic and narrative patterns characteristic of oral narrative (see Ong 31–77). The final authorial acknowledgment to Father Joaquín Barrales, the compiler and translator of informa-

tion on the Machiguengas' culture that Vargas Llosa claims to have incorporated into the novel (237/247), suggest that the hablador's performance should be taken as essentially authentic (at least truthful, if not exactly real) rather than as merely verisimilar. (It would also identify the author's role as that of a copyist rather than originator of the chapters in which that material appears.) However, the appearance of authenticity produced is in fact but an effect of verisimilitude. For Vargas Llosa's reader could only recognize such a performance through its resemblance to other written texts—those produced by linguists and anthropologists who have recorded their speech in writing, and not through its correspondence with the Machiguenga's actual speech, to which the reader of course has no direct access. See Blanco for some related points.

25. See Benveniste 217–30.

26. See especially his references to learning from and knowing things through the *seripigari*, the authoritative figures of tribal knowledge in relation to whom the hablador becomes situated as both subordinate and superior figure (e.g., 122/125–26, 189–90/198, 195/202, 201–3/208–10). It might be noted that such techniques for establishing credibility are similar to those used by most narrators of realist fiction, and that the distance between the one and the other tradition may not be as great as the appearance of the hablador initially suggests.

27. See also the comparison of the hablador, the Bahian *trovero*, and the Irish *seanchaí*, all figures previously encountered by the narrator (159–60/164–65). The detailed description of the *seanchaí* indirectly tells more about the presumed functions of the hablador, which it most resembles, as the narrator substitutes the latter for the former in that description (160/165).

28. Vargas Llosa's novel might be read as a repetition (in the mode of fiction) of Benjamin's recuperative critical gesture in "The Storyteller," the essay that, in focusing on the storytelling figure so as to note its inexorable disappearance, also preserves the disappearing figure of oral tradition in its text (*Illuminations* 220–38); cf. Franco 14.

29. The conversations between the narrator and his friend thematize these issues in the novel. The narrator's ruminations summarize the so-called psychological interpretation, which he presents to his friend: "¿Se había inconscientemente identificado con esos seres marginales [Amazon natives, perceived as exceptional, abnormal to Peruvian society] debido a su lunar que lo convertía también en un marginal cada vez que ponía los pies en la calle?" ["Had he unconsciously identified with those marginal beings because of the birthmark that made him, too, a marginal being, every time he went out on the streets?"] (30/28). The "Judaic reading" is developed, according to Mascarita, by his father Don Salomón, whose proposition he summarizes: "yo identifico a los indios de la Amazonía con el pueblo judío, siempre minoritario y siempre perseguido por su religión y sus usos distintos a los del resto de la sociedad" ["I am identifying the Amazonian Indians with the Jewish people, always a minority and always persecuted for their religion and their mores that are different from those of the rest of society"] (30/28).

30. See also Franco ("¿La historia de quién?") on the novel's literary plundering of oral culture and the author as a figure of appropriation.

31. The privilege granted to the Kafka text by Mascarita is noted early in the novel (18/16, 19/17, 22/20, 27/25); this text is a singularly authoritative text (as

noted above), from which he draws the name "Gregorio Samsa" to name his parrot (12/10, 17/15) and to create a generic name for "monster," the description applied to himself as a disfigured character as well as to other deformed figures with whom he would identify (e.g., 27/25). The name Gregorio Samsa and the name "Kafka" (which may derive from the Czech word for jackdaw) also become names that identify (the first directly, the second indirectly) both Mascarita and the hablador (e.g., 200/207–8).

32. The last story told by the hablador is the story that explains to his listeners the presence of his parrot-companion and the identification between their two figures (219–24/228–34). It follows patterns of traditional etiological myths, and thus appears both to authenticate the connection between the hablador and the parrot and to incorporate them, as figures of a traditional story, into the collectivity's narratives. If the telling of this story is viewed as a narrative strategy, the etiological narrative becomes a device of verisimilitude: Saúl authors an etiological myth so as to give an appearance of authenticity both to his own performance and to that of his pet parrot. The techniques of this telling may also figure Saúl as a figure of Vargas Llosa, or of any author that aims to produce a verisimilar story.

33. Saúl's family's position within the social, if not also cultural, order would be further established if he were also to "make a name for himself." It is precisely Saúl's responsibility to the family name that his father would emphasize (15/12, 31/29), and from which Saúl would be released upon his father's death. In fact, when his father dies (his mother is already deceased), so it seems does the family name; for it is then that Saúl effaces himself as his father's son (by giving up his name) and takes on another identity, through which he would also recuperate his indigenous (and maternal) origins (his mother is a native Peruvian). However, as noted, the recuperation of this indigenous origin is at the same time a kind of recovery of Jewish heritage. For it is precisely his identification with the latter that makes it possible for him to recover (or construct) the former. Each is a history of both marginalization and survival that becomes a story to be relived, and also retold, by Saúl/Mascarita/the hablador. On Saúl's divided family history, see 11–15/9–12; and on the thematized connections between the Jewish and the indigenous histories, and/or Saúl's reading of them, see 29–31/27–29, 97/99, 231–33/241–43.

34. The parrot's association with Saúl/Mascarita is established early in the text in scenes that prefigure the traditional narrative setting that will later become associated with the hablador: he is seen with his "lorito hablador" on his shoulder, as he tells stories about the native tribes to the novel's narrator (e.g., 12/10, 17/15).

35. The name "Tasurinchi," which the hablador uses to identify his different interlocutors (i.e., the members of the tribe with whom he has spoken and from whom he learns the stories he tells), functions as a provisional tag for every member of the tribal community, none of whom has a proper name. In his narratives it is a kind of Jakobsonian "shifter" that identifies but also masks the identity of each individual. (The Schneils' brief explanation of the system of naming—or non-naming—is repeated by the narrator-author on 81/83).

36. Vargas Llosa would appear to inscribe himself in the text of El hablador, either as a personal or a literary figure, not only through the autobiographical details shared with the narrator-author, as noted above. He also may appear to unmask himself in a cryptic reference to another of his titles (the narrator-author uses the

Notes

phrase "contra viento y marea" ["against wind and tide"] [234/244], which readers familiar with Vargas Llosa's work will recognize as that of a collection of his essays, written between 1962 and 1988). In addition, there is also the final authorial "Reconocimiento" ["Acknowledgments"] (237/247), through which the empirical author would appear to speak directly to his reader (see note 24).

37. See Alonso "The Writing Subject's Fantasy of Empowerment."

Bibliography

Abrams, M. H. *The Mirror and the Lamp: Romantic Theory and the Critical Tradition*. New York: Oxford UP, 1953.

Alazraki, Jaime. Prólogo. *Rayuela*. By Julio Cortázar. Caracas: Biblioteca Ayacucho, 1980. ix–lxxv.

———. "*Terra nostra*: Coming to Grips with History." *World Literature Today* 57 (1983): 551–58.

Alazraki, Jaime, ed. *Critical Essays on Jorge Luis Borges*. Boston: G. K. Hall, 1987.

Alonso, Carlos J. "Julio Cortázar: The Death of the Author." *Revista de estudios hispánicos* (Vassar) 21.2 (1987): 61–71.

———. "*La tía Julia y el escribidor*: The Writing Subject's Fantasy of Empowerment." *PMLA* 106 (1991): 46–59.

Alter, Robert. Rev. of *The Storyteller*, by Mario Vargas Llosa. *The New Republic* 8, 15 January 1990: 41–42.

Arendt, Hannah. *Between Past and Future: Six Exercises in Political Thought*. New York: Viking, 1961.

Bacarisse, Pamela. "The Projection of Peronism in the Novels of Manuel Puig." *The Historical Novel in Latin America. A Symposium*. Ed. Daniel Balderston. Gaithersburg,

MD: Ediciones Hispamérica/The Roger Stone Center for Latin American Studies, Tulane U, 1986. 185–99.

Bakhtin, Mikhail. *The Dialogic Imagination: Four Essays*. Trans. Caryl Emerson and Michael Holquist. Ed. Michael Holquist. Austin: U of Texas P, 1981.

——. *Problems of Dostoevsky's Poetics*. Trans. and ed. Caryl Emerson. Minneapolis: U of Minnesota P, 1984.

——. *Speech Genres and Other Late Essays*. Trans. Vern W. McGee. Ed. Caryl Emerson and Michael Holquist. Austin: U of Texas P, 1986.

Bal, Mieke. *Narratology: Introduction to the Theory of Narrative*. Toronto: U of Toronto P, 1985.

Barnes, Julian. *Flaubert's Parrot*. New York: Alfred A. Knopf, 1985.

Barnet, Miguel. "La novela testimonio. Socioliteratura." *Unión* 6.4 (1969): 99–122. Rpt. in Jara and Vidal 280–302.

——. "The Documentary Novel." Trans. Paul Bundy and Enrico Mario Santí. *Cuban Studies* 11.1 (1981): 19–32.

Barrenechea, Ana María. "La estructura de *Rayuela* de Julio Cortázar." *Textos hispanoamericanos: De Sarmiento a Sarduy*. Caracas: Monte Avila, 1978. 195–220.

——. "Estudio preliminar." Cortázar and Barrenechea 9–138.

——. "Los dobles en el proceso de escritura de *Rayuela*." *Revista iberoamericana* 49 (125) (1983): 809–28.

Barthes, Roland. *Writing Degree Zero and Elements of Semiology*. Trans. Annette Lavers and Colin Smith. Boston: Beacon, 1967.

——. *Critical Essays*. Trans. Richard Howard. Evanston: Northwestern UP, 1972.

——. "The Death of the Author." *Image-Music-Text*. Trans. Stephen Heath. New York: Hill and Wang, 1977. 142–48.

——. "From Work to Text." Harari 73–81.

——. *The Rustle of Language*. Trans. Richard Howard. New York: Hill and Wang, 1986.

Benjamin, Walter. *Illuminations*. Trans. Harry Zohn. Ed. Hannah Arendt. New York: Schocken Books, 1969.

Benveniste, Emile. *Problems in General Linguistics*. Trans. Mary Elizabeth Meek. Coral Gables: U of Miami P, 1971.

Bernal, A. Alejandro. "La dictadura en el exilio: *El jardín de al lado* de José Donoso." *Inti* 21 (1985): 51–58.

Bersani, Leo. "The Subject of Power." *Diacritics* 7.3 (1977): 2–21.

Beverley, John. "The Margin at the Center: On *Testimonio* (Testimonial Narrative)." *Modern Fiction Studies* 35.1 (1989): 11–28.

Blanco, Pedro E. "*El hablador*: elementos para un discurso oral." *Antípodas*: 1 (1988): 183–89.

Bloom, Harold, ed. *Jorge Luis Borges*. New York: Chelsea House, 1986.

Boling, Becky. "A Literary Vision of History: Marxism and Positivism in *Terra nostra* by Fuentes." *Latin American Research Review* 19.1 (1984): 125–41.

Booth, Wayne C. *The Rhetoric of Fiction*. 2nd ed. Chicago: U of Chicago P, 1983.

Borges, Jorge Luis. *Obras completas*. Buenos Aires: Emecé, 1974.

——. *Borges: A Reader. A Selection from the Writings of Jorge Luis Borges*. Ed. Emir Rodríguez Monegal and Alastair Reid. New York: E. P. Dutton, 1981.

Borinsky, Alicia. "Repetition, Museums, Libraries." Bloom 149–60.

Braudy, Leo. *The Frenzy of Renown: Fame and Its History*. New York: Oxford UP, 1986.

Brody, Robert. *Julio Cortázar: Rayuela.* London: Grant and Cutler/Tamesis, 1976.

Bruce-Novoa, Juan. "Elena Poniatowska: The Feminist Origins of Commitment." *Women's Studies International Forum* 6 (1983): 509–16.

Bruns, Gerald L. "Intention, Authority, and Meaning." *Critical Inquiry* 7 (1980–81): 297–309.

———. *Inventions: Writing, Textuality and Understanding in Literary History.* New Haven, CT: Yale UP, 1982.

Burgos, Fernando. "Exilio y escritura: *El jardín de al lado.*" *Revista interamericana de bibliografía/Inter-American Review of Bibliography* 35.1 (1987): 57–61.

Carter, E. D., Jr. "Bibliografía de y sobre Julio Cortázar." *Explicación de textos literarios* 17.1–2 (1988–89): 251–327.

Castro-Klarén, Sara. "Desire, The Author and the Reader in Cortázar's Narrative." *Review of Contemporary Fiction* 3.3 (1983): 65–71.

Caughie, John, ed. *Theories of Authorship: A Reader.* London: Routledge and Kegan Paul, 1981.

Cavallari, Héctor M. "Ficción, testimonios, representación." Jara and Vidal 73–84.

Chatman, Seymour. *Story and Discourse: Narrative Structure in Fiction and Film.* Ithaca, NY: Cornell UP, 1978.

Chenu, M.-D. "Auctor, Actor, Autor." *Bulletin du Cange* 3 (1927): 81–86.

Chevigny, Bell Gale. "The Transformation of Privilege in the Work of Elena Poniatowska." *Latin American Literary Review* 13 (26) (1985): 49–62.

Cixous, Hélène. "The Laugh of the Medusa." Trans. Keith Cohen and Paula Cohen. *Signs* 1 (1976): 875–93.

Coover, Robert. "Our Old New World." Rev. of *Terra nostra,* by Carlos Fuentes. *New York Times Book Review* 7 November 1976: 3, 48–50.

Corbatta, Jorgelina. *Mito personal y mitos colectivos en las novelas de Manuel Puig.* Madrid: Orígenes, 1988.

Cortázar, Julio. *Rayuela.* Buenos Aires: Sudamericana, 1963.

———. *Hopscotch.* Trans. Gregory Rabassa. New York: Pantheon, 1966.

Cortázar, Julio, and Ana María Barrenechea. *Cuaderno de bitácora de "Rayuela."* Buenos Aires: Sudamericana, 1983.

Culler, Jonathan. *Structuralist Poetics: Structuralism, Linguistics, and the Study of Literature.* Ithaca, NY: Cornell UP, 1975.

Curtius, Ernst Robert. *European Literature and the Latin Middle Ages.* Trans. Willard R. Trask. New York: Harper and Row, 1953.

Damisch, Hubert. "La partie et le tout." *Revue d'esthétique* 23 [23] (1970): 168–88.

———. "Le gardien de l'interprétation." *Tel quel* 44 (1971): 70–84.

———. "Le gardien de l'interprétation" (fin). *Tel quel* 45 (1971): 82–96.

Dante Alighieri. *The Convivio of Dante Alighieri.* Trans. and ed. Philip Wicksteed. 3rd ed. London: J. M. Dent and Sons, Aldine House, 1912.

Davis, Lisa. "An Invitation to Understanding Among Poor Women of the Americas: *The Color Purple* and *Hasta no verte Jesús mío.*" *Reinventing the Americas: Comparative Studies of Literature of the United States and Spanish America.* Ed. Bell Gale Chevigny and Gari Laguardia. New York: Cambridge UP, 1986. 224–41.

De George, Richard T. *The Nature and Limits of Authority.* Lawrence: UP of Kansas, 1985.

Deleuze, Gilles, and Félix Guattari. *Kafka: Toward a Minor Literature.* Trans. Dana Polan. Minneapolis: U of Minnesota P, 1986.

Bibliography

de Man, Paul. "A Modern Master." Bloom 21–27.

———. *Allegories of Reading: Figural Language in Rousseau, Nietzsche, Rilke, and Proust.* New Haven, CT: Yale UP, 1979.

———. "Autobiography as De-facement." *MLN* 94 (1979): 919–30.

Derrida, Jacques. *Of Grammatology.* Trans. Gayatri Chakravorty Spivak. Baltimore, MD: Johns Hopkins UP, 1976.

———. "Signature Event Context." Trans. Samuel Weber and Jeffrey Mehlman. *Glyph* 1 (1977): 172–97.

———. "Limited Inc abc. . . ." Trans. Samuel Weber. *Glyph* 2 (1977): 162–254.

Docherty, Thomas. *On Modern Authority: The Theory and Condition of Writing, 1500 to the Present Day.* Sussex: Harvester/New York: St Martin's, 1987.

Donoso, José. *Historia personal del "boom."* Barcelona: Anagrama, 1972.

———. "Chronology." *Review* 9 (1973): 12–19.

———. *Casa de campo.* Barcelona: Seix Barral, 1978.

———. *La misteriosa desaparición de la marquesita de Loria.* Barcelona: Seix Barral, 1980.

———. *El jardín de al lado.* Barcelona: Seix Barral, 1981.

———. *Poemas de un novelista.* Santiago: Ediciones Ganymedes, 1981.

Durán, Gloria. "*Terra nostra* or 'It Seems to Me I've Heard That Song Before.' " *The American Hispanist* 3 (24) (1978): 4–7.

Eco, Umberto. *The Role of the Reader: Explorations in the Semiotics of Texts.* Bloomington: Indiana UP, 1979.

Ehrlich, Victor. *Russian Formalism: History - Doctrine.* 3rd ed. New Haven, CT: Yale UP, 1981.

Eliot, T. S. "Tradition and the Individual Talent." Lambropoulos and Miller 145–51.

Engelbert, Jo Anne. *Macedonio Fernández and the Spanish American New Novel.* New York: New York UP, 1978.

Escala, María. "Aspectos de una estética negativa: 'El jardín de al lado' de José Donoso." *Studi de letteratura ibero-americana offerti a Giuseppe Bellini.* Ed. Mariateresa Cattaneo, Carlos Romero, and Silvana Serafin. Rome: Bulzoni, 1984. 291–99.

Everman, Welch D. *Who Says This? The Authority of the Author, the Discourse, and the Reader.* Carbondale: Southern Illinois UP, 1988.

Feal, Rosemary Geisdorfer. *Novel Lives: The Fictional Autobiographies of Guillermo Cabrera Infante and Mario Vargas Llosa.* Chapel Hill: North Carolina Studies in the Romance Languages and Literatures, 1986.

———. " 'In my end is my beginning': José Donoso's Sense of an Ending." *Chasqui* 17.2 (1988): 46–55.

———. "Veiled Portraits: Donoso's Interartistic Dialogue in *El jardín de al lado.*" *MLN* 103 (1988): 398–418.

———. "Spanish American Ethnobiography and the Slave Narrative Tradition: *Biografía de un cimarrón* and *Me llamo Rigoberta Menchú.*" *Modern Language Studies* 20.1 (1990): 100–111.

Felman, Shoshana. "Turning the Screw of Interpretation." *Literature and Psychoanalysis. The Question of Reading: Otherwise.* Ed. Shoshana Felman. Special issue of *Yale French Studies* 55/56 (1977): 94–207.

———. *La folie et la chose littéraire.* Paris: Seuil, 1978.

Fernández Muñoz, María T. "El lenguaje profanado (*Terra nostra*, de Carlos Fuentes)." *Cuadernos hispanoamericanos* 359 (1980): 419–28.

Fernández Olmos, Margarite. "El género testimonial: Aproximaciones feministas." *Revista/Review Interamericana* (San Juan) 11.1 (1981): 69–75.

Fish, Stanley. *Self-Consuming Artifacts: The Experience of Seventeenth-Century Literature.* Berkeley: U of California P, 1972.

———. "What Is Stylistics and Why Are They Saying Such Terrible Things About It?" *Approaches to Poetics.* Ed. Seymour Chatman. New York: Columbia UP, 1973. 109–52.

Flaubert, Gustave. "Un coeur simple." *Trois Contes.* Paris: Gallimard, 1966. 17–61.

Flores, Ralph. *The Rhetoric of Doubtful Authority: Deconstructive Readings of Self-Questioning Narratives, St. Augustine to Faulkner.* Ithaca, NY: Cornell UP, 1984.

Fokkema, Douwe, and Hans Bertens, eds. *Approaching Postmodernism.* Amsterdam/Philadelphia: John Benjamins, 1986.

Foley, Barbara. *Telling the Truth: The Theory and Practice of Documentary Fiction.* Ithaca, NY: Cornell UP, 1986.

Foster, David William. "Latin American Documentary Narrative." *PMLA* 99 (1984): 41–55.

Foster, Hal, ed. *The Anti-Aesthetic: Essays on Postmodern Culture.* Port Townsend, WA: Bay, 1983.

Foucault, Michel. *Discipline and Punish: The Birth of the Prison.* Trans. Alan Sheridan. New York: Pantheon, 1977.

———. *The History of Sexuality.* Vol. I: *An Introduction.* Trans. Robert Hurley. New York: Pantheon, 1978.

———. "What Is an Author?" Harari 141–60.

Franco, Jean. "Narrador, autor, superestrella: la narrativa latinoamericana en la época de cultura de masas." *Revista iberoamericana* 47 (114–15) (1981): 129–48.

———. "Memoria, narración y repetición: la narrativa hispanoamericana en la época de la cultura de masas." Viñas et al. 111–29.

———. *Plotting Women: Gender and Representation in Mexico.* New York: Columbia UP, 1989.

———. "¿La historia de quién? La piratería postmoderna." *Revista de crítica literaria latinoamericana* 33 (1991): 11–20.

Freccero, John. "The Fig Tree and the Laurel: Petrarch's Poetics." *Diacritics* 5.1 (1975): 34–40.

Freud, Sigmund. *Character and Culture.* New York: Collier, 1963.

Fuentes, Carlos. *Terra nostra.* Mexico City: Joaquín Mortiz, 1975.

———. *Cervantes o la crítica de la lectura.* Mexico City: Joaquín Mortiz, 1976.

———. *Terra Nostra.* Trans. Margaret Sayers Peden. New York: Farrar, 1976.

———. "A Talk with Carlos Fuentes." Interview with Frank McShane. *New York Times Book Review* 7 November 1976: 3, 50.

———. "Terra nostra o la crítica de los cielos. Entrevista a Carlos Fuentes." Interview with Marcelo Coddou. *American Hispanist* 3 (24) (1978): 8–10.

García Núñez, Fernando. "Herejías cristianas y superposición en *Terra nostra.*" *Cuadernos americanos* 240 (1980): 94–110.

Gass, William. *Habitations of the Word: Essays.* New York: Simon and Schuster, 1985.

Genette, Gérard. *Narrative Discourse: An Essay in Method.* Trans. Jane E. Lewin. Ithaca, NY: Cornell UP, 1980.

———. *Figures of Literary Discourse.* Trans. Alan Sheridan. New York: Columbia UP, 1982.

Bibliography

Gertel, Zunilda. "Semiótica, historia y ficción en *Terra nostra.*" *Revista iberoamericana* 47 (116–17) (1981): 63–72.

Ghisalberti, F. "Mediaeval Biographies of Ovid." *Journal of the Warburg and Courtauld Institutes* 9 (1946): 10–59.

Gilbert, Sandra M., and Susan Gubar. *The Madwoman in the Attic: The Woman Writer and the Nineteenth-Century Literary Imagination.* New Haven, CT: Yale UP, 1979.

———. *No Man's Land: The Place of the Woman Writer in the Twentieth Century.* Vol. 1. New Haven, CT: Yale UP, 1988.

Ginzburg, Carlo. "Morelli, Freud, and Sherlock Holmes." *The Sign of Three: Dupin, Holmes, Peirce.* Ed. Umberto Eco and Thomas A. Sebeok. Bloomington: Indiana UP, 1983. 81–118.

Giordano, Enrique. "Algunas aproximaciones a *Rayuela,* de Julio Cortázar, a través de la dinámica del juego." *Homenaje a Julio Cortázar.* Ed. Helmy F. Giacoman. Madrid: Anaya, 1972. 95–129.

Goldmann, Lucien. *Towards a Sociology of the Novel.* Trans. Alan Sheridan. London: Tavistock, 1975.

———. *Cultural Creation in Modern Society.* Trans. Bart Grahl. St. Louis: Telos, 1976.

González, Ann Brashear de. "'La novela totalizadora': Pynchon's *Gravity's Rainbow* and Fuentes' *Terra nostra.*" *Kañina* 5.2 (1981): 99–106.

González, Eduardo. "Fuentes' *Terra nostra.*" *Salmagundi* 41 (1978): 148–52.

González Echevarría, Roberto. Rev. of *Cervantes o la crítica de la lectura,* by Carlos Fuentes. *World Literature Today* 52.1 (1978): 84.

———. *The Voice of the Masters: Writing and Authority in Modern Latin American Literature.* Austin: U of Texas P, 1985.

———. "Borges and Derrida." Bloom 227–34.

———. *La ruta de Severo Sarduy.* Hanover, NH: Ediciones del Norte, 1987.

Goodman, Nelson. "The Status of Style." Lambropoulos and Miller 254–66.

Goodrich, Diana Sorensen. Rev. of *Cuaderno de Bitácora de Rayuela,* by Julio Cortázar and Ana María Barrenechea. *Poetics Today* 7 (1986): 571–74.

Goytisolo, Juan. "Our Old New World." *Review* 19 (1976): 5–24.

Green, James Ray, Jr. "*El beso de la mujer araña:* Sexual Repression and Textual Repression." *LA CHISPA '81: Selected Proceedings.* Ed. Gilbert Paolini. New Orleans: Tulane U, Louisiana Conference on Hispanic Languages and Literatures, 1981. 133–39.

Guillory, John. *Poetic Authority: Spenser, Milton, and Literary History.* New York: Columbia UP, 1983.

Gutiérrez Mouat, Ricardo. "Aesthetics, Ethics, and Politics in Donoso's *El jardín de al lado.*" *PMLA* 106 (1991): 60–70.

Gyurko, Lanin A. "Novel into Essay: Fuentes' *Terra nostra* as Generator of *Cervantes o la crítica.*" *Mester* 11.2 (1983): 16–35.

Harari, Josué V., ed. *Textual Strategies: Perspectives in Post-Structuralist Criticism.* Ithaca, NY: Cornell UP, 1979.

Hayman, David. *Re-forming the Narrative: Toward a Mechanics of Modernist Fiction.* Ithaca, NY: Cornell UP, 1987.

Hirsch, E. D., Jr. *Validity in Interpretation.* New Haven, CT: Yale UP, 1967.

———. *The Aims of Interpretation.* Chicago: U of Chicago P, 1976.

Hobbs, Jerry R. "Against Confusion." *Diacritics* 18.3 (1988): 78–92.

Holsten, Ken. "Notas sobre el 'Tablero de dirección' en *Rayuela.*" *Revista iberoamericana* 39 (84–85) (1973): 683–88.

Hutcheon, Linda. *A Poetics of Postmodernism: History, Theory, Fiction.* Boston: Routledge and Kegan Paul, 1988.

Huyssens, Andreas. *After the Great Divide: Modernism, Mass Culture, Post-modernism.* Bloomington: Indiana UP, 1986.

Iser, Wolfgang. *The Implied Reader: Patterns of Communication in Prose Fiction from Bunyan to Beckett.* Baltimore, MD: Johns Hopkins UP, 1974.

———. *The Act of Reading: A Theory of Aesthetic Response.* Baltimore, MD: Johns Hopkins UP, 1978.

Jaen, Didier T. "La neopicaresca en México: Elena Poniatowska y Luis Zapata." *Tinta* 1 (5) (1987): 23–29.

Jakobson, Roman. *Selected Writings II.* The Hague: Mouton, 1971.

Jameson, Fredric. "Postmodernism and Consumer Society." H. Foster 111–25.

Jara, René, and Hernán Vidal, eds. *Testimonio y literatura.* Minneapolis: Institute for the Study of Ideologies and Literature, 1986.

Jauss, Hans Robert. *Toward an Aesthetic of Reception.* Trans. Timothy Bahti. Minneapolis: U of Minnesota P, 1982.

Jefferson, Ann, and David Robey, eds. *Modern Literary Theory: A Comparative Introduction.* 2nd ed. Totowa, NJ: Barnes and Noble, 1986.

Josephs, Allen. "The End of *Terra Nostra.*" *World Literature Today* 57 (1983): 564–67.

Juhl, P. D. *Interpretation: An Essay in the Philosophy of Literary Criticism.* Princeton, NJ: Princeton UP, 1980.

Kadir, Djelal. *Questing Fictions: Latin America's Family Romance.* Minneapolis: U of Minnesota P, 1986.

Kamuf, Peggy. *Signature Pieces: On the Institution of Authorship.* Ithaca, NY: Cornell UP, 1988.

Kerr, Lucille. "Leaps Across the Board." *Diacritics* 4.4 (1974): 29–34.

———. *Suspended Fictions: Reading Novels by Manuel Puig.* Urbana: U of Illinois P, 1987.

———. "Conventions of Authorial Design: José Donoso's *Casa de campo.*" *Symposium* 42 (1988): 133–52.

Kiddle, Mary Ellen. "The *Novela Testimonial* in Contemporary Mexican Literature." *Confluencia* 1.1 (1985): 82–89.

Knapp, Steven, and Walter Benn Michaels. "Against Theory." *Critical Inquiry* 8 (1982): 723–42.

Kofman, Sarah. *L'enfance de l'art. Une interprétation de l'esthétique freudienne.* Paris: Payot, 1975.

Krauss, Rosalind. "Originality as Repetition: Introduction." *October* 37 (1986): 35–40.

Kristeva, Julia. *Séméiotiké: Recherches pour un sémanalyse.* Paris: Seuil, 1969.

Kushigian, Julia A. "Transgresión de la autobiografía y el Bildungsroman en *Hasta no verte Jesús mío.*" *Revista iberoamericana* 53 (140) (1987): 667–77.

Lagos-Pope, María Inés, "El testimonio creativo de *Hasta no verte Jesús mío.*" *Revista iberoamericana* 56 (150) (1990): 243–53.

Lambropoulos, Vassilis, and David Neal Miller, eds. *Twentieth-Century Literary Theory: An Introductory Anthology.* Albany: State U of New York P, 1987.

Lang, Berel. "Style as Instrument, Style as Person." *Critical Inquiry* 4 (1977–78): 715–39.

Laurenson, Diana (T.). "The Writer and Society." *The Sociology of Literature.* Ed. Diana T. Laurenson and Alan Swingewood. New York: Schocken Books, 1972. 91–166.

Lemaître, Monique. "Jesusa Palancares y la dialéctica de la emancipación femenina." *Hispamérica* 30 (1981): 131–35.

Lewis, Bart L. "*Pubis angelical:* la mujer codificada." *Revista iberoamericana* 49 (123–24) (1983): 531–40.

Lindstrom, Naomi. *Macedonio Fernández.* Lincoln: Society of Spanish and Spanish-American Studies, U of Nebraska, 1981.

Linenberg-Fressard, Raquel. "La motivation des noms de personnage dans *Pubis angelical* de Manuel Puig." *Imprévue* 1 (1986): 99–109.

Lukács, Georg. *Writer and Critic and Other Essays.* Ed. and trans. Arthur D. Kahn. New York: Grosset and Dunlap, 1970.

Lyotard, Jean-François. *The Postmodern Condition: A Report on Knowledge.* Trans. Geoff Bennington and Brian Massumi. Minneapolis: U of Minnesota P, 1984.

Mac Adam, Alfred J. *Modern Latin American Narratives: The Dreams of Reason.* Chicago: U of Chicago P, 1977.

———. "*Rayuela:* la cuestión del lector." *Explicación de textos literarios* 17.1–2 (1988–89): 216–29.

McGann, Jerome J. "The Significance of the Biographical Context: Two Poems by Lord Byron." Martz and Williams 347–64.

McHale, Brian. *Postmodernist Fiction.* New York: Methuen, 1987.

Macherey, Pierre. *A Theory of Literary Production.* Trans. Geoffrey Wall. London: Routledge and Kegan Paul, 1978.

Magnarelli, Sharon. *The Lost Rib: Female Characters in the Spanish-American Novel.* Lewisburg, PA: Bucknell UP, 1985.

Manzor-Coats, Lillian. "Borges/Escher, *Cobra*/CoBrA: Un encuentro posmoderno." Dissertation. U of Southern California, 1988.

Martz, Louis L., and Aubrey Williams, eds. *The Author in His Works: Essays on a Problem in Criticism.* New Haven, CT: Yale UP, 1978.

Meléndez, Priscilla. "Writing and Reading the Palimpsest: Donoso's *El jardín de al lado.*" *Symposium* 41 (1987): 200–213.

Méndez Rodenas, Adriana. *Severo Sarduy: el neobarroco de la transgresión.* Mexico City: UNAM, 1983.

Merrim, Stephanie. "For a New (Psychological) Novel in the Works of Manuel Puig." *Novel* 17 (1984): 141–57.

———. "Desire, and the Art of Dehumanization: Macedonio Fernández, Julio Cortázar and João Guimarães Rosa." *Latin American Literary Review* 16 (31) (1988): 45–64.

Mignolo, Walter, and Jorge Aguilar Mora. "Borges, el libro y la escritura." *Caravelle/Cahiers du monde hispanique et luso-brésilien* 17 (1971): 187–94.

Miller, Jacqueline T. *Poetic License: Authority and Authorship in Medieval and Renaissance Contexts.* New York: Oxford UP, 1986.

Minnis, A. J. *Medieval Theory of Authorship.* 2nd ed. Philadelphia: U of Pennsylvania P, 1988.

Molloy, Sylvia. *Las letras de Borges.* Buenos Aires: Sudamericana, 1979.

Montenegro, Nivia. "Las novelas de Mario Vargas Llosa: La retórica de la duplicidad." Dissertation. U of Southern California, 1982.

Bibliography

Montero, Oscar. "*El jardín de al lado*: la escritura y el fracaso del éxito." *Revista ibero-americana* 49 (123–24) (1983): 449–67.

Morello-Frosch, Marta. "The New Art of Narrating Films." *Review* 4–5 (1971–72): 52–55.

———. "La sexualidad opresiva en las obras de Manuel Puig." *Nueva narrativa hispanoamericana* 5 (1975): 151–57.

Mukařovský, Jan. *The Word and Verbal Art: Selected Essays*. Trans. and ed. John Burbank and Peter Steiner. New Haven, CT: Yale UP, 1977.

Muñoz, Elías Miguel. *El discurso utópico de la sexualidad en Manuel Puig*. Madrid: Pliegos, 1987.

Ong, Walter J. *Orality and Literacy: The Technologizing of the Word*. London: Methuen, 1982.

Ortega, Julio. "Morelli on the Threshold." *Review of Contemporary Fiction* 3.3 (1983): 45–47.

Ostria González, Manuel. "*Rayuela*: poética y práctica de un lector libre." *Cuadernos hispanoamericanos* 364–66 (1980): 431–48.

Oviedo, José Miguel. "Fuentes: sinfonía del nuevo mundo." *Hispamérica* 16 (1977): 19–32.

———. "*Terra Nostra*: historia, relato y personaje." *Latin American Fiction Today*. Ed. Rose S. Minc. Takoma Park, MD: [Ediciones] Hispamérica; Upper Montclair, NJ: Montclair State College, 1980. 19–31.

———. *Mario Vargas Llosa: la invención de una realidad*. 3rd ed. Barcelona: Seix Barral, 1982.

Pease, Donald E. "Author." *Critical Terms for Literary Study*. Ed. Frank Lentricchia and Thomas McLaughlin. Chicago: U of Chicago P, 1990. 105–17.

Peden, Margaret Sayers. "A Note on an Early Published Fragment of *Terra Nostra*." *Mester* 11.1 (1982): 75–80.

Pellón, Gustavo. "Manuel Puig's Contradictory Strategy: Kitsch Paradigms versus Paradigmatic Structures in *El beso de la mujer araña* and *Pubis angelical*." *Symposium* 36 (1983): 186–201.

Pérez Blanco, Luciano. "*El jardín de al lado* o del exilio al regreso." *Cuadernos americanos* 239 (1981): 191–216.

Peters, R. "Authority." Quinton 83–96.

Poniatowska, Elena. *Hasta no verte Jesús mío*. Mexico City: Era, 1969.

———. "*Hasta no verte Jesús mío*: Jesusa Palancares." *Vuelta* 24 (1978): 5–11.

———. "Entrevista con Elena Poniatowska." Interview with Lorraine Roses. *Plaza* (Cambridge, MA) 5–6 (1981–82): 51–64.

———. "Testimonios de una escritora: Elena Poniatowska en Micrófono" (1982). *La sartén por el mango: encuentro de escritoras latinoamericanas*. Ed. Patricia Elena González and Eliana Ortega. Río Piedras, PR: Ediciones Huracán, 1984. 155–62.

———. "Entrevista con Elena Poniatowska." Interview with Teresa Méndez-Faith. *Inti* 15 (1982): 54–60.

———. "Elena Poniatowska: De periodista a escritora de cuentos y novelas." Interview with Manuel Durán and Gloria Durán. *Autorretratos y espejos*. Boston: Heinle and Heinle, 1988. 59–63.

Poulet, Georges. "Criticism and the Experience of Interiority." *The Structuralist Controversy: The Languages of Criticism and the Sciences of Man*. Ed. Richard Macksey and Eugenio Donato. Baltimore, MD. Johns Hopkins UP: 1970. 56–72.

Bibliography

Prada Oropeza, Renato. "De lo testimonial al testimonio: notas para un deslinde del discurso-testimonio." Jara and Vidal 7–21.

Previtali, Giovanni. "A propos de Morelli." *Revue de l'art* 42 (1978): 27–31.

Puig, Manuel. *Pubis angelical*. Barcelona: Seix Barral, 1979.

———. *Pubis Angelical*. Trans. Elena Brunet. New York: Vintage/Aventura, 1986.

———. "Growing Up at the Movies: A Chronology." *Review* 4–5 (1971–72): 49–51.

———. "El folletín rescatado." Interview with Emir Rodríguez Monegal. *Revista de la Universidad de México* 27.2 (1972): 25–35.

———. "Entrevista [a Manuel Puig]." Interview with Saúl Sosnowski. *Hispamérica* 3 (1973): 69–80.

———. Interview with Jean-Michel Fossey. *Galaxia Latinoamericana*. Las Palmas: Inventarios Provisionales, 1973. 137–52.

———. "Conversación con Manuel Puig: La redención de la cursilería." Interview with Danubio Torres Fierro. *Eco* 28 (1975): 507–15.

———. "An Interview with Manuel Puig." Interview with Ronald Christ. *Partisan Review* 44 (1977): 52–61.

———. "Interview with Manuel Puig." Interview with Ronald Christ. *Christopher Street* April 1979: 25–31.

———. "Entrevista con Manuel Puig: una narrativa de lo melifluo." Interview with Nora Catelli. *Quimera* April 1982: 22–25.

———. "Encuentros con Manuel Puig." Interview with Jorgelina Corbatta. *Revista iberoamericana* 49 (123–24) (1983): 591–620.

Quint, David. *Origin and Originality in Renaissance Literature: Versions of the Source*. New Haven, CT: Yale UP, 1983.

Quinton, Anthony, ed. *Political Philosophy*. Oxford: Oxford UP, 1967.

Rabinowitz, Peter J. *Before Reading: Narrative Conventions and the Politics of Interpretation*. Ithaca, NY: Cornell UP, 1987.

Rama, Angel. *La novela en América Latina: panoramas 1920–1980*. Montevideo: Fundación Angel Rama; Xalapa Universidad Veracruzana, 1986.

Rivas, José Andrés. "*El hablador*: metáfora de una autobiografía nostálgica." *Antípodas* 1 (1988): 190–200.

Robbe-Grillet, Alain. *For a New Novel: Essays on Fiction*. New York: Grove, 1965.

Rodríguez Monegal, Emir. "A Literary Myth Exploded." *Review* 4–5 (1971–72): 56–64.

———. "Borges and La Nouvelle Critique." *Diacritics* 2.2 (1972): 27–34.

Said, Edward W. *Beginnings: Intention and Method*. Baltimore, MD: Johns Hopkins UP, 1975.

Sarlo, Beatriz. "Releer *Rayuela* desde *El cuaderno de bitácora*." *Revista iberoamericana* 51 (132–33) (1985): 939–52.

Schor, Naomi. *Reading in Detail: Aesthetics and the Feminine*. New York: Methuen, 1987.

Siegle, Robert. *The Politics of Reflexivity: Narrative and the Constitutive Poetics of Culture*. Baltimore, MD: Johns Hopkins UP, 1986.

Siemens, William L. "Celestina as *Terra Nostra*." *Mester* 11.1 (1982): 57–66.

Sklodowska, Elzbieta. "Hacia una tipología del testimonio hispanoamericano." *Siglo XX/Twentieth Century* 8 (1990–91): 103–20.

Smith, Paul. *Discerning the Subject*. Minneapolis: U of Minnesota P, 1988.

Bibliography

Solotorevsky, Myrna. "El cliché en *Pubis angelical* y *Boquitas pintadas*: Desgaste y crea-tividad." *Hispamérica* 38 (1984): 3–18.

Spector, J. J. "The Method of Morelli and Its Relation to Freudian Psychoanalysis." *Diogenes* 66 (1969): 63–83.

Spires, Robert C. *Beyond the Metafictional Mode: Directions in the Modern Spanish Novel.* Lexington: UP of Kentucky, 1984.

Stallybrass, Peter, and Allon White. *The Politics and Poetics of Transgression.* Ithaca, NY: Cornell UP, 1986.

Steiner, Peter. *Russian Formalism: A Metapoetics.* Ithaca, NY: Cornell UP, 1984.

Suleiman, Susan Rubin. *Authoritarian Fictions: The Ideological Novel as a Literary Genre.* New York: Columbia UP, 1983.

Suleiman, Susan R., and Inge Crosman, eds. *The Reader in the Text: Essays on Audience and Interpretation.* Princeton, NJ: Princeton UP, 1980.

Swietlicki, Catherine. "Doubling, Reincarnation, and Cosmic Order in *Terra Nostra.*" *Hispanófila* 79 (1983): 93–104.

Tatum, Charles. "Elena Poniatowska's *Hasta no verte, Jesús mío* [*Until I See You, Dear Jesus*]." *Latin American Women Writers: Yesterday and Today.* Ed. Yvette E. Miller and Charles M. Tatum. Pittsburgh, PA: Latin American Literary Review P, 1977. 49–58.

Thiher, Allen. *Words in Reflection: Modern Language Theory and Postmodernist Fiction.* Chicago: U of Chicago P, 1984.

Todorov, Tzvetan. *The Poetics of Prose.* Trans. Richard Howard. Ithaca, NY: Cornell UP, 1977.

———. "Point of View in Fiction." *Encyclopedic Dictionary of the Sciences of Language.* Ed. Oswald Ducrot and Tzvetan Todorov. Trans. Catherine Porter. Baltimore, MD: Johns Hopkins UP, 1979. 328–33.

———. *Mikhail Bakhtin: The Dialogical Principle.* Trans. Wlad Godzich. Minneapolis: U of Minnesota P, 1984.

Tomashevsky, Boris. "Literature and Biography." Trans. Herbert Eagle. *Readings in Russian Poetics: Formalist and Structuralist Views.* Ed. Ladislav Matejka and Krystyna Pomorska. Cambridge, MA: MIT P, 1971. 47–55.

Tompkins, Jane P., ed. *Reader-Response Criticism: From Formalism to Post-Structuralism.* Baltimore, MD: Johns Hopkins UP, 1980.

Vargas Llosa, Mario. *La orgía perpetua: Flaubert y "Madame Bovary."* Madrid: Taurus, 1975.

———. *El hablador.* Barcelona: Seix Barral, 1987.

———. *The Storyteller.* Trans. Helen Lane. New York: Farrar Straus Giroux, 1989.

Viñas, David. "Pareceres y digresiones en torno a la nueva narrativa latinoameri-cana." Viñas et al. 13–50.

Viñas, David, et al. *Más allá del boom: literatura y mercado.* Mexico City: Marcha, 1981.

Wellek, René, and Austin Warren. *Theory of Literature.* 3rd ed. New York: Harcourt, Brace and World, 1956.

West, David, and Tony Woodman, eds. *Creative Imitation and Latin Literature.* Cambridge: Cambridge UP, 1979.

Whinnom, Keith. "*Autor* and *tratado* in the Fifteenth Century: Semantic Latinism or Etymological Trap?" *Bulletin of Hispanic Studies* 59 (1982): 211–18.

Wimsatt, W. K., Jr. *The Verbal Icon: Studies in the Meaning of Poetry.* Lexington: UP of Kentucky, 1954.

Winch, Peter. "Authority." Quinton 97–111.

Bibliography   **221**

Wind, Edgar. *Art and Anarchy. The Reich Lectures* 1960. Rev. and enl. London: Faber and Faber, 1963.

Wollheim, Richard. *On Art and the Mind*. Cambridge, MA: Harvard UP, 1974.

Yúdice, George. "*El beso de la mujer araña* y *Pubis angelical*: Entre el placer y el saber." *Literature and Popular Culture in the Hispanic World: A Symposium*. Ed. Rose S. Minc. Gaithersburg, MD: Montclair State College and Ediciones Hispamérica, 1981. 43–57.

Zerner, Henri. "Giovanni Morelli et la science de l'art." *Revue de l'art* 40–41 (1978): 209–15.

Index

Index

Cortázar, Julio, 26, 29–36 passim, 39–45 passim, 161, 167, 182 n. 30, 182 n. 31, 182 n. 32, 194 n. 10, 202 n. 15; figured by Morelli, 28; name of, 33–34; writings by, 178 n. 1, 194–95 n. 10. *See also* Barrenechea-Cortázar; Cortázar-Barrenechea; Cortázar-Morelli; Morelli-Cortázar

Cortázar-Barrenechea, 44. *See also* Barrenechea; Barrenechea-Cortázar; Cortázar

Cortázar-Morelli, 35. *See also* Cortázar; Morelli; Morelli-Cortázar

Critic, figure of, 90, 127, 193 n. 1

Cuaderno de bitácora de "Rayuela" (Cortázar and Barrenechea), 41, 44, 182 n. 30, 182 n. 31; authorship of, 43; and *Rayuela*, 42; "pre-textos" in, 42

Dante, 140–41, 205 n. 12

"Death of the Author, The" (Barthes), 5–7, 10, 13, 193 n. 28, 193 n. 1, 202 n. 14

Details, significance of, 37, 40, 180 n. 23

Discourse, 7, 9, 13, 51–53, 56, 59, 61, 91, 93, 106, 108, 109, 125, 146, 147, 173 n. 10, 185 n. 12, 186 n. 17, 201 n. 9; hierarchy of, 73, 77, 132; storyteller as function of, 148

Documentary fiction, 46, 182 n. 1. *See also* novela testimonial

Donoso, José, 113, 115, 117–19, 122–26 passim, 129–33 passim, 162–63, 168, 201 n. 7, 201 n. 11, 202 n. 15, 203 n. 20; as author, 201 n. 9; and boom authors, 201–2 n. 12; experience as exile, 200 n. 5; as implied author, 132; writings by, 199 n. 1

Felipe (*Terra nostra*). *See* El Señor

Fiction, 46, 70, 74, 91–93, 97, 110, 149, 164; modernist, 19; poetics of, 4, 15, 19, 20; postmodernist, 19–20. *See also* Spanish American fiction

Flaubert, Gustave, 154–55

Foucault, Michel, 1, 5, 7–10, 12, 18,

30, 201 n. 9; theory of power of, 190–91 n. 6, 192 n. 26

Freud, Sigmund, 38; "Moses of Michelangelo, The," 38–39; relation to Giovanni Morelli, 39, 40, 41, 45. *See also* Freud-Morelli; Morelli-Freud

Freud-Morelli, as composite author, 39. *See also* Morelli, Giovanni; Freud; Morelli-Freud

"From Work to Text" (Barthes), 5, 6, 202 n. 14

Fuentes, Carlos, 66, 68–71, 74, 76, 78, 79, 87, 88, 162, 167, 194 n. 10; authorial power play of, 86; as author-figure, 85; as author-schemer, 191 n. 12; as magus, 72; writings by, 190 n. 1, 194–95 n. 10

Gestor, 62, 189 n. 33; as *auctor*, 63; and author, 63; as *scriptor*, 62

Gloria Méndez (*El jardín de al lado*), 112, 113, 116, 118, 127; as author, 117, 200 n. 7; authority of, 124, 129; narration of, 123, 130; as narrator and author, 114–15, 117, 132; notebooks of, 131; novel of, 129, 131–32; as reader, 125–26; relation to husband of, 119, 120–22, 128, 203 n. 17; refusal of discourse of, 121, 202 n. 13; as *scriptor*, 131

Hablador (*El hablador*), 135–39, 146, 148, 151, 155–56, 158, 163, 168, 204 n. 5, 207 n. 23, 207 n. 24, 208 n. 27, 209 n. 35; appearance of, 140–43; authority of, 149; as collective voice, 147; as figure of identity and difference, 144; as figure of indirection, 140, 143; as figure of repetition, 141, 149, 151; identity of, 144, 146, 149, 156; and modern author, 138, 157; naming of, 152; as "narrative-man," 142; and narrator-author, 138; and parrot, 154–55; photograph of, 143; as storyteller, 149, 151; as word, 137, 145–48, 204 n. 5, 206–7 n. 19, 207 n. 21; and written culture, 151

Index

Spanish American fiction, 11, 15–16, 20–21, 24–25, 45–47, 110, 158, 160–61, 168, 170, 177 n. 53; diversity of authorial images in, 165; figure of author in, 1, 3, 27, 164; image of "Spanish American author" in or around, 167, 169
Storyteller, the [El hablador]. See hablador
Style, 13, 14, 20, 90, 92, 103–4, 105–6, 108, 162, 197–98 n. 28; as generic convention, 107; as idiosyncratic performance, 107; as image or voice, 109. See also Puig
Stylization, 106–7. See also parody

"Tablero de dirección" (Rayuela). See Rayuela
Terra nostra [Terra Nostra] (Fuentes), 65–70, 78–79, 82–83, 85, 87, 88, 162, 167; as attack on nature of literature, 86–87; authorial project in, 86; Celestina in, 78, 83, 85, 192 n. 23; Cronista in, 78, 84; Escorial in, 68, 69, 77, 80–82, 84; figures of authority in, 87; first and last chapters of, 75–77; focalization in, 75–76; Fray Julián in, 78; narrative structure of, 71, 74, 86; narrator(s) and narration in, 70, 71, 73–76, 79; Polo Febo as author-reader in, 77; reader's relation to, 74, 77–80, 83–86, 89; reading in, 69–70, 73, 78,

80, 84; structures of power in, 68–71, 74, 80–87 passim, 190–91 n. 6, 192 n. 26; three identical youths in, 71–73, 77, 79–80, 83–84; title of, 65, 88, 190 n. 2; truth in, 70, 73, 78–79, 84–85
Testimonial novel, 62, 161. See novela testimonial
True, the ["le vrai"], 51–53, 56, 185 n. 12, 186 n. 17. See also Real; Verisimilar

Vargas Llosa, Mario, 135, 136, 138, 140–41, 144, 146, 150–53, 159, 163–64; 205 n. 9, 208 n. 24, 209 n. 36; as auctor, 157; as author, 167; on becoming an author, 158; as figured by Saúl, 209 n. 32; as "real" figure in El hablador, 156; as political figure, 157; as scriptor, 157; writings of, 195 n. 10, 203–4 n. 2
Verisimilar, the ["le vraisemblable"], 49, 52, 55, 61, 144, 185 n. 12. See also Real; True; Verisimilitude
Verisimilitude, 55, 56, 59, 206 n. 16, 208 n. 24; generic, 189 n. 32. See also Verisimilar

"What Is an Author?" (Foucault), 5, 7–8, 10, 16, 18

Zuratas, Saúl (El hablador). See Saúl Zuratas

About the Author

Lucille Kerr is a professor of Latin American literature at the University of Southern California where she teaches in the Department of Spanish and Portuguese and in the Program in Comparative Literature. She is the author of *Suspended Fictions: Reading Novels by Manuel Puig*.

Library of Congress Cataloging-in-Publication Data

Kerr, Lucille, 1946–

    Reclaiming the author : figures and fictions from Spanish America / Lucille Kerr.

    p.   cm.

    Includes bibliographical references and index.

    ISBN 0-8223-1227-1 (alk. paper). — ISBN 0-8223-1224-7 (pbk. : alk. paper)

    1. Spanish American fiction—20th century—History and criticism.   I. Title.

PQ7082.N7K47   1992

863—dc20   91-36087

                                                      CIP